T0311169

Democracy and
Civil Society
in the Third World

Democracy and Civil Society in the Third World

Politics and New Political Movements

JEFF HAYNES

Polity Press

Copyright © Jeff Haynes 1997

The right of Jeff Haynes to be identified as author of this work has been asserted in accordance with the Copyright, Designs and Patents Act 1988.

First published in 1997 by Polity Press in association with Blackwell Publishers Ltd.

Transferred to Digital Print 2003

2 4 6 8 10 9 7 5 3 1

Editorial office:
Polity Press
65 Bridge Street
Cambridge CB2 1UR, UK

Marketing and production:
Blackwell Publishers Ltd
108 Cowley Road
Oxford OX4 1JF, UK

Published in the USA by
Blackwell Publishers Inc.
Commerce Place
350 Main Street
Malden, MA 02148, USA

All rights reserved. Except for the quotation of short passages for the purposes of criticism and review, no part of this publication may be reproduced, stored in a retrieval system, or transmitted, in any form or by any means, electronic, mechanical, photocopying, recording or otherwise, without the prior permission of the publisher.

Except in the United States of America, this book is sold subject to the condition that it shall not, by way of trade or otherwise, be lent, re-sold, hired out, or otherwise circulated without the publisher's prior consent in any form of binding or cover other than that in which it is published and without a similar condition including this condition being imposed on the subsequent purchaser.

ISBN 0-7456-1646-1
ISBN 0-7456-1647-X (pbk)

A catalogue record for this book is available from the British Library and has been applied for from the Library of Congress.

Typeset in 10 on 12 pt Palatino
by Best-set Typesetter Ltd., Hong Kong

This book is printed on acid-free paper.

Contents

List of Tables   vi
Preface   vii
Acknowledgements   ix

1 Introduction   1
2 Action Groups in Regional Focus   24
3 Macroeconomic Decline and Action Groups   51
4 Democracy and Indigenous Peoples   75
5 Environmental Protection   95
6 Women and Empowerment   120
7 Islamist Action Groups   142
8 Conclusion   165

Notes   183
Bibliography   186
Index   208

Tables

2.1 Action groups in the Third World   26
3.1 Average annual growth rate of GNP per capita, by region,
     1980–1993   53
5.1 Production of tropical timber in Brazil and Malaysia, 1987
     (million m^3)   101

Preface

It was the events of the early 1990s – especially the end of the Soviet bloc and Eastern European communist systems more generally and the emergence of a (putative) New World Order – which stimulated the writing of this book. Initially, I set out to examine links between local and transnational actors in the Third World in the context of a (re)turn to democracy and the growth of civil society. Early drafts were, however, discouraging: certainly, there *were* such links, but little had been formulated in the way of models to comprehend them fully. As time went on, I decided that such a project would have to wait until a later date.

The book which *did* result has a narrower focus than initially envisaged. It is concerned with the development of contemporary Third World sociopolitical and economic movements – which I refer to as 'action' groups for reasons explained in the book's introduction. The book's aim, then, is to examine what I believe to be one of the most important contemporary developments in the Third World in the post-Cold War 1990s: the rise of mostly anti-system, mostly grassroots, movements with a variety of political, social and economic goals. I believe that in general they are A Good Thing – because they (sometimes implicitly) seek to wrest power from (often) undemocratic ruling elites and pass it to those historically without it. Yet this will lay me open to the charge from liberals and socialists – for example in relation to Islamist groups – that I am ignoring such actors' allegedly anti-democratic aspects. But that, I believe, is not the main point. Why *should* such groups necessarily conform to what is expected of them by people steeped in often very different cultures and life experiences?

Second, a lack of space has meant that I have had (virtually) to ignore two theoretical issues of importance. How likely is it that such groups will endure and thrive under their own steam? Or are they simply 'flashes in the pan', likely to die – or be coopted – as soon as regimes under whose jurisdiction they must live manage to assert control? While speculating about such issues in the book's conclusion, I am aware that more might have been done in this regard. Finally, little comparison is made between the rise of contemporary Third World groups and the comparative historical role and functions of similar groups at an earlier stage in Western development. The issue of whether they are derivative or *sui generis* is not fully confronted. Once again, space limitations were the chief obstacle.

Acknowledgements

Many thanks to my editor at Polity, Andy Winnard, who retained his enthusiasm for the project through thick and thin! I also want to thank Polity's anonymous reader whose comments and suggestions on several drafts of the book meant that it is better than it would have been without them. As is usually stated at this juncture, I alone am responsible for errors of fact and interpretation that remain.

The author and publishers wish to thank Oxford University Press for permission to reproduce table 5.1, 'Production of tropical timber in Brazil and Malaysia, 1987' from *Third World Atlas* (second edition), Alan Thomas and Ben Crow et al., Open University Press, 1994.

1
Introduction

It appears that many Third World[1] peoples are once again at the beginning of an era of significant political and economic changes. Not since nationalist political movements led demands for independence during the closing period of European colonialism has popular demand for political and economic transformation been so deep or widespread. In the 1950s, 1960s and 1970s nationalist movements in Africa, Asia, the Middle East and the Caribbean demanded and attained an end to colonial rule and the establishment of independent countries. Most Latin American nations had gone through the same process over a hundred years earlier.

There was considerable optimism at the new countries' economic and political prospects which seems, with hindsight, in many cases misplaced: many were small, economically underdeveloped and beset by potential or existing ethnic and/or religious schisms. For Huntington (1968), such cultural mistrust between peoples feeling no affinity with each other yet forced to coexist in states with inflexible boundaries normally leads to an incapacity to build strong, durable political structures. What was crucial were skilful governments to establish and then preside over prolonged progress. It was nearly always a prerequisite for colonial handovers of power for Third World nationalist politicians to adopt the trappings and outward forms of Western models of democracy. However, some did not necessarily feel a close affinity with a form of politics that had rarely been encouraged during colonial rule; no doubt for some leaders the acquisition of power itself was by far the most significant reward. Yet the wielding of that power was frequently problematic: ethnic and religious unrest, military insurgencies and coups d'état, combined with the difficulty of achieving often elusive economic development, served to derail many Third World governments' progress towards political liberation and socio-economic improvement.

Governments of Third World countries faced two main problems, one social and political, the other economic. First, how to establish and then maintain control over their citizens – that is, how to build *nation-states* from often disparate congeries of people, thrown together for the most part through the whims of imperial administrators. As already noted, such a goal was often difficult due to societal polarization. Second, it is no doubt easier for many citizens to be satisfied with their governments if they are perceived to be presiding over acceptable levels of economic growth, relatively equitably shared. Yet the fact is that the vast majority of Third World countries emerged at a time when the global economic system was already established. How could they hope to prosper in an economic system not of their making and whose 'rules' they could not change? Some – a few – managed it by skill, care and flexibility; many others did not.

Third World governments have not only had to deal with an often hostile, or at least uncertain, international economic environment. They have also had to try to win the trust of their citizens by policies perceived to be in the 'national interest'. Many governments have found both sets of tasks beyond their capabilities. The result has been that initial loyalty and belief in government's efficacy has often drained away, replaced by popular cynicism regarding the state's competence and probity. In short, it is highly probable that many Third World peoples no longer regard their governments as the champion of society's collective interests at home and abroad, a set of institutions working for the common good. Instead, governments may well be widely perceived as vehicles for the self-interest of tiny elites and their ethnic, religious or class allies.

What many Third World peoples lack – and, in many cases, fiercely desire – is both development[2] and democracy. Despite a great deal of expressed concern about development and the problems of the rural and urban poor, the position of the lower stratum is in many places steadily worsening (UNDP 1996: 1). 'Development' is often more rhetoric than reality and on present indications – with a concentration of economic power and a generally narrow base of the political system – there seems little chance of matters improving in the short term. Despite the spread of elections to Latin America, Africa and Asia in recent times, there is generally little discernible diminution in the power of the urban-based elite and its rural allies.

None the less, hundreds of thousands of ordinary people in the Third World – in both rural and urban areas and displaying different degrees of militancy – are attempting to articulate and pursue what they see as their interests through collective effort. While they are involved in a range of activities, economic development and the sociopolitical empowerment[3] of subordinate groups – the poor, the young, women, religious and ethnic minorities – are frequent aims. Despite great diversity, what such endeavours have in common is that they are often beyond the control of the state or institutionalized political parties. For the great majority (Islamist groups in the Middle East, discussed in chapter 7, are a notable exception) there is no primary focus on the capture of state power. In short, the growth of ordinary people's development and empowerment groups – which I will label 'action' groups, for reasons to be explained shortly is a popular Third World response to growing poverty and lack of power.

This book is concerned with an examination of what happens when ordinary people in the Third World band together in an attempt to deal with a range of material and existential problems. Are there any parallels in the political history of social and economic change in the West, or earlier, in the Third World? Are such movements and groups simply defensive reactions to rapid change, where the subordinate are especially damaged? Sometimes these movements take on apparently strange forms – the religions of the oppressed – and of course their forms and particulars may be unique, but are there fundamental deeper principles that we can recognize from comparable times elsewhere? What particular variations and features do the action groups demonstrate? Is this how civil society gets to be born? Are the Third World action groups discussed in this book contributing to the slow emergence of the democratic process? These hypotheses, provide an introduction to the chapters and cases which follow. In the book's conclusion I attempt to provide some answers.

By locating the struggles of subordinate people in the growth of civil societies, the aim is to understand better how the latter grow in significance in the contemporary Third World. Yet we must not overlook the fact that a range of institutionalized groups within civil society – such as trade unions, professional associations, student groups and religious bodies – may have different aspirations and goals from those of subordinate people's action groups. How action groups and their institutionalized counterparts interact – and with what results – is an important question which is unfortunately beyond the scope of this book.

But the fact that the point is a relevant one analytically is suggested by what is happening in India. India is a country with a huge number of action groups and a vibrant civil society, yet the former may well 'oppose an exploitative section within the [civil] society, whether conceived of as upper castes . . . urban-industrial sections or whatever' (Omvedt 1994: 40). The point is that while action groups' aims are not always identical with those of some of the institutional organizations, it does not mean that action groups are not contributing to the growth of a richer, denser civil society. At this point five questions need addressing:

1 Why use the term 'action' groups?
2 How many action groups are there?
3 Were are they to be found?
4 What is the organizational variety among action groups?
5 Why are the action groups politically significant?

Third World Action Groups

Why use the term 'action' groups?

There are a range of terms to refer to non-institutionalized socioeconomic and political bodies in the Third World, including grassroots, popular and local groups, associations and organizations. Having pondered over what to call the bodies examined in this book, I have settled on action group.[4] I am aware that this term is not without its problems and limitations, but it seems to me that these are fewer than with other possible forms of nomenclature. I rejected 'popular' groups because the adjective has a socioeconomic class connotation which I do not wish to imply. However, this is not to suggest that action groups are somehow 'classless'. In fact, they usually attract those lacking in power, especially the poor, women, young people, and ethnic and religious minorities.

Some action groups have links with foreign nongovernmental organizations – and outlooks which reflect this. Thus, the adjectives 'local' or 'grassroots', suggesting an orientation exclusively concerned with narrow, parochial issues, is often inappropriate. A process of elimination leads me to use the term 'action' group for the following reasons. First, the groups I focus on are characterized by a desire to achieve goals through their own activities and deeds – that is, by their own actions and activities – sometimes with the help of domestic or foreign allies. Second, members see themselves as part of a *group* because they are related in some palpable way – by poverty, gender, religious beliefs, ethnicity or whatever. Third, they often consciously link their personal struggles to the creation of a more democratic and just society – that is, they regard themselves, perhaps implicitly, as building blocks of civil society and democratic polities. Yet the term 'action' group cannot hope to convey a precise meaning because not all groups so labelled pursue identical goals involving the same kinds of people. On the contrary, they are in some respects very different, albeit concerned with how to increase development and/or empowerment for their members. The action groups examined in the chapters of this book are always 'channels for promoting economic and social development, [or] contributing to democratization of the economy, society and polity' (Uphoff 1993: 618).

There is a growing literature devoted to such groups – analysing them, prescribing what they should do to achieve their goals – and to many case studies (Camilleri and Falk 1992; Stiefel and Wolfe 1994). It is not possible here to provide a comprehensive insight into and review of this literature; the works cited in the bibliography nevertheless offer those who want them entry points.

To sum up: the argument is that many ordinary Third World peoples are mobilizing in pursuit of a range of developmental, social and political goals. The common background is generally grim economic performances and demands for democratic space, providing their raison d'être. Third World action groups, I believe, are at the cutting edge of a democratic revolution whose central themes are liberty, equality and autonomy. This is a major claim, one requiring justification – which I hope to provide in the chapters of the book – that action groups are at the forefront of efforts to democratize Third World societies.

How many action groups are there?

Many have noted that there is an 'organizational explosion' in many parts of the Third World, 'fueled ... by escalating demands from below' (Fisher 1993: 29). It is widely believed that the collective size of action groups' memberships has 'proliferated rapidly in recent years' (Ergas 1986: 323). Yet, their precise number is impossible to determine – no one has counted them. None the less, Durning (1989: 55) has plausibly calculated that there are hundreds of thousands of extant action groups at any one time, with an average collective membership of over 100 million people.

Where are the action groups?

Whereas, as we shall see in the chapters that follow, action groups are common in Latin America, sub-Saharan Africa and parts of Asia, two groups of countries have relatively few: the Asian communist states and the Middle Eastern Muslim nations. There are very few in China, Laos, North Korea and Vietnam because these are polities where the state has achieved a high degree of dominance over its citizens; as a result, social impetus for collective organization – outside of official institutional channels – is weak. Second, there are politically important Islamist groups in the Muslim countries of the Middle East, but few action groups of other kinds.[5] Why should this be? Apart from the fact that, like the Asian communist countries, strong states are common in the Middle East, Fisher argues that Quranic 'culture emphasizes the duty of the individual to assist Islamic charities, not the importance of organizing for social change' (1993: 25). Yet probably the most zealous advocates of sociopolitical change in the Middle East and North Africa are the Islamist organizations, especially Algeria's Islamic Salvation Front, the Muslim Brotherhood in Egypt and Hamas in Israel's Occupied Territories. The point is that such groups emerge because, where democracy is forbidden and civil society extremely embryonic, many Muslims – especially the young and alienated – consider that an Islamic state is the only way to achieve a satisfactory social and political arrangement.

Organizational variety among the action groups

Action groups proliferate by the thousand in Latin America, sub-Saharan Africa and South Asia. Not all are new, but since the early 1970s traditional development organizations have been augmented by new action groups stimulated by various factors, including declining macroeconomic conditions, environmental degradation, a lack of democracy or, especially in the case of women, status as second-class citizens.

There has also been international encouragement for action group formation. The concept of 'popular participation' entered the vocabulary of many development experts, endorsed in various United Nations declarations and resolutions, during the 1980s. This dovetailed with demands, enunciated by critics of the state on both the left and the right, for wide-ranging reforms of the state's activities. Leftist critics called for the empowerment of societal groups and organizations, and a reduction of the state's power (A. Scott 1990). Right-wingers, riding on the crest of the wave which produced the Reagan, Thatcher and Kohl governments, claimed that there was an objective need to move to what they called an 'enabling' state, that is, one which focused on maximum political and administrative decentralization, privatization of state-owned assets and the freeing of the 'market' from excessive bureaucratic meddling. In short, what many on the left and the right exhibited was a hostility to big, remote government, to overbureaucratization, and to the apparent inability of ordinary people to influence politics except – momentarily – by voting in periodic national elections once every four or five years (Held 1987, 1993; Beck 1994; Crook and Manor 1995).

It is not apparent to what extent such arguments reflected what was already happening or whether they helped to stimulate demands. What seems plausible is that both international and domestic factors encouraged action group formation in the Third World. A rich body of experience of subordinate people's mobilization has evolved in pursuit of three broad aims: alleviating poverty, achieving greater social justice, preserving the environment. Increasing poverty and inequality, landlessness and unemployment, coupled with a growing centralization of power, are a feature of many Third World countries – hence the demands for more democracy. There is a wide array of organizational forms among action groups. Whereas some are in embryonic, experimental stages, others have been around for one or two decades, or even longer, allowing them to develop into groups of significant proportions with clear objectives, programmes and organizational structures. Such mobilization may be large, medium or small in scale. Some of the resulting activities amount to movements involving considerable numbers of people over a wide geographical area. At the other end of the spectrum are grassroots experiments confined to a particular locality or a few villages. At this point in their development it would be premature to highlight sharp distinctions or give precise definitions: the position is rather fluid. In sum, there is a great deal of variety: some action groups are autonomous, community-level organizations; some operate at national level with links to government for technical and financial support; others interact with like-minded transnational bodies elsewhere in the world. In many cases, support from international sources promotes local organization (Fisher 1993: 29). Often strong organizational initiatives are based on partnerships between local people and technically trained professionals. All that can be stated with certainty is that, in the late 1990s, Third World action groups are mobilizing people for change; where it will lead to is not yet clear. I will return to this issue in the book's conclusion.

Why are the action groups politically significant?

One of the main reasons for action groups' formation is a defensive reaction to increasingly intolerable conditions. Responses involve a varied mix of activities, scales of operation, world-views and operational methodologies. But all the groups I examine in the chapters of this book have in common attempts to empower the poor and vulnerable in some way(s). Some start with protests against the existing social, economic or political system, others start with small development activities. In short, what the action groups examined in this book share is that

1 They are nearly always defensive in orientation;
2 The great majority are concerned with strategies for the long-term defence of sources of livelihood or enhancing the sociopolitical position of subordinate groups;
3 Most are in the short term unable to attain their goals, often because powerful interest groups prevent them.

But why is this important for politics in the Third World? Part of the reason for the contemporary growth of action groups is simply that for many ordinary people in the Third World material conditions are getting worse and governments appear to be able to do little to improve the situation. Under such circumstances it makes sense for ordinary people to organize themselves to try to improve things. The growing polarization of income distribution in many Third World societies is reflected in an array of statistics: 1 per cent of the world's people controls 60 per cent of its resources; 80 per cent of human beings struggle for 15 per cent of its resources (Vidal 1996). While a handful of Third World countries has seen a 'dramatic surge in economic growth' since 1980, dozens more have been hard hit by economic decline, reducing the incomes of over 1.5 billion people (UNDP 1996: 1). Half the world's rural poor – more than a billion people, heavily concentrated in the Third World – have insufficient land to provide for themselves (Harrison 1993: 317). Then there is increasing environmental degradation and destruction, forcing the poorest to compete for declining resources. Put together, these developments amount to the emergence of a new global dispossessed class. This hints at the political importance of some action groups: they challenge the status quo, sometimes force-fully, consistently and with real determination.

Demands for democracy have also encouraged action group forma-tion. Gurr (1993: 184) argues that mobilization for protest was higher in the Third World in the 1980s than in earlier decades. Why should this be? Part of the answer may be that the political climate produced by demands for democracy helps provide the 'space' for action groups openly to organize, mobilize and demand change. Yet, as I shall argue in chapter 4, the inauguration of what I call 'formal' democracies – involving regular elections yet with power remaining in more or less the same hands – helps to stimulate the formation of action groups, especially among groups (for example, indigenous peoples in Latin America or women nearly everywhere) who perceive that they do not benefit from such a form of democracy.

While some subordinate groups may feel they do not gain much from formal democracy, it is the very opening up of the political agenda that may help to stimulate action groups to organize, mobilize and act. The point is that once a regime allows increasing questioning of the status quo – following a promise to democratize – it may find that it is very difficult to keep the bounds of political debate within narrow parameters. What tends to happen instead is that powerless groups take the opportunity to widen the political debate into areas of their own choosing.

This is not to imply that all action groups are politically strident or that they are necessarily a simple, effective developmental panacea. Often they face crises of survival, of growth, of identity. How does a small group survive the onslaughts of the local vested interests or the state? Where does one make links and forge alliances? There are dan-gers of localism: a group may lose its ability to stay out of local factional fights, ceasing to have the wider perspective that impelled it to under-take activity in the first place; small is not necessarily beautiful in this context. As Sethi (1993: 237) describes, attempts to combat the problems of excessive localism commonly take one of three forms:

1 *To join with a major political party* The advantages are that this offers allies one can count on: it may become easier to resist repression as a part of a larger, institutionalized group. On the downside, how-ever, incorporation by a political party – as happened to many wom-en's groups in Latin America following redemocratization in the 1980s – often means that the action group and its activity lose whatever distinctive character they had in the first place.

2 *To remain autonomous but have a working relationship with one or a number of political parties* The main problem here is that the two sides

are of unequal strength: the party may swallow up the action group. As most action groups have a popular base but no electoral ambitions, larger parties are often interested in forming alliances with them during elections – but only then. And after the election? It is likely that the action group would be ignored until the next time.

3 *To try to form an autonomous federation with other non-party action groups* This move has succeeded to a certain extent at regional level (in India) when the ideology and objectives of the groups have been similar enough to give them a joint stake in cooperation. But even then such federations often work only to attain or attempt to attain a specific objective, and only for a limited period.

Yet because their concerns may radically affect the status quo and hence the interests of incumbent elites, action groups may find that none of the conventional political parties will be willing to endorse their demands. They have three choices if this happens: to downgrade their demands and follow one of the parties; to set up their own party; to pursue change through their own efforts. To follow the first option will almost inevitably lead to the pursuit of a different political agenda than the one they wish to pursue. To pursue the second option may well be fruitless because it will very often prove to be impossible to appeal to a wide enough cross-section of society to translate group concerns into votes. Thus the third may be the only reasonable option.

Popular demands in the Third World are often funnelled through conventional political parties or nationalist/separatist movements. Yet more spontaneous outbursts are also now common. For example, during the early 1990s there was the uprising of the Ogonis in oil-rich Nigeria, the Zapatista rebellion in southern Mexico and the civil war launched by the Islamic Salvation Front in Algeria when it was denied electoral victory by a military coup d'état. Then there are the continuing protests by Indians in the Brazilian rain-forest and campaigns in India to protect trees and to protest against huge dams. Food riots in Haiti, Central America and the Philippines in the 1990s add to a picture reflecting a global development model which, some consider, ruthlessly pursues profits and ignores people (Harriet Lamb of the World Development Movement, quoted in Vidal 1996).

From these examples it would seem that the 1990s are characterized by something new: the tendency is to reject power imposed without consultation or responsibility and to demand a fair share of resources for all. The differences between the Zapatista rebels of Chiapas, demanding both development and democracy, the angry young men of Papeete, Tahiti, burning their own capital in response to the French decision to resume nuclear testing at Mururoa Atoll in 1995, the Islamists in Algeria, expressing their alienation from the political process by launching a civil war killing around 60,000 people, and the domestic and international outcries at the hangings of nine Ogoni activists in late 1995 are not as large as distance, and professed political objectives, might at first suggest.

What links such anti-system outbursts are three main characteristics. First, there is a feeling of alienation from rulers, with responses that are both diverse and politically ambivalent. This is especially apparent among young people: throughout the Third World there is a generation of often illiterate young people who lack role models, who are without hope or real contact with the traditions of their societies, and who are unlikely to nurture a sense of participation, discipline and principles. Many Third World countries – for example, Algeria and the Gaza Strip, where Islamist groups are strong – have populations with 60 per cent of people under the age of 16 years (Heikal 1995). Political leaders often completely fail to address this constituency; very few even appear to appreciate its importance. It is scarcely surprising that the young see a recourse to a variety of solutions to deal with their existential dilemmas. Students in higher and further education – in the past, elites-in-waiting, but now finishing their studies to find no jobs – rebel against the elders, taking to the streets (Bennett 1992; Castaneda 1993: 225). Political rigidities and forced conformism often generate in young people a powerful sense of resentment against the social barriers which prevent them from gaining both status and employment. Frustrations and exclusions produced from domestic circumstances combine with the global cultural currents influencing youth, leading them to reject the conventions of their parents and of older people generally. As a result, many young, disaffected people, on the one hand, join action groups with a variety of social and political aims while, on the other, some seek solutions in crime, drink, drugs or violence (Stiefel and Wolfe 1994: 173).

Second, there is a widespread refusal to accept the decisions of ruling groups, whether democratically elected or not, because they are frequently perceived to be out of touch with the feelings and aspirations of ordinary people for whom democracy is *supposed* to lead to enhanced representation and societal influence.

Social and economic difficulties are at the root of the political action groups' raison d'être, problems which are especially severe in many of the fast-growing cities of the Third World. In a rapidly urbanizing world, the cost of fuel, shelter, food and water is escalating as the environmental conditions in cities – the so-called 'brown agenda' of pollution, sanitation and inadequate water supplies – grow worse.

Two-thirds of Africa's urban population – and a slightly smaller proportion in Latin America and Asia – are under the age of 25 years. Yet,
as the process of urban decay accelerates, authorities are proving unable to meet the expectations of the young. The latter seem to be quick
to denounce the abuses of the state, yet uncertain that the ballot box –
if available – will change things for the better. Such people are the
natural followers of action groups, especially the highly political Islamist groups.

In sum, the political significance of the action groups stems from (1)
the varied responses to a lack of development and empowerment; (2)
demands to reduce the state's influence; (3) the effects of economic
decline, and (4) the spread of demands for 'real', what I call 'substantive', democracy. Thus the overall political significance of the action
groups is that collectively they challenge the postcolonial Third World
status quo usually dominated by a small urban–rural elite coalition.

'Politics' in the Third World is about competition or collaboration
among politically and economically powerful elites. Whether regimes
are characterized as leftist or rightist authoritarian or as oligarchic
democracies, power monopolies at the apex traditionally form the political superstructure in virtually all Third World countries. Organski
(1965) described this power monopoly as a 'syncratic' alliance – that is,
one that pulls together a variety of urban-located and rural-domiciled
individuals to defend a shared class position. The resulting alliance
unites traditional agrarian interests too strong to be destroyed with
those of a modernizing industrial elite. In exchange for obtaining the
political support of agrarian interests, powerful urban sectors agree not
to disturb the often semifeudal conditions of the countryside. The
consequence is that class structures in many Third World countries
remain largely traditional, with the impact of industrialization being in
the main accommodated to traditional patterns of dominance and subordination. In Latin America and parts of Asia, large landowners represent the rural side of the coalition. For example, a succession of
democratically elected Indian governments, despite socialist rhetoric,
failed to break with powerful rural elites. The latter managed to use
their continued social standing to 'pursue the democratic route to
power as a very successful alternative' to their former position of
inherited predominance (Calvert and Calvert 1996: 111). In short, while
the bases of power of countries in the Third World differ, a coalition of
urban and rural elites often control both the basis of economic wealth
and the direction of political development.

My main thesis is that the action groups discussed in this book
should be perceived as a new stimulus to the growth of Third World

civil societies. The central thrust is, first, that in all the spheres I deal with there is increasing disaffection and dissatisfaction with states' developmental abilities, and second, that action groups are a function and expression of this. In short, generally grim economic performances and opening democratic space provide the basis for action groups in the Third World.

Action Groups and Civil Society

While action groups are of only relatively recent importance in many Third World countries, there have been various attempts to assess their significance, with differing points of emphasis. Some see them as examples of a wider global trend towards 'new social movements', some as the progenitors of a transition to socialism, and others as contributors to the emergence of civil society.

Action groups as new social movements

Numerous studies began to appear in the 1980s concerned principally – but not exclusively – with Western 'new social movements' (NSMs), especially in the areas of feminism, 'green' issues and peace (Cohen 1985; Touraine 1985; Melucci 1985; Wignaraja 1993b). Touraine defines NSMs as

> culturally oriented actors involved in social conflict, whose goals and strategies have a social coherence and rationality of their own. [Their functions] cannot be understood within the logic of the existing institutional order, since their overriding function is precisely to challenge that logic and transform the social relations which it mirrors and reinforces. (1985: 749)

To Touraine, it seems that a 'new social movement' is about three main things. They are (1) *new*, qualitatively different from *old* social movements, such as labour and peasant organizations, which were primarily concerned with economic and sociopolitical justice, (2) concerned with *social* issues, and (3) individual groups but forming elements of larger *movements*. Auda claims that NSMs *always* challenge the status quo – they are anti-system, articulating and aggregating demands for change of the social, political and/or economic order (1993: 404). Thus NSMs seek to achieve a high degree of change, infused with and derived from perceptions of what is right and wrong in society. Escobar and Alvarez claim that the chief characteristic of NSMs is that they *contest* the political ground with the state: they do not develop 'in isolation from other social and political actors' but are 'organised collective actors who engage in sustained political or cultural contestation through recourse to institutional and extrainstitutional forms of action' (1992b: 320).

The theme of challenging the status quo is also emphasized by Cohen (1985). According to her, NSMs attempt to construct new social identities, to create democratic spaces for autonomous social action and to reinterpret norms and reshape institutions. NSMs should be regarded, she believes, as reactions to the cultural, technological and institutional manifestations of modernization seeking to dominate sociopolitical vistas in most parts of the world.

In short, from the perspectives of Auda, Cohen, Escobar and Alvarez, and Touraine, new social movements seek to mobilize sections and groups oppressed or exploited in 'new' or different ways, especially by the 'processes of modern capitalism' (Omvedt 1994: 38). For them, NSMs emerge as primarily 'single issue' movements, although many may well hope that resolving a single issue, for example, the poor societal position of women, will lead to progressive trends in society more generally.

The action groups I examine in this book are different from the types of NSMs discussed by Auda and the others in a number of ways. First, while many of the groups examined in this book do wish to change the status quo, not all do. For example, the development-oriented groups discussed in chapter 3 do not have overtly political or social goals. While some – for example, the Islamist groups examined in chapter 7 – have clear agendas of *system* change, others do not. Second, not all of them are *new*; many are, but some – including a variety of development groups and Islamist groups – have been around for two decades or more. What they have in common, however, is that there are recent catalysts for their growth, especially macroeconomic decline and a global move towards democracy. Third, few of the groups examined are part of regional, national or transnational *movements*, whereas many Western NSMs are. Instead, most of the groups I focus on are relatively autonomous, grassroots-level groups, often loosely coordinated within a national umbrella organization. At the same time, many will be content to accept foreign assistance in pursuit of their goals. In sum, the action groups I discuss are not synonymous with the NSMs discussed by these authors. They need to be seen as something qualitatively different.

Action groups and the 'transition to socialism'

But how should they be understood? An influential article by Fuentes and Gunder Frank seeks to analyse the recent growth of action groups in the Third World. Using a very inclusive definition that includes practically any movement that is not a traditional class or national/ separatist organization, they define such groups as 'grassroots (locally-based), transitional to socialism (in the sense of being efforts to delink from capitalism), [and] anti-political, in the sense of not seeking to achieve power at the institutional level, but broadly democratic movements' (1989: 179). In addition, they believe that they are 'cyclical': not really 'new', but actually 'older' than historically recent working-class movements. In short, for Fuentes and Gunder Frank, they are age-old instruments and expressions of people's struggle against exploitation and oppression and for survival and identity, attempts at, and instruments of, democratic self-empowerment.

While having merit in the way that they seek to generate broad theoretical insights to cover a myriad of movements over space and time, their analysis falls down in several ways. First, many action groups *are* political, if we understand the term in a broader sense than merely a concern with *institutional* politics. Second, there is no evidence at all that many groups wish to build socialism. Third, many of the groups are new, having been established over the last 20 years or so – especially those concerned with environmental protection and the societal position of women. There is simply no evidence that such concerns were of social or political concern historically in the vast majority of Third World countries. For these reasons, we can reject Fuentes and Gunder Frank's account.

Action groups and civil society

A better way of perceiving Third World action groups is to see them as constituent elements in emerging civil societies. In my view, this is where their real significance lies – that is, wittingly or unwittingly, Third World action groups, by seeking to protect, protest and promote members' interests, are contributing to the slow emergence of the democratic process by strengthening and enlarging civil society.

As already noted, movements for change have arisen in many Third World countries in recent times. Pressure from civil societies has frequently forced governments to announce programmes of democracy, to articulate political reform agendas, and to plan and preside over multiparty elections, monitored for fairness by teams of international observers. Not at all clear, however, is the ultimate depth, breadth and direction of these incipient movements for political reform. Multiparty elections do not by themselves produce or sustain democracy. They do not thereby institutionalize broad participation in political life. Nor do democracy and parallel transitions from state-dominated to market-driven economies – often via structural adjustment programmes – always peacefully coexist.

This is where civil society comes in – to protect the interests of citizens vis-à-vis the state, especially during times of transition. The term 'civil society' has crept quietly and largely unexamined into the literature on political economy in the Third World over the last decade. To some extent it has also seeped into the discourse of leaders of movements for political reform in many countries. The idea of civil society, of course, has been of central importance in much of the literature of Western political philosophy since the emergence of the modern nation-state in the eighteenth century. It has reappeared at a point in history when the capabilities of existing states to satisfy even minimally the political and economic aspirations of nationalities and ethnic communities is increasingly in question.

While there are many extant conceptions of civil society and its relationship with the state, I shall employ one which understands civil society as encompassing the collectivities of non-state organizations, interest groups and associations – such as trade unions, professional associations, further and higher education students, religious bodies, and the media – which collectively help maintain a check on the power and totalizing tendency of the state. I follow Stepan (1988) in this regard. He defines civil society as that arena where numerous social movements (including community associations, women's groups, religious bodies, and intellectual currents) and civic organizations (of lawyers, journalists, trade unions, entrepreneurs and so on) strive to constitute themselves into an ensemble of arrangements to express themselves and advance their interests. Thus civil society aims to balance the state's tendency to seek ever greater amounts of power, by achieving a measure of power in its own right. Civil society, in short, functions as the citizen's curb on the power of the state.

Civil society is linked to, but separate from, political society. The former comprises civil institutions not directly involved in the business of government or in overt political management. They are not political parties either. Yet this does not prevent civil society from exercising profound political influence, on matters ranging from single issues to national constitutions. By political society is meant 'that arena in which the polity specifically arranges itself for political contestation to gain control over public power and the state apparatus' (Stepan 1988: 3). At best, civil society can destroy an authoritarian regime – witness the events in Eastern Europe in the late 1980s. However, a full democratic transition of necessity concerns political society. This is because the make-up and consolidation of a democratic polity entails a great deal of serious thought and action about its core institutions – that is, political parties, elections, electoral rules, political leadership, intraparty alliances and legislatures. It is through these establishments that civil society can constitute itself politically to select and monitor democratic government.

Civil society is embedded in the conception of free associations of individuals, independent of the state, self-organizing in an array of autonomous and politically significant activities. Sturdy civil societies nearly always stem from strong societies. For Risse-Kappen (1995: 22), ' "strong societies" are characterized by a comparative lack of ideological and class cleavages, by rather "politicized" civil societies which can be easily mobilized for political causes, and by centralized social organizations such as business, labor or churches.' Thus civil society and the state should – ideally – form mutually effective counterweights. The former should be a stalwart defender of society against state dominance, comprising organizations which both limit *and* legitimate state power. In other words, the institutions and supporting bodies which make up civil society will ideally be strong enough to keep the state within substantive and procedural confinement.

This conception of civil society is de facto a description of civil societies in Western democracies. Third World civil societies, on the other hand, are often rather ineffectual counterbalances to the power of the state, not up to the job of controlling it, because they are often weak and fragmented. This problem is pronounced in Africa. As Robert McNamara, a former president of the World Bank, puts it, 'Africa faces problems of governance which are ... far more severe than those of other regions,' despite extensive movement in the region towards more democratic forms of government (Harsch 1996: 24). In particular, popular participation, transparency in government operations and accountability are all inadequate. Villalón (1995: 24) argues that the failure or inability 'of social groups [in Africa] to organize in such a way as to defend and promote their interests has often crippled their ability to counter the state's hegemonic drives'. The accuracy of such an assessment is demonstrated, I believe, when we bear in mind how very few African civil societies were able to prevent long periods of authoriarian rule in the 1960s and 1970s.

Civil societies want democracy in order to turf out unsatisfactory governments. Bromley (1994: 166) notes, however, that in the Middle East this is problematic: 'assuming the persistence of a powerful state apparatus, the weakness of and divisions within civil society seem likely to be a major problem in the future process of democratization.' Said (1996) asks rhetorically why 'real' – that is, effective – civil societies are lacking in Arab societies. He claims that civil society is frail in the Middle East for reasons similar to those in Africa: widespread societal and religious divisions, coupled with a low level of industrialization, serve to dissipate the ability to confront the power of often strong, nearly always centralized, states. Governments in the Middle East – and in Africa – are often adept at buying off or crushing dissent if it does appear.

This is not to argue that all Third World regions have civil societies as weak as those in Africa and the Middle East. In fact, three broad categories suggest themselves. In general, Third World civil societies are weak and insubstantial in Africa and the Middle East; of only embryonic importance in Asia – although India is a notable exception; and stronger, yet often dominated by powerful institutionalized interest groups – trade unions, professional organizations, and the Catholic Church – in Latin America.

Why are there varying degrees of effectiveness of civil society across the Third World? Broadly, the effectiveness of civil society is dependent on (1) its cohesiveness, (2) a country's level of economic development, (3) the length of time a country has been independent, and (4) the extent of ethnic or religious schisms in the society. Civil society had much longer to develop in Latin America – independent since the early nineteenth century – than elsewhere in the Third World. In addition, Latin American countries are less fragmented by ethnic and religious schisms than other Third World regions, while for the most part its countries are relatively industrialized and urbanized (Remmer 1993; World Bank 1995: 166–7, table 3; UNDP 1996: 176–7, table 20). This helps explain the strong growth of politically active working classes and well-organized trade unions in the region. Such growth was evident from the 1950s and 1960s as increasing industrialization and urbanization, coupled with swift population growth, combined to generate strong popular pressures for increased social spending and greater mass political participation. The result, however, was not – in the short term – more democracy but the reverse: between 1964 and

1976 democratic regimes in a number of countries, including Brazil, Peru, Uruguay, Chile and Argentina, fell to military coups.

The resulting bureaucratic authoritarian governments guaranteed and organized the political and economic domination of a small, exclusivist group whose chief loyalty was to itself rather than to the nation (O'Donnell 1979). This oligarchy managed to exclude the mass of people from political decision-making by banning elections and by directing state spending to build up infrastructure attractive to foreign capital and the military. There was a distinct separation between state and civil society during the bureaucratic authoritarian era (Philip 1993).

During the 1960s and 1970s, developmental imperatives focused on the utilization of capital to fuel industrialization. This ran contrary to the perceived interests of sectors of the vocal urban working and lower-middle classes who instead demanded increased spending on welfare-oriented projects. The military and its state allies believed, however, that the way out of a growing economic crisis was for a small elite to retain power, to exclude popular sectors from pressurizing policy-makers via democracy. The governing coalition comprised large-scale landowners and capitalists and the military, that is, the sectors of society who felt threatened by popular demands. In the late 1970s and early 1980s, however, Latin America's economic fortunes declined in the wake of growing foreign indebtedness. A series of political and economic crises threatened the position of the ruling elites. Moves towards democracy were spearheaded by a bottom-up process rooted in civil society and by international pressure led by the United States government. By the late 1980s all Latin America's countries were democratic.

As elsewhere, the state in Asia is characterized by a pursuit of a central role vis-à-vis both society and the international environment. Distinctive social, cultural, ethnic, linguistic and religious mixes in Asia have produced a variety of post-colonial states and an assortment of civil societies, from 'weak' ones (for example, in the Philippines) to 'strong' ones (for example in India). The variety in this regard is largely a consequence of (1) comparative levels of industrialization and economic development, and (2) the importance of specialized interest groups, a consequence of modernization.

In sum, differences in the strength of civil society in the Third World are due to a number of factors. First, when society is divided by ethnicity and religion, then civil society's putative impact will normally – but not always, India is a notable exception – be dissipated. Second, representative organizations in civil society – the media, trade unions, professional associations, religious bodies and so on – may not be autonomous in relation to the state (Bromley 1994; Monga 1995; Sylvester 1995). When the institutions of civil society are collectively weak it is usually easy for the state to incarcerate, coopt or buy off troublesome opponents. The result is that the state is often able to 'shape, define, create or suppress civil society and popular reactions hereto' (Manor 1991: 5). In other words, the state is frequently able to ensure that civil society remains pliable and under its control. Or so it was thought until recently.

Civil society and democracy in the Third World

Beginning in the 1970s in southern Europe, a wave of democracy swept through the Third World. No region was immune. Buoyed by redemocratization in Greece, Spain and Portugal, Third World democrats began to question the legitimacy of non-democratic governments. The end of dictatorial governments in Latin America came a decade later. At the end of the 1980s democracy was given a further fillip by the demise of communist governments in Eastern Europe. The number of democratic countries rose from 44 in 1974 to 107 in 1994 (Shin 1994: 136). As there are now about 190 countries this means that about 56 per cent are democracies.

In 1996 all 23 Latin American countries were democratic. In Asia, seven formerly non-democratic regimes – Pakistan, Bangladesh, Nepal, the Philippines, Taiwan, South Korea, Mongolia – had recently democratized. In Africa there are clear signs of moves towards greater democratization: of the continent's over 50 countries, more than half held democratic elections between the late 1980s and the mid-1990s. Only the Middle East seems to be apart from the democracy trend, although there were some encouraging signs, especially the recent reintroduction of democracy in Lebanon after two decades of civil war and deepening democratization in Jordan.

In seeking to explain and account for this wave of democracy, explosions of 'people power' – from Eastern Europe to Africa and Asia – cannot be ignored. Following mass demonstrations, sometimes involving millions of people, apparently stable governments collapsed, sometimes literally overnight. Clearly, popular pressure – coupled with international persuasion – led to the recent wave of democratization in the Third World. It was not merely pressure from the institutions of civil society, but also from millions of ordinary people, toppling authoritarian regimes.

If multiparty elections are one facet in the evolution of a more receptive state and a more powerful civil society, ordinary people's organizations for socioeconomic and political change – that is, action groups – are another. Such organizations amount to the ordinary person's attempt to ameliorate their life chances in the face of a state system which seems to many to be unable to deal with their socioeconomic needs and demands, even if it is formally democratic. The evidence I present in this book suggests that action groups are important components of emerging civil societies in the Third World. The general ramifications of this for politics in the Third World will be examined in the book's overall conclusion.

The Book's Structure

The purpose of chapter 2 is to describe the various categories of action groups that I examine – and illustrate with case studies – in the chapters of the book. It is my intention to answer the following questions: What do they do? Who is doing it? What do they hope to achieve? To what extent do they contribute to the growth of civil society and democracy? In the second chapter I present a taxonomy – that is, a system of categorization – according to the locus of action groups and their various concerns: economic development; democratic reform; environmental protection; increases in women's status; and the Islamic state.

Chapter 3 investigates the impact of recent macroeconomic weakness and decline on action group formation. It examines the impact of structural adjustment programmes, arguing that such economic reforms were not in themselves often a progenitor of action groups. I focus on Ghana's state-supported 31 December Women's Movement as one of the few major development-oriented groups which grew as a direct result of the consequences of structural adjustment. The point, however, is that the state in Ghana was able to pass some of its developmental responsibilities to a collectivity of women's action groups which had no political ambitions in the sense of wishing to change the distribution of power in society.

Many development-oriented action groups – especially in Africa – have arisen in response to declining environmental conditions. Others, especially in Latin America, emerge because of poor material conditions in the burgeoning shanty towns – many lacking basic services. Yet macroeconomic decline was not caused by structural adjustment *per se*.

As a recent definitive analysis of structural adjustment puts it, 'living standards have evidently fallen in many developing countries, including those which have undergone structural adjustment' (Mosley et al. 1991b: 302). The point is that declining living standards were one of the main impulses for many action groups to emerge – but they cannot be taken in isolation.

Structural adjustment came simultaneously with democratization in many Third World countries. Chapter 4 seeks to explain the reasons for the spread of formally democratic systems to much of the Third World over the last 20 years, by reference to a combination of international and domestic factors. Second, it explains that two forms of democracy are common in the Third World: 'formal' and 'facade' democracy. The former allows regular, often relatively 'free and fair' elections; the latter incorporates periodic elections, but they are not competitive. However, what both have in common is that subordinate groups cannot achieve empowerment *whatever* the election result; power nearly always stays in the hands of a broad elite class. A third type of democracy – I call it 'substantive' democracy – would facilitate the empowerment of the subordinate. Yet nowhere in the Third World, I maintain, is such a system in operation. As a result, those at the bottom of the social and economic pile – such as indigenous peoples in Latin America – seek other ways of achieving empowerment, illustrated by case studies of, first, the Zapatista rebellion in Chiapas state, Mexico, and second, the fight of Brazil's Indians to place their concerns on the national political agenda.

In chapters 5–7 I turn to explanations for and examples of action groups primarily concerned with (1) environmental protection, (2) the socioeconomic position of poor women, and (3) the creation of an Islamic state and society. I discuss the action groups not only in terms of their origins, membership, activities, successes and failures but also in relation to how they contribute to the growth of civil society. In short, the aim is to describe what they look like, how they work, what they do. Yet, comprehensiveness *per se* is not the purpose; rather, I hope to offer a representative range of examples to demonstrate that there are common threads and themes to the case studies, even when they seem to be addressing quite different problems in different fields. Such a broad framework seems necessary given the pervasiveness and interdependence of the issues involved. In short, I aim to show that the concerns of many action groups are connected in a variety of ways and that successful approaches in one area are often of great relevance to another. In the conclusion, chapter 8, I discuss the general arguments and comparative implications of the material presented in the earlier chapters, and also outline a few suggested areas for further research, predictions as to the future for action groups in the Third World and, finally, implications for our wider understanding of political change.

2
Action Groups in Regional Focus

Because there are so many Third World action groups, I will only attempt to separate them into two broad categories. The first is concerned principally with development – that is, aiming for increases in members' 'quality of life' – while the second seeks a range of sociopolitical goals. Since development action groups are fundamentally involved in seeking to improve the economic position of their members, the critical question for them is not how to redistribute economic resources for greater equality more generally; their concerns are apolitical because they do not wish to change the distribution of power in society.

In contrast, sociopolitical action groups seek, *inter alia*, to contribute to the growth of a heightened sensitivity and debate among members, drawing conventionally apolitical citizens into expressing and fighting for the right to further their social and political interests. In other words, they offer an opportunity for those lacking in power to take their life chances into their own hands, that is, to have a voice in the *arrangement* of society. From the vantage point of traditional power holders this will be unwelcome because, if successful, it will result in a reduction of their power. Sociopolitical action groups tend to have success in democratic – or democratizing – societies because they have the 'space' to pursue their goals, space lacking in closed – that is, authoritarian – systems.

However, not all the types of action groups examined in this and following chapters fall neatly into either 'development' or 'sociopolitical' categories. Groups with, for example, environmental or gender-oriented goals may well have both developmental and sociopolitical agendas. Some women's groups, especially in Latin America, aim overtly to improve societal perceptions of females as well as to increase their material – that is, developmental – position. Many others, however, are 'merely' concerned to increase women's developmental and economic position. Groups of this kind are common in sub-Saharan Africa. There is a similar division in the realm of the environment protection groups. Some – such as the Ogoni people's organization in Nigeria and anti-nuclear protesters in Tahiti – clearly regard environmental issues as part and parcel of a wider agenda of sociopolitical change. Others – such as India's Chipko movement – appear to perceive environmental protection as integral to advancing members' developmental positions, but without an overtly sociopolitical thrust. The point is that there is a variety of positions identifiable among the categories of action groups that I describe and assess in this book. A broad separation into 'development' and 'sociopolitical' categories will, I hope, aid the analysis; the price is that such an analytical framework necessarily oversimplifies.

In this chapter I present the range of action groups to be examined. I analyse them by their regional spread, and by how important they are in each region. Table 2.1 presents a taxonomy according to their objectives; perception of the role of state in development; role in the political process; members' social profile; tactics employed to achieve goals; and regional location.

Development Action Groups

Sub-Saharan Africa

Numbers of development action groups have grown swiftly in the region below the Saharan desert in recent times, a consequence of drought and deepening poverty. At the same time, trust in the ability of the state to improve things may have diminished. There is a contrast in this respect between, on the one hand, sub-Saharan Africa and, on the other, Latin America and South Asia. In the latter regions the powerless tend to establish cohesive cooperatives and self-help groups on the basis of opposition from distant, powerful aggregations, such as landlords and the state. In sub-Saharan Africa, by contrast, development action groups are usually apolitical (Hamer 1984: 278).

Analyses of politics in sub-Saharan Africa are often informed by an understanding of a more or less fundamental division between state and society in many countries. Civil societies are generally weak and

Table 2.1 Action groups in the Third World

	Development groups	Representation groups	Environmental protection groups	Women's empowerment groups	Islamist groups
Objective	More development	To achieve greater political voice for indigenous peoples	Protect local environment – land, water, air – from outside interests	To seek enhanced social, economic and political status	Islamic state and society
Organizational levels	Local, national and transnational	Local and national	Local, national and transnational	Local and national	Local and national
Perceptions of government	As not doing enough to facilitate development	As not doing enough to help indigenous peoples	Seen as being in cahoots with big business to take away or degrade local people's land	As dominated by men not concerned with women's interests	As secularising society and politics
Role in political process	Variable – dependent on a range of factors including regional location	Aiming to be central	Variable	Often marginal	Often central

Membership profile	Poor, especially women	Indigenous peoples	Those affected by environmental degradation or loss of land	Women of various social classes – especially the poor	The young, jobless and alienated
Tactics to achieve goals	Self-help; seeking outside assistance	Lobbying and campaigning	Direct action, lobbying and campaigning	Direct action, lobbying and campaigning	Variable: from ballot box to terrorism
Where found					
Many	Latin America, Sub-Saharan Africa, South Asia	Latin America	Latin America, South Asia	Latin America, India	Middle East
Some	South-East Asia	South-East Asia, Sub-Saharan Africa	Sub-Saharan Africa, South-East Asia	Sub-Saharan Africa	Sub-Saharan Africa
Few	Middle East, Asian communist countries	Middle East, Asian communist countries	Middle East, Asian communist countries	Middle East, Asian communist countries	Non-Muslim countries

inchoate. None the less, states usually fail to attain a comprehensive penetration of society. It is the state's inability to penetrate society fully which demonstrates what has been called its weakness or 'softness' in Africa. Many African citizens, it is argued, are disaffected and disillusioned by the falsity of developmental promises and by the arbitrariness of modes of rule. They take their 'revenge', in Bayart's (1993) terminology, on the state in a number of ways. Distrust of the state extends, in many cases, to suspicion regarding the desirability or usefulness of political institutions *per se*. As a result, independent political parties, when they exist, are frequently shunned or ignored; tax collection is evaded; state-run development programmes are ridiculed. This is not to claim that most ordinary Africans do not seek to *use* the state and its resources when opportunity presents itself; it is merely to note that the African state, for the most part, functions without the support and trust of a significant proportion of its citizens. At the same time, when state aid is forthcoming African development groups will often welcome it.

Because deepening poverty is a powerful stimulus for action groups in the Third World, it is unsurprising that development-oriented action groups are common in sub-Saharan Africa, the world's poorest region (Pradervand 1989; Fisher 1993). Collectively, they are probably the most significant driving force behind development in many parts of sub-Saharan Africa, largely because most states have been unable to fulfil development obligations. Development action groups in sub-Saharan Africa tend to be either (1) autonomous and village-level; (2) structured by the state into national development networks, for example, in Kenya, Tanzania and Ghana; or (3) transnational in scope. While the first two categories are common, few groups have managed to establish durable transnational networks. One that did – West Africa's Six-S movement (Se Servir de la Saison Sèche en Savane et du Sahel: the Association for Self-Help during the Dry Season in the Savannahs and the Sahel) – became defunct in 1995 after 20 years. Until then, Six-S was widely perceived as a rare example of a large movement: it involved about 12,000 groups, with a membership of around 400,000, located in nine West African countries. Why it failed will be discussed below.

Local-level development groups   There are two main forms of local development bodies in Africa: village-level groups formed to combat the effects of drought and environmental degradation; and credit unions, that is, groups which collect small regular sums from members for disbursement of small loans to the latter. Both kinds are traditional features of rural African society. Sub-Saharan Africa has a long tradition of cooperatives and self-help groups, based on effective, local organization, aimed at improving living standards (Hailey 1957: 14–54). Some are voluntary, others are compulsory cooperatives. Both types, according to Winans and Haugerud (1977), possess similar local orientations, requiring a certain amount of local initiative, resources, leadership and indigenous legitimizing principles.

Periodic drought is one of the most important progenitors of development action groups in West and East Africa. Pradervand (1988: 7) discusses the village of Zom in Senegal, almost devoid of cultivable soil in the early 1980s, the result of drought and soil erosion. Through self-help, the village development organization managed to add 30 centimetres of top soil to village land in three years, enabling it to plant and harvest sufficient rice to feed the local community. Another Sahelian village, Tintam in Mali, was first devastated by drought in 1984; two years later a plague of locusts arrived, stripping the vegetation from the village land. All the local fruit trees died. Without solidarity and the will to organize to turn things around, it is difficult to imagine how the local community would have dealt with the double catastrophe. The leader of the village assembly put it like this: 'We are not discouraged. So long as there rests in us any energy, and that God has given us intelligence, we believe we can overcome our difficulties' (Fisher 1993: 29–30).

Many of the countries of East Africa are also afflicted with periodic shortages of rainfall. Unlike West Africa, pastoralist societies are common in the region. Socially, they are often strongly non-hierarchical, based on communal pasture ownership. During periods of climatic emergency, local pastoral units traditionally join together into groups of perhaps several hundred people. Water storage areas are created, grass is burnt to promote fresh growth and collective searches are made for food, such as edible roots and various animals (Dyson-Hudson 1985).

Another common form of development group in sub-Saharan Africa is the credit union. From small beginnings in the 1960s, by the late 1980s there were more than three million members of more than 12,000 credit unions (Dichter and Zesch 1989: 4). They are nearly always independent of the state, with an average membership of around 250, predominantly poor people. Over 70 per cent of all loans granted by credit unions to members go for purposes of development, as opposed to consumption; 80 per cent of development loans are spent in rural areas (1989: 2–3).

In sum, the macroeconomic developmental impact of credit unions has been considerable: credit union members had deposited over $500 million in their accounts by the late 1980s. Credit union movements have been particularly successful in certain countries, including Kenya, where over three-quarters of a million members of credit unions had deposits in excess of $120 million in the mid-1980s. Growth has also been swift in Cameroon and Zimbabwe. Launched in both countries in 1983, within half a dozen years the credit union sector in each had over 200 constituent groups, memberships of over 50,000 people, and savings in excess of $15 million.

National-level development groups: the harambee *groups of Kenya* Most governments in post-independence Africa have actively encouraged local development groups as a means of promoting local enthusiasm and participation in the modernization process, at the same time linking local, usually rural, endeavours to national socioeconomic objectives. Such forms of association may be especially appropriate because of relatively small and limited capital investment, which means that they fit more easily with local knowledge and organizational abilities and use up a minimum of scarce capital resources (Hamer 1984: 276). In Kenya, such bodies are known as *harambee* ('popular participation in development') groups.

Harambee groups are voluntary bodies providing the organizational framework facilitating popular participation. Despite the continued reliance on foreign donors for development, the reality of strong central government control over almost every aspect of local-level developments in Kenya means that although local communities are required to initiate development projects based on their perceived needs, whether they get any state resources is decided at national level.

Thousands of *harambee* groups emerged following independence in 1963. Their growth was particularly fast during the 1980s, when the speed of Kenya's economic development began to falter after a promising start (Mosley 1991). From around 4,000 in 1980, numbers increased fourfold to about 16,000 in 1984, rising to over 20,000 by the early 1990s (Wanyande 1987: 96; Fisher 1994: 140). By the latter date, over two-thirds of a million people (about 1 in 10 of the country's 6 million adult population) belonged to the *harambee* groups.

Membership size of an 'average' *harambee* group is between 30 and 80 people. Most are found in rural areas, are organized around the village community, comprise mostly poor farmers, and have a majority of women members (Wanyande 1987). What do *harambee* groups do? With members contributing much of the finance and all of the labour, they carry out a range of developmental tasks, including tree planting, credit provision, literacy drives and well, road and bridge construction

(1987: 101). Government supplies technical expertise and supervision when necessary – and if available. Thus the *harambee* strategy emphasizes the need for cost sharing between the people and the government.

The emphasis on cost sharing between local people and government is an important strategy on the part of the latter to avoid blame for lack of development. Winans and Haugerud (1977) argue that a high rate of participation in *harambee* groups is a means of expressing resentment at the national political leadership's failure to provide for the expectations of a high material standard of living; it is a means of tapping into state resources. Because it is the responsibility of the people to initiate development, and the government only gets involved once this stage is reached, then any failure to initiate development is, according to government, the fault of the people alone. On the other hand, there is little doubt that the *harambee* concept is a popular one among Kenyans, encouraging a feeling of self-reliance for development. Given that the Kenyan government is consistently strapped for cash, then it is by no means a bad policy to follow a development strategy which relies on the energies and commitment of local communities. Yet it would be incorrect to suggest that the *harambee* philosophy is based on the idea of an equal partnership. Clearly government controls the process because of its overall dominance of the management of *harambee* schemes. There is virtually no chance of spontaneous formation of cooperatives, as the government's regulatory measures very severely curtail autonomy. As a result, it is sometimes argued that *harambee* groups are little more than government bureaucracies. In addition, the state not only aims to coordinate planning on a district or regional basis so that projects are not unnecessarily duplicated, but also to limit the misappropriation of *harambee* funds by some local leaders (Winans and Haugerud 1977: 335; Hamer 1984; Wanyande 1987).

Transnational development groups: Six-S of West Africa An example of a transnational development group in sub-Saharan Africa is the recently defunct Six-S movement. Although it is dealt with at length in chapter 3, I briefly examine the movement here because of the lessons to be learned from its unexpected demise in 1995. The Six-S movement grew in the 1970s in West Africa from a network of traditional organizations – known as Naam groups – in the Yatenga area of Burkina Faso (Ekins 1992: 115; Fisher 1993: 24; Hintjens 1996). By mobilizing local farmers, Six-S was able to encourage crop diversification and changes in food consumption habits by promoting new, more drought resistant species. The organization was not only involved in the construction of health posts, pharmacies, and schools, but also in encouraging women to get more involved in development: for the first time in local people's memory, activist women organized local microenterprises under the auspices of Six-S (Pradervand 1988: 8).

Yet swift growth in the number of groups affiliated to Six-S led to an overreliance on foreign funds and the growth of a stultifying bureaucracy. The outcome was that the movement became overfunded, overbureaucratized and politicized, eventually collapsing under its own weight in 1995. The founder of Six-S, Bernard Lédéa Ouédraogo, found his own political profile had been greatly raised by his leadership of the organization. As a result, he became the state-appointed mayor of Burkina Faso's capital, Ouagadougou – that is, a highly important political figure.

Since its demise, Six-S/Naam has been replaced by a host of small *'groupements'*, primarily concerned, like the Naam groups in their infancy, with promoting collective actions to ensure food security. Other, less donor-dependent associations of farmers have also emerged. It will be interesting to see whether this second wave of local development groups manages to endure. The lesson of the Six-S movement is that growth that is too swift – enabling participant groups to tap into international funds – may not be in the long-term interests of such developmental groups.

Despite the successes noted above in terms of dealing with drought and shortages of finance for small projects, the shortcomings of development action groups in Africa are noteworthy. First, the state will sometimes attempt to control local initiative, substituting a bureaucracy for the participatory control common in local associations. Second, individuals join cooperatives and self-help groups to increase their standard of living, but a preference for funds from outside sources may take precedence over local initiatives. In short, there may be a strong concern for short-term benefits, conflicting with the long-term ideals of reciprocity and cooperation necessary for development groups to prosper over time.

Latin America

While Latin America is not collectively as poor as sub-Saharan Africa, there are nevertheless tens of millions of poor people who are every bit as poverty-stricken as their counterparts in Africa. As in sub-Saharan Africa, development action groups have proliferated in recent years, stimulated by increasing poverty. Unlike sub-Saharan Africa, developmental problems in Latin America are widely regarded as social prob-lems which sooner or later become political (Navarro 1996).

The most important types of local development groups are the Basic Christian Communities (BCCs), the *favela* (slum development) organi-zations of the shanty towns, and the urban development associations, all of which emerged in the 1960s and early 1970s. This was an impor-tant period in Latin America's modernization, urbanization and indus-trialization (Stiefel and Wolfe 1994: 74–98). BCCs in particular grew in many countries in the region during the years of military dictatorship, of the 1960s and 1970s. In Brazil, for example, there are about 100,000 BCCs, with at least 3 million members (Haynes 1995a), while, *inter alia*, Chile, Nicaragua, El Salvador and Colombia have thousands. Many countries in the region also have large numbers of urban development organizations and *favela* groups: Chile has some 12,000 and Brazil about 10,000, Costa Rica has in the region of 6,000 and Guatemala around 800; Peru has about 1,500 'community kitchens' (Fisher 1993: 24).

Unlike sub-Saharan Africa's development groups, those in Latin America tend to regard developmental problems as intimately con-nected to social and political problems. Resolving development obsta-cles necessarily involves challenging the status quo, a status quo which often enriches a small elite at the expense of the mass of people. In short, Latin America's development groups are significant elements in building civil societies and facilitating the return to democracy.

Basic Christian Communities BCCs have engendered a large literature (Levine 1984; Medhurst 1989; Casanova 1994). Usually they came into being as the result of Catholic priests working at local level identifying a need to organize local people for broad development purposes in the absence of sufficient state initiatives. For developmental progress, de-pendence and passivity had to be replaced by self-help initiatives.

BCCs are found in both rural and urban environments. Because of their large numbers – probably more than 200,000 groups in the region – it is difficult to identify closely what they have in common. Generally, however, BCCs are face-to-face neighbourhood groups of between 10 and 20 families (20–60 people), bonded by physical proximity and poverty, and meeting periodically, perhaps fortnightly or monthly. Many undertake a range of self-help development projects, including the provision of schools, health posts, clean water, roads and latrines (Medhurst 1989: 25).

Because of the nature of Latin America's political arrangements – long periods of military rule interspersed with shorter intervals of civilian government and with relatively dense civil societies – it is unsurprising that many BCCs became highly politicized. The most dynamic period in many BCCs' existence was during the years of military rule, that is, from the 1960s to the 1980s. In El Salvador, for example, BCCs began as development vehicles which evolved into politicized organizations with the tacit blessing of the Catholic hierarchy (Cardenal 1990: 245). In Colombia, on the other hand, local conservative bishops vigorously attacked liberation theology, the ideology of many BCCs (Levine 1990: 26). Socialist Nicaragua was also the home of numerous BCCs during the 1980s, the period of Sandinista rule. The Sandinistas saw the BCCs as political allies and as a result encouraged them (Serra 1985: 151–74).

BCCs were routinely regarded as communist front groups by the conservative military governments. In Chile, where leftist political parties were banned after the military takeover in 1973, they became a haven for a leftist radicals incensed by what they saw as a series of politically repressive and economically stringent measures whose net effect was seriously to disadvantage the poor. During the rule of General Pinochet (1973–90), it was not uncommon for BCCs, especially in the capital Santiago, to incur the wrath of the regime. Verbal attacks began to appear in the government-controlled media by 1977, charging that the umbrella group of the Chilean BCCs, the Vicaria de la Solidaridad (the Vicariate of Solidarity), harboured communist sympathizers and received foreign money to support political dissidents in Chile. As a result, many local BCC members were harassed. Foreign priests were also frequently perceived as politically undesirable: between 1973 and 1979, 400 foreign priests were expelled from Chile, precipitating a net decline of over 10 per cent in the total clergy (Smith 1982: 343).

Over time, however, military governments in Latin America were gradually forced on to the defensive by a combination of domestic and international pressures for democracy. The BCCs were important in this regard because, by helping to establish a sense of community empowerment, they were able to take a leading role in the growth of civil society (Mainwaring and Viola 1984; Hewitt 1990). By actively seeking to ameliorate a poor development position – by pressing for infrastructural improvements such as sewers, streetlights and electricity – BCC activists learnt that the best way to achieve their goals was not by appealing as individuals to powerful figures and bureaucratic authorities, but by coordinating the community in pursuit of developmental goals that is, by gaining power through a collective search for group goals.

The return of democracy to Latin America in the 1980s coincided with a decline in the political profile of many BCCs, although the majority maintained an interest in development initiatives. Focusing on 22 BCCs in Brazil's large and dynamic Archdiocese of São Paulo, Hewitt (1990) showed them to be maintaining an effective developmental presence. On the other hand, he suggests that the role of the BCCs in São Paulo is changing: they are no longer agents of social and economic transformation. Such a change is probably attributable to the rejuvenation of democracy in Brazil whereby many erstwhile BCC activists look to the political parties, especially the radical Workers' Party, as the main route to sociopolitical and economic improvements.

Neighbourhood developmental associations and favela *groups*   Basic Christian Communities grew swiftly in numbers during Latin America's period of swift modernization and military governments. Two further forms of local development bodies – neighbourhood development associations and *favela* (slum development) groups – also emerged and grew in numbers from the 1960s. Whereas neighbourhood developmental associations are commonly found in established residential districts, which however frequently lack many basic services, *favela* groups in Brazil – known as *pueblos jovenes* in Peru, and *barrios* in Venezuela – have grown in the fast-expanding shanty towns. As all Latin America's cities have grown in size over the last three decades, the poor have been pushed to the margins. Falling real wages, rising unemployment and soaring prices for land in the cities combine to force a growing proportion of low-income families to seek shelter in shanty towns. Smith (1990: 261) estimates that a majority of the 20,000 squatter settlements in Latin America have developed their own self-help associations. The Mexican city of León is thought to be typical, with at least 350 voluntary groups, one for every 2,000 people in a population of 700,000 (1990: 261). *Favela* and neighbourhood development associations attract both men and women – as with development groups in Africa, the latter are often very well represented. Some groups have exclusively female memberships. I describe and analyse such groups in chapter 6.

In sum, in the polarized societies of Latin America development is a contentious – a highly political – issue. The poorest members of society – that is, the bottom 40 per cent – have very low incomes compared to the richest stratum of society, the top 20 per cent. Democracy has done little to ameliorate things. For example, in Brazil the bottom 40 per cent receive just 7 per cent of the national income. In Chile, the corresponding figure is 10 per cent, in Costa Rica 13.1 per cent, in Panama 8.3 per cent, in Mexico 11.9 per cent, and in Guatemala 7.9 per cent (UNDP 1996: table 17, pp. 170–1). The point is that in the relatively educated and class-conscious societies of Latin America, unlike in sub-Saharan Africa, many development-oriented groups regard development as a social, economic and political problem.

South Asia

Like Latin America and sub-Saharan Africa, South Asia has a huge number of development action groups. The poorest countries in the region – Bangladesh, India and Sri Lanka – have thousands; most are located in the rural areas (Sethi 1993; Fisher 1993: 23). Like Latin America, South Asia also has many examples of women-only and women-dominated development groups.

Paralleling the situation in sub-Saharan Africa, there are both village-level and larger regional and transnational development organizations, often coordinated by national umbrella organizations. Unlike the *harambee* groups of Kenya, many are not state controlled. Of especial note because of their size and record of long-term development success are the Bangladesh Rural Advancement Committee, India's Self-Employed Women's Association and Sri Lanka's Sarvodaya Shramadana Movement – all of which are discussed below. Like West Africa's Six-S movement, each has stimulated networks of local development action groups, with initial growth primarily due to the energies and talents of key individuals. Yet Sarvodaya nearly collapsed in the early 1990s, like Six-S, and for similar reasons: a large influx of funds from foreign donors, leading to a massive expansion of the bureaucracy, eroded the informal, village-based structures, the movement's main strength.

The Bangladesh Rural Advancement Committee   BRAC was founded in 1972 by Fasle H. Abed, shortly after the country won its independence from (West) Pakistan. BRAC's raison d'être is to strive to ameliorate the plight of the poor 'by developing their ability to mobilise, manage, and control local and external resources themselves' (BRAC 1988: 1–2). BRAC's growth has been swift: it is now the largest nongovernmental organization (NGO) in Bangladesh, employing over 4,000 people. It has a budget of $22 million, a membership of 350,000 (60 per cent women) in 210,000 households in 3,200 villages, organized into nearly 6,000 groups (Ekins 1992: 116). BRAC focuses its efforts on the largest group among the poor in Bangladesh: the rural landless, mobilizing them into cooperatives. The latter, as autonomously as possible, plan, initiate, manage and control their activities. This helps to build greater self-reliance. BRAC works as a facilitator, organizing and encouraging projects in a variety of areas, including functional and non-formal education, training in vocational skills, health care, the paralegal service and employment and credit support (1992: 117–18). BRAC's enterprises also extend to shops, a women's production centre and a bank. In short, BRAC is a highly successful development umbrella organization helping the rural poor to help themselves.

Sarvodaya Shramadana Movement (Sri Lanka) The SSM was founded in 1958 by a 26-year-old teacher, A. T. Ariyaratne. Like BRAC, the organization aims to help people to help themselves; its philosophy is embodied in its name, which means the 'awakening of all by voluntarily sharing people's resources, especially their time, thoughts and efforts' (Fisher 1993: 146). Sarvodaya sees development as a means, not an end: 'Material wellbeing is no more than the vehicle necessary for spiritual awakening' (Lean 1996). Over the past 40 years it has worked in about 8,000 of the country's 23,000 villages – where 3 million people live – growing to be the most important national development organization, employing about 7,000 people. Over 30,000 trained village youths work in their local communities. SSM's areas of interest include nutrition, health, education, housing, water supply and sanitation, agriculture, savings and credit, rural industries and marketing. In short, as Ariyaratne puts it, millions of rural people in Sri Lanka 'are participant-beneficiaries of an integrated rural awakening programme' (quoted in Ekins 1992: 101).

India's Self-Employed Women's Association SEWA is a good example of a women's development group which, perceiving the slow pace of social change, decided to try to speed it up. SEWA, based in Ahmedabad, was established in 1972 as a women-only trade union and credit organization for females working in the informal sector. Such women would, typically, have to borrow 50 rupees ($1.50) every morning from a money-lender. With the money they would buy produce – fruit, vegetables or grain – and then sell it. At the end of the day they would have to repay the 50 rupees plus 10 per cent interest. From their meagre profits they would often have to find bribes to pay the local police to overlook their selling without a licence. At the end of the working day they might show a net profit of seven rupees ($0.21), quite insufficient to buy the essential items they needed. To combat such poverty, SEWA established its own 'bank', providing loans at a very low 12 per cent annual interest. The organization soon saw its membership grow as working women flocked to join. By the late 1980s SEWA had more than 13,000 members. In order to get over the problem of bribes, SEWA successfully lobbied to the Supreme Court in Delhi to pressurize the authorities to set up a municipal market for the women (Clark 1991: 109–10).

While it is difficult to generalize, the most successful national-level development groups in South Asia seem to occupy an organizational position midway between those of sub-Saharan Africa and those of Latin America. While in the former they tend to be under the control of government, in the latter they do not. In South Asia, umbrella development groups tend to be dominated by key individuals who enjoy a good relationship with the state. Development groups – except in India and Latin America – tend not to have an overtly political focus to their activities. A key point is that South Asia's civil societies similarly occupy a position midway between those of Africa and those of Latin America. While India's development action groups often have an important political voice, in Sri Lanka and Bangladesh particular political configurations – civil war in the former, military government in the latter – seem to have stymied the development of civil society to the same extent. The governments in Sri Lanka and Bangladesh, rather like that of Kenya, seem to be happy for private development initiatives to thrive – as long as they are not in any way vehicles of popular mobilization like the BCCs and urban development groups of Latin America.

The development action groups described by region above employ a variety of methods to pursue their goals. Sometimes they work overtly with the state, sometimes against it, while some work in a third way: that is, they alternate between periods of close involvement with the state and times of at least quasi-autonomy. It is, however, the nature of the political arrangements of society which, at root, explains Third World development action groups' perceptions of the causes of their lack of development or, more prosaically, impoverishment. Many Latin American countries have a range of politicized development action groups, reflectling the region's relatively developed civil societies. The position is reversed in sub-Saharan Africa, where the impoverishment of large sections of society is matched by a seeming inability to deal with their development problems. South Asia falls somewhere between these two extremes: India has a range of politicized development action groups, while its neighbour, Bangladesh, does not.

Sociopolitical Action Groups

While necessitating a large measure of generalization, it is useful analytically to separate out Third World action groups into two broad categories: those concerned primarily with economic development, and those working towards sociopolitical change. As we have already seen, I believe that whether development is regarded by the members of action groups as a sociopolitical issue or not is largely a function of the level of ordinary people's political awareness and of the density of civil society in the various regions and countries of the Third World. It is in the democratic or democratizing Third World countries that action groups tend to have the most overtly sociopolitical goals. As we saw in the case of India's Self-Employed Women's Association, a sociopolitical goal is not necessarily one which is geared to changing a country's government; for many women's groups it is the societal perception of females which is of most importance.

When a country is democratic it implies that there is at least a degree of 'space' within which civil society and opposition groups can function and pursue their goals. The recent spread of democracy to the Third World has allowed such space to open up in a growing number of countries. The result, Rau (1991) claims, is a 'silent revolution' emanating from the grassroots and increasingly influencing organizations and policies at both regional and national levels in the Third World. In a similar vein, Hong sees grassroots participatory organizations as the very foundations of democratic society in the Third World. Their impact, he suggests, is leading to a 'fundamental restructuring of the institutional field of development' as a result of the extension of processes of self-development (Hong 1991, quoted in Stiefel and Wolfe 1994: 197).

Triumphalist conclusions about the impending advent of true participatory democracy in the Third World is, in my view, over-optimistic or at least premature. Reality is more complex and, for the subordinate, much grimmer. It is true that in a number – perhaps a majority – of Third World countries new and often unexpected institutional and political spaces have opened for the kinds of organized efforts that I discuss in this book. On the other hand, large and heterogeneous groups of the poor and otherwise excluded find it increasingly difficult to defend their positions. Yet, in some respects, what is happening *is* a 'quiet' revolution. Relative to what was there before, an organizational explosion *is* occurring in the Third World; very often, however, it is *defensive* in orientation. As Fisher puts it, 'relative to the magnitude of the ... task, this is a revolution stumbling through its early stages'; action groups 'are making inroads but are still far from overthrowing the old order of poverty and inequality' (1993: 8). The point is that sociopolitical action groups tend to make progress when they are able to exploit the spaces provided by democracy. As a result, sociopolitical action groups are plentiful in democratic

India and Latin America. They are less common in Africa or the Middle East.

Four categories of sociopolitical action groups are common. Broadly, they seek to promote the empowerment of indigenous peoples and of women, to protect and defend the natural environment, and to heighten perceptions of an appropriately Islamic state and society. In Latin America, the first three are common, while in India women's sociopolitical groups have a high profile. The goal of creating a more Islamic society is common among action groups in many Muslim countries in the Middle East and Africa.

Latin America

In Latin America, the concerns of sociopolitical action groups encompass a vast range, from 'squatters to ecologists, from popular kitchens in poor urban neighbourhoods to Socialist feminist groups, from human rights and defense of life mobilizations to gay and lesbian coalitions' (Escobar and Alvarez 1992a: 2). And that's not all, there are also 'black and indigenous peoples' [groups], new modalities of workers' cooperatives, peasant struggles, middle- and lower-middle-class civil movements . . .' (1992a: 2). The recent growth in numbers of sociopolitical action groups in Latin America is partly linked to the crisis of the traditional left which, following a wave of successful military coups in the 1960s and 1970s, disappeared from sight for more than a decade. However, when political parties were banned, political action groups tended to mushroom. The point is that the left's political defeat was not followed by popular passivity and resignation. Instead, many people in 'practically every country of the region' became involved in projects of resistance to and collective struggle against military rule (1992a: 1). The same thing happened in India: one of the main catalysts to the growth of political action groups was the period of heightened social tensions which preceded the period of 'emergency' – that is, non-democratic – rule between 1975 and 1977 (Omvedt 1994: 35).

When democracy returns what happens if the political parties are perceived not to represent the interests of your group? You can start another, but you are likely to discover that it is extremely hard to displace established parties from people's affections. If the extant political parties do not appear to represent the interests of marginal and underrepresented groups, the latter may well use sociopolitical action groups to pursue their goals; this is especially clear in the case of women.

Women's empowerment Years of military dictatorship helped to politicize millions of women in Latin America. Wives, mothers and daughters remained free when their husbands, sons and fathers were abducted, jailed or killed by military regimes. Many became political activists. Following the return to democracy, many women retained their political awareness, eschewing the political parties and instead seeking to improve the societal position of women vis-à-vis men through their own action groups.

One of the best known of the women's groups is the Madres de la Plaza de Mayo of Argentina, a group discussed fully in chapter 6. These 'mothers of the disappeared', who rallied for years in Buenos Aires from the early 1970s, became an international symbol of both human and women's rights. On the one hand, they symbolized the emergence of women as an important political constituency, while on the other they manifested the need for the country to come to terms with the 'dirty war' fought by the state against alleged terrorists and subversives (Castaneda 1993: 227).

A second example of a women's rights group is Conavigua (Confederation of Widows of Guatemala), founded in 1988. By 1992 its membership had grown to 10,000 women. It is a more broadly based group than the Madres of Argentina. Conavigua's concerns and membership, reflecting the characteristics of repression in Guatemala, extends from 'indigenous peoples in the highlands, labour leaders, and peasant activists, [to] middle-class intellectuals' (Schirmer 1993: 50).

The emergence and growth of women's groups in Latin America does not, of course, occur in a social vacuum. Where the Catholic Church is strong and conservative, as in Colombia, women's movements find it hard to take off. In countries where the church is more socially progressive – such as Brazil, Chile and Peru – the concerns of women's groups include human rights, the cost of living, poor quality housing, insufficient urban services and domestic violence at the hands of their partners. Four developments seem to have encouraged feminist consciousness in Latin America. First, where the church is progressive, women tend to participate in community struggles. Second, the defeat of the left in Brazil, Chile and elsewhere in the 1960s and 1970s encouraged militant women to work with local groups. Third, political liberalization from the 1970s and democracy in the 1980s increased the political space available to women to organize. Finally, non-democratic regimes tended to allow women to organize while they simultaneously cracked down hard on other nascent civil society organizations (Alvarez 1990: 262).

Environmental protection	The fight for a more protected environment is just beginning in Latin America. The 1992 Earth Summit held in Rio di Janeiro helped to focus environmental concerns. Like women's groups, environmental protection groups often have sociopolitical agendas, and for the same reasons. As Ricardo Navarro (1996), head of Cesta, El Salvador's Friends of the Earth organization, puts it: 'Our ecological problems are already social problems and are becoming political.' Environmental protection groups – aiming to preserve access to water supplies and clean air, and to prevent soil erosion and the dumping of developed countries' toxic waste – have goals fundamentally opposed to many governments and their friends with business interests. The environmental groups see many of the region's governments pursuing a highly destructive developmental model opposed to the interests of the poor, who rely on access to land for farming. Like women's groups, environmental protection groups have managed to thrive in democratic spaces; on the other hand, some of the region's governments see the environmentalists as the 'new communists', intent on subverting the state (Navarro 1996; Lamb 1996).

It would be incorrect, however, to portray all of the region's environmental protection groups as pursuing an overtly sociopolitical agenda against the state or business interests. Costa Rica is one of the few countries in Latin America to have been a continuous democracy for nearly 40 years. The Asociación ANAI was founded by a 37-year-old American, Dr Bill McLarney, in 1973, aiming 'to further the cause of earth stewardship in the tropical lowland environment of Atlantic Costa Rica' (McLarney, quoted in Ekins 1992: 153). From small beginnings – agricultural diversification from cacoa (cocoa) on a seven hectare site – ANAI's operation grew over the next 20 years to include the entire 3,000 sq km of the poor canton of Talamanca with a population of 25,000 people. ANAI, with a membership of some 6,000 local people, enjoys the help both of volunteers and of $600,000 local funding annually from the state-run ACCORDE (Asociación Costarricense de Organizaciones de Desarrollo) and others. Over the years, it diversified into forest protection, agroforestry, tree planting and the development of disease-resistant crops. In 1984, in addition, it founded a 10,000 hectare wildlife refuge, now protected by presidential decree. Local people also benefit from a further project: a land titling exercise whereby some 500 families have gained the title deeds for land around the refuge. The aim is to manage the area more sustainably and to conserve pockets of privately managed forest. By the early 1990s, ANAI was well on the way to achievement of its goals: on the one hand, the transformation of the country's poorest canton into an ecologically stable, prosperous farming area, and on the other, appreciable environmental benefits through the conversion of local farms to agroforestry systems which could be expected to decrease the pressure for the clearing of natural forests (Ekins 1992: 156).

As we have seen, ANAI works closely with government to pursue its programmes, seeking to exploit the opportunities that Costa Rica's democratic environment offers. Democracy does not, of course, ensure that environmental protection groups will be successful. Like women's groups, many environmental protection groups seek to change the prevailing societal view of an issue area. Environmental protection groups in Latin America and elsewhere are likely to come into conflict with government and business interests because of their differing perceptions of what development entails. Organizations like the late Chico Mendes' Rubber Tappers of Brazil, the Chipko tree-protection movement in India, and the Green Belt movement in Kenya – discussed in detail in chapter 5 – all pursue goals of sustainable development[1] which may bring them into conflict with vested interests.

As in the field of development, individual environmental protection groups are likely to increase the power of their voice if they unite. In Venezuela, for example, more than 100 environmental groups, Guadilla argues, share an 'eco-socialist view which criticizes the style of capitalist development' (1993: 72). The latter is regarded by the groups as a primary cause of the gradual worsening of living conditions, the marginalization and impoverishment of large sectors of the population and the growing deterioration of the physical and natural environment. Solutions offered by one of the leading groups, the Grupo de Ingeniera de Arborización (GIDA: Group of Forestation Engineering and Habitat), aim at transforming the prevailing economic and sociopolitical model into one which is more socially egalitarian and technologically rational. GIDA is opposed to large-scale projects such as the exploitation of the Orinoco Oil Belt, and the petrochemical, coal and gas industries (Gaudilla 1993: 72). During the 1980s many of Venezuela's environmental groups, most of which have small, educated memberships, joined together in the Federación de Organisaciones de Juntas Ambientalistas (FORJA: Federation of Environmental Organizations). One of FORJA's successes has been to assume a corporate role as technical adviser to the Congressional Commission on the Environment. This is important because it allows the combined force of the leading environmental groups a voice in national environment policy-making.

Indigenous peoples   The original inhabitants of countries are often the ones who miss out on developmental benefits. Conflicts relating to their rights revolve round defence of land, cultures and languages. European migration to Australasia and the Americas, and the subsequent development of the world market, often devastated the lives of indigenous peoples. Those who survived warfare and disease frequently saw their land and other resources confiscated. Today most of their descendants live on the margins of society, poor, uneducated and politically powerless. Their numbers continue to fall: they now constitute only 10 per cent of the population in Latin America and an even smaller proportion in Australasia and South and South-East Asia. In Latin America, they face two major problems: first, they find it very difficult to pursue their demands through the vehicle of conventional political parties; second, because they feel unprotected by the state they seek to gain their goals through their own efforts..

The most bitter confrontations are over land. For many indigenous peoples, land is not only necessary for physical survival, it is also important for spiritual, cultural and psychological well-being. Yet their remaining lands in Latin America are under constant threat both from the state and transnational or national corporations keen to profit from forest and mineral resources. Concerns relating to the natural environment are described and analysed in chapter 5.

In addition to environmental issues, indigenous peoples in Latin America – like their counterparts in Canada, the USA, Australia and New Zealand – are struggling to gain a measure of control over their own lives, campaigning to retrieve land lost historically to European settlers. They also want greater autonomy – perhaps even the right to govern themselves using their own laws, traditions and institutions. Such goals are potentially achievable in vibrant democracies. But what happens when the political system is not conducive to dealing with such demands? What can indigenous peoples do then? In chapter 4, I relate the struggle of the Indians of Chiapas state, Mexico, and others in Brazil to reform the quality of their country's democracy to allow them a greater say.

India

Women's rights   There are thousands of women's empowerment groups in India with sociopolitical goals (Omvedt 1994: 35). I examined the Self-Employed Women's Association (SEWA) of Ahmedabad above, while the Socio-Legal Aid, Research and Training Centre located in Calcutta is analysed briefly below. Until recently, India was an exception among Asian countries in that it had – except for the 1975–7 'Emergency' period – opted for and maintained a parliamentary system since independence (Shah 1988: 262). Yet, while formally democratic, India does not seem to be especially good at enhancing the material position of half the country's population – girls and women.

Most women's groups emerged in the early 1970s, a time when the political-economic system and ideologies were in crisis (Omvedt 1994: 35). Many have chosen direct action as a way of expressing popular aspirations and grievances in the context of a political system which, while outwardly democratic, is in fact highly resistant to granting the demands of subordinate citizens. Popular aspirations and requirements are, as a result, regularly expressed through the extraconstitutional methods of protest and mass mobilization.

Like SEWA, the Calcutta-based Socio-Legal Aid, Research and Training Centre (SLARTC) helps women to help themselves. Whereas SEWA aids women seeking to gain a measure of economic independence, SLARTC organizes women across north-east India into legal groups to monitor and confront abuses against those who are unable to defend themselves. SLARTC's main effort is involved in arming poor women to help themselves by informing them about the law and their rights. With a network of 200 volunteer lawyers, SLARTC works assiduously to uncover and redress violence against women, long tolerated in India (Durning 1989: 60).

Sub-Saharan Africa

Women's rights   Reflecting the paucity of democracy, the underdevelopment of civil societies and widespread societal perceptions that women are of less importance than men, there are very few women's sociopolitical action groups in sub-Saharan Africa with any clout. When they do exist, they tend to be the domain of small groups of educated women. Women in Nigeria (WIN), for example, was founded by a coalition of university and professional women in Kaduna in 1982. Its aim is to bring together women regardless of which religious, class or ethnic group they belong to. In attempting to be a national organization, WIN, with a membership of only a few hundred, is outspoken on a number of issues, which paradoxically has reduced its appeal for many uneducated women. WIN's arguments against child marriage and the low priority given to women's health in Nigeria by state bodies led to it being accused by some religious figures as 'too radical' and 'pro-Western' (Callaway and Creevey 1994: 156).

In Senegal, another rather exclusive feminist group, Yewwi Yewwu ('raise consciousness for liberation'), aims to liberate women by creating a 'crisis of conscience and a mobilization to transform the situation of women and the relations between them and men' (1994: 166). Yewwi Yewwu, like WIN, is not a mass organization, but one that appeals to a fairly small group of educated women. Neither is Yewwi Yewwu supported by the main religious groups: it is regarded as too radical (Haynes 1996a). The women of Yewwi Yewwu are widely regarded – at least in Senegal – as irredeemably corrupted by their contacts with Western feminists (Callaway and Creevey 1994: 166).

Religious opposition   Militant Muslim groups – that is, Islamist organizations – have emerged in recent years in response to perceived injustice against Muslim minorities at the hands of the state. Next I examine two such groups from Kenya and Tanzania. The aim is to explain why and how such groups emerge from among religio-ethnic minority peoples in response to what they perceive as serious economic and political injustices at the hands of the state. Such groups function as collective voices of the marginalized groups in civil society.

My first example is the Islamic Party of Kenya (IPK). The consequences of a lack of democracy and economic decline are important factors in the rise of Islamist groups in Kenya. The country has a minority Muslim population of about 10 per cent – about 2.5 million people – located in areas influenced over centuries by Arabic culture, that is, the coastal, north-eastern and eastern provinces. Many Muslims regard themselves as economically marginalized, believing that non-Muslim ethnic groups, such as the Luhya, Kamba and Kalenjin, benefit disproportionately under the ruling regime, which is perceived by them as a pro-Christian government (Gifford 1996: 15).

The legalization of political activity in December 1991 was the main catalyst for the Islamist opposition in Kenya. Islamist parties were not, however, allowed to register for the 1992 elections. As a result, the Islamic Party of Kenya, led by Khalid Salim Ahmed Balala, could not compete. In response to the government's decision, the IPK instigated riots in Mombasa, Voi and several other coastal cities during 1992.

The IPK was founded by a group of Asian intellectuals and businessmen to tap popular Muslim discontent on two main issues. The first was the question of the introduction of Islamic (Sharia) law for the country's Muslim population, many of whom feel discriminated against by the wholesale application of 'Christian' – that is, European-style – laws; the second was resentment on the part of many Muslim Mombasans, chiefly over land issues (Haynes 1996a: 163–4). Many Mombasans saw that local land was being bought up by outsiders, including whites and Christian Kikuyus. In an attempt to head off the advance of the IPK, the ruling party KANU sponsored its own Muslim movement, known as the United Muslims of Africa (UMA). UMA, led by Abdullahai Kiptonui, a Muslim and prominent government figure, was created to split the Muslim constituency along ethnic lines in order to diminish its collective political impact. Young African Muslims were encouraged by UMA to fight their co-religionists of Asian origin.

As in Kenya, resentment at perceived political and economic discrimination stimulates Muslim opposition in neighbouring Tanzania. About a third of mainland Tanzania's population, and 97 per cent of the people of the island of Zanzibar, are Muslim (Gifford 1989). On the mainland, Muslims are scattered among the country's numerous ethnic groups. The greatest concentrations are found, as in Kenya, in the coastal areas, where there have been centuries of interaction with Muslim Arabs from the Middle East. Also as in Kenya, a main catalyst for the growth of an Islamist constituency was the fracturing of the one-party system and the tentative beginnings of political pluralism in the early 1990s. Tanzania's Muslims on the mainland claim they are economically discriminated against. Yet until recently there was little tension between Tanzania's Muslim communities and the government. This is in part explicable by the fact that Muslims have enjoyed senior political positions in Tanzania, while there was little religious tension between Muslims and Christians, a reflection of the social consensus achieved under the country's first president, Julius Nyerere, in power from 1963 to 1985.

If a major catalyst for the emergence of Islamist opposition was the announcement of multiparty democracy, it was the government's mistake in transferring the country's health and education system to the control of the Catholic Church which is usually credited with fanning the flames of Muslim anger. Focusing such concerns, Balukta (Council for the Propagation of the Quran in Tanzania) complained about the silence of the national Muslim organization, Baraza Kuu ya Waislamu wa Tanzania (Bakwata), on the matter. Balukta, enjoying the support of dozens of youthful radicals, not only accused the leaders of Bakwata of corruption but also denigrated their attempts to promote Islam. Anti-Christian sentiment was whipped up by a series of inflammatory sermons broadcast from Dar-es-Salaam's central mosque in March 1992, triggering street battles in the capital between Christian and Muslim youths (Shaikh 1992: 240). Balakta was banned a year later, following a further riot when supporters went on the rampage attacking shops which sold pork.

I have shown how in Kenya many coastal Muslims regard outsiders as taking disproportionate economic influence in their country, and in Tanzania how minority Muslims regard the Catholic Church as building its significance at their expense. The point is that in each of these examples religious-based opposition, closely linked with ethnic concerns, is one of the main symbols of dissatisfaction with the state and its allies in their attempts to increase their power in relation to subordinate groups.

The Middle East

Women's rights   The subordinate socioeconomic position of women in many Middle Eastern countries effectively prevents their organizing for sociopolitical goals. While certain regions and countries – Latin America and India, notably – have experienced a growth of women's political organizations in recent times, sociocultural conditions and a lack of democracy have often prevented the opening up of 'space' within which women can organize themselves to redress their often lowly societal position in the Middle East.

Religious opposition   While in sub-Saharan Africa Islamist groups are beginning to focus concerns of alienated Muslims, in the Middle East they are widely ensconced as the most prominent critics of ruling regimes. Several of the most politically significant, including Algeria's Islamic Salvation Front, the Muslim Brotherhood in Egypt and Hamas in Israel's Occupied Territories, are examined in chapter 7. Like many other Third World regimes, governments in the Middle East frequently rely on centralist and centralizing development strategies and modes of non-democratic government from which many people feel excluded; importantly, many regimes have also failed to deliver acceptable levels of development for most of their people. In the absence of significant civil societies and democratic political environments, Islamist opposition de facto emerges as the chief voice of protest, focusing the energies of the youth, the unemployed and the alienated.

Authoritarian systems of rule are still the norm in the countries of the Middle East, despite the international spread of democracy. As in sub-Saharan Africa, the virtual absence of civil societies in the Middle East renders the development of more accountable systems highly unlikely in the near future (Esposito and Piscatori 1991). Societies and political cultures there are often 'patriarchal or patrimonial', and 'loyalties to religious sects, clans, or ethnic groups tend to vitiate any incentive toward the individual initiative and choice necessary to the democratic process' (Dorr 1993: 132). In terms of Islamist action groups, their emergence is best explained as a result of social and economic changes related to modernization, and in particular to the internal migration of large numbers of people to population centres, growing unemployment and declining living standards for many.

Conclusion

The emergence of development-oriented and sociopolitical action groups in the Third World over the last quarter century reflects, on the one hand, increasing poverty and falling levels of development among subordinate groups and, on the other, the effects of the recent wave of democracy. The effect has been, in some cases, to strengthen civil societies, encouraging a variety of action groups to pursue sociopolitical demands by campaigning, lobbying and direct action.

The result is that millions of people in the Third World now organize themselves in pursuit of development and/or sociopolitical change. While development-oriented groups are chiefly vehicles for the rural and urban poor, those with sociopolitical goals tend to attract the young, women and religious and ethnic minorities. What they have in common, Touraine claims, is a shared sense of 'exclusion, labelling, stigmatisation' by the state (1985: 749). I suggest that it is in democratic or democratizing societies that sociopolitical groups have the best chances of achieving their objectives. The problem, however, is that while an increasing number of Third World countries have formally democratic systems – that is, where governments are chosen by regular, relatively 'free and fair' elections – subordinate peoples often find that their concerns fail to be those of the institutionalized political parties. Thus democracy gives such groups the space within which to organize because, paradoxically, most current political parties do not give full weight to subordinate groups' concerns. This is especially clear in relation to indigenous peoples in Latin America, who seem not to have benefited greatly by the return to democracy. In chapter 4 I examine the emergence of democratic systems in the Third World, arguing that they are often deficient becuse they do not satisfy the aspirations of many subordinate groups. However, before that, in chapter 3, I explore the impact of macroeconomic decline and its putative palliative – structural adjustment – on the formation and goals of Third World action groups.

3
Macroeconomic Decline and Action Groups

Having examined the raisons d'être of Third World action groups in chapter 2, I turn, in chapters 3 and 4, to an examination of how their existence was facilitated by two specific features of the 1980s: macroeconomic decline and demands for democracy. I argued in chapter 1 that action groups should be seen as constituent elements in emerging civil societies in the Third World. In my view, this is where their real significance lies: that is, wittingly or unwittingly, action groups – by seeking to protect, protest and promote members' economic and/or sociopolitical interests – are contributing to the slow emergence of the democratic process in the Third World by strengthening and enlarging civil society.

This chapter examines how macroeconomic decline stimulated action group formation. Attempts at economic structural adjustment almost always failed to resolve prior developmental failures. Some macroeconomic goals may have been achieved, yet social inequality frequently grew. Structural adjustment programmes (SAPs) involved privatization, cutbacks in state provision, price increases in commodities and the commercialization of new spheres of activity. Along with demands for democracy, they helped to stimulate action groups because many people considered they were the best way to defend their interests. In short, this chapter argues that structural adjustment policies were important in stimulating the explosion of action groups. The evidence presented gives support to Hintjens's assertion that 'microlevel experiences are vitally affected by state-level macro-political [and economic] strategies' (1996: 598). That is, macroeconomic policies, along with democratic openings, the subject of the next chapter, have promoted and allowed the expression of dissent in ways that were not available before; the result was that civil society was strengthened.

First I describe the general Third World economic picture since the 1960s. As the argument is that declining economic performances has helped to stimulate action groups, it will be useful to show how widespread macroeconomic failure has been across many Third World regions. Second, I discuss development initiatives in West Africa, Bangladesh and Thailand, assessing how far success is dependent on the extent to which local, autonomous action groups are coordinated by a dynamic umbrella organization. Yet this is only part of the story. During the 1980s many Third World countries adopted SAPs. Conditions attached to international development loans often hit the poor and powerless rather hard. Such people had two choices: suffer in silence or do something about it. While some undoubtedly chose the former course of action, others refused to be resigned to their fate. In Latin American countries with relatively developed civil societies – such as Mexico – responses to structural adjustment – dovetailing with demands for greater democracy – stimulated a variety of action groups. In Algeria, on the other hand, the absence of democratic openings and of a developed civil society meant that economic decline and structural adjustment encouraged the strongest section of opposition – the Islamists. A different outcome occurred in Ghana, where the leading national women's development group – the 31 December Women's Movement – used the lever of structural adjustment to push for greater economic and social justice for poor and working women. The conclusion is (1) that macroeconomic decline and SAPs – along with demands for democracy – helped to focus dissatisfaction with the status quo, encouraging many action groups to organize, and (2) that while SAPs hurt the poor and vulnerable, their responses were variable – in part dependent on available avenues to protest in reaction to their grievances.

Third World Economies since the 1960s

During the 1960s and early 1970s economic growth rates across the regions of the Third World were reasonably uniform at around 3 per cent a year (Callaghy 1993: 185). Growing economic divergence appeared in the second half of the 1970s, before widening in the 1980s (Thomas et al. 1994: 76). During the 1980s, as table 3.1 indicates, there were considerable discrepancies in regional economic performance: the East Asian and Pacific region did best, the Middle East and North

Table 3.1 Average annual growth rate of GNP
per capita, by region, 1980–1993

Region	% growth
East Asia and Pacific	6.4
South Asia	3.0
Latin America and Caribbean	−0.1
Sub-Saharan Africa	−0.8
Middle East and North Africa	−2.4

Source: World Bank 1995: 163, table 1.

Africa worst. While it is necessary to bear in mind that these are *average* performances which obscure country variations, the trend is nevertheless clear: the 'average' East Asian country managed annual growth in GNP per capita between 1980 and 1993 that was 8.8 per cent better than the 'average' Middle Eastern and North African state (Callaghy and Ravenhill 1993: 542). In the latter, GNP per capita declined by an average 2.4 per cent per annum, while for sub-Saharan Africa the average fall was 0.8 per cent a year. The 1980s and early 1990s were also disappointing for Latin America and the Caribbean – average GNP per capita dropped by 0.1 per cent per annum. South Asia, on the other hand, performed relatively well with 3.0 per cent growth during the same period, although mass poverty was a problem in all the countries of the region, including Bangladesh, Nepal, Bhutan and India (Lane and Ersson 1994: 94; Goldenberg 1996).

There were various reasons for poor economic performances. The oil-producing countries of the region of the Middle East and North Africa experienced economic downturn as the world price of oil fell, halving from $26 to $13 between 1985 and 1986, before settling down to around $17 a barrel in the early 1990s (Bill and Springborg 1994: 423). As a result, many of the region's states sought to reform their economies, although some had begun an economic reform process earlier (Owen 1992: 138). The results, however, were generally disappointing.

The reformist trend had begun with the Tunisian government's attempt to reverse the process of state-led development in the late 1960s. This was followed by Egypt's *intifah* ('liberalization' or 'opening up') policy introduced by President Sadat in 1974, by the challenge to 'socialist' planning which resulted from Chadli Benjedid's accession to power in Algeria in 1978 and by the structural adjustments begun in

Turkey just before the military coup of 1980. Later, during the 1980s, 'many more regimes, including oil producers, began a process of attempting to reduce the state's share of national resources consumption' (1992: 138).

Attempts to alter statist systems of economic management in the Middle East and North Africa ran into problems. Both 'demand side' – involving changes in the exchange rate or reduction of budget deficits – and 'supply side' – concerning attempts to increase exports – ran up against a web of vested interests which made fundamental change very difficult to achieve (1992: 141).

The 'quality of life' indicators for the region of sub-Saharan Africa are far below those of the West or even of more affluent Third World areas such as East Asia. Angola, Benin, Ethiopia, Guinea, Liberia, Mozambique, Niger, Sierra Leone, Somalia and Zaire are among the poorest states in the world. The need for socioeconomic change in sub-Saharan Africa is obvious: each year in the region more than 4 million children die before they reach the age of five, a third of all African children are malnourished, one in eight is disabled and one in three receives no primary education. Yet, despite widespread poverty, many of the region's governments were very slow to embark on systematic economic reforms; the power of vested interests helped to prevent change.

To improve the poor developmental position, the region's share of global aid more than doubled from the early 1970s. Despite this, the vast majority of its economies performed poorly. The problem is that increased aid flows on their own are not enough: without better governance and substantial debt relief – neither, for the most part, forthcoming – there is little hope of an economic turnround. With gross debts now more than 100 per cent of annual export output, and with service payments over three times annual export earnings, the continent is stuck in a debt vice from which it cannot easily escape. Sub-Saharan Africa, increasingly peripheral to the world economy, is suffering most in the harsh international climate of the 1990s because it is by far the weakest region economically (Callaghy 1993: 180).

The region of Latin America and the Caribbean was in the middle of the range of the Third World's regional economic performances in the 1980s and early 1990s. Those years were relatively poor for the region, largely because of a foreign debt crisis which reversed the previously positive trend in per capita income and brought about a general and severe setback. Yet the debt crisis was partially brought under control in the early 1990s, the result of a reduction in the foreign debt of most Latin American countries in return for adoption of market-oriented reforms (Haynes 1996b: ch. 4). One result was to save governments money; another was to bolster both national and international confidence. By the early 1990s the general trend was for the majority of the region's economies to show some signs of economic recovery, at least at the macro level (Philip 1993: 555).

Like Latin America, most of the countries of the South Asia region embarked on extensive economic reforms in the 1980s or 1990s. Reform focused on rethinking the role of the state. Such a turn of events was especially surprising in India, where state control was for many years the core of economic policy. After many years of prevarication India began to engage in serious economic reform from the late 1980s. Ruled at that time for 40 years by the Congress Party, India was characterized by a very inward-looking, heavily statist economy whose direction was justified and defended by a dominant ideological mix of 'socialism, self-reliance, nationalism and Third World pride' (Callaghy 1993: 194). The immediate cause of the reforms was a debt crisis, although larger economic pressures had been building.

Even though the rate of economic growth in India in the 1980s had been respectable, it was little more than a third of that recorded by South Korea, one of the most economically successful of Third World countries in recent times. While both India and South Korea had had the *same* per capita income in the mid-1950s, three decades later South Korea had surged ahead with a figure *ten times* that of India. With exports accounting for less than 5 per cent of GDP, the Indian government began to realize that – as with its counterpart in South Korea – the best way forward was to focus on export-led growth. A succession of weak governments in the 1980s, however, lacked the ability and political will to reorientate the economy. Balance of payments imbalances and inflation grew, while foreign exchange reserves dropped; as a result a debt crisis loomed. By the early 1990s, India's foreign debt – $83 billion – was the third highest in the world; only those of Brazil and Mexico were greater. The country's debt service ratio – that is, the proportion of export earnings devoted to paying the interest on foreign debt – was 30.1 per cent, four times South Korea's manageable 7.1 per cent on a debt of $35 billion (World Bank 1995: 200–1, table 20). On top of this came the Gulf Crisis of 1990–1 which (temporarily) led to higher oil prices and hence increased price inflation. India's reluctance to restructure economically was finally dispelled in mid-1991 when $600 million was due to be repaid in debt servicing which the government did not have. The result was serious economic restructuring which, while leading to rapid growth, nevertheless did very little to diminish already serious socioeconomic divisions between rich and poor.

The best economic performance of any Third World region in the 1980s and early 1990s was that of East and South-East Asia. South Korea, Taiwan, Hong Kong and Singapore – the 'tiger' economies – all performed particularly well, managing to offset shortfalls in raw materials' earnings by substantial increases in exports of manufactured goods. In order to appreciate South Korea's success as the region's leading economy (in terms of overall output), it will be useful to compare its economic performance with countries which were at the same developmental stage a few decades ago.

As noted above, Korea's economic situation was similar to India's in the 1950s; it was also akin to two sub-Saharan African countries, Kenya and Nigeria. In 1950, Korea had a GNP per capita of $146, while Kenya and Nigeria managed $129 and $150 respectively. By 1993, South Korea's per capita GNP had grown to $7,660, while Nigeria's and Kenya's were a mere $340 each (Callaghy 1993: 185). In other words, in little more than 40 years South Korea's per capita GNP had grown from parity to a figure *more than 18 times* greater than that of Kenya and Nigeria. It is plain that South Korea enjoyed impressive economic success, while Nigeria and Kenya fell far behind. What explains the difference in economic outcomes?

One factor in the success of South Korea was that the country received 6 per cent of global aid in 1960, when its population was less than 1 per cent of that of the Third World. Aid was used to build up local industry, while the approval signified by relatively large resource transfers from Western donors encouraged foreign investors to risk long-term commitments. On the other hand, Nigeria had extensive oil deposits, yielding to date over $150 billion, which South Korea lacked (Naanen 1995). The disparity in performance between Nigeria and South Korea or between the latter and India cannot be explained by natural resource endowment or levels of foreign aid alone. Rather, the crucial issue is how *effective* government is in pushing through its policies. The more expert government is in directing the national economy towards its developmental goals, the more likely it is that there will be not only (1) sustained economic growth, but also (2) relative equity in the distribution of resources. The main lesson of the spectacular economic growth of the Asian tigers over the last few decades is the unsurprising one that it is crucial that governments deal expertly with actors both inside and outside their country's borders if they want to oversee sustained economic growth and development.

In conclusion, Third World regional economic outcomes in the 1980s and early 1990s differed widely, ranging from 'highly disappointing' in the Middle East and Africa, to 'poor' in Latin America and the Caribbean, 'satisfactory' in South Asia, and 'highly satisfactory' in East and South-East Asia. The newly industrializing countries of the latter region are especially noteworthy because they are the paradigmatic cases of both rapid local industrialization and effective adjustment to a changing international economic situation. Apart from the ability to deal with international actors, the external dimension, their success also shows that it is crucial for Third World governments to exhibit clear signs of purpose and capability internally.

On the other hand, where state development efforts are inadequate, local development action groups may be a partial solution. Next I offer three case studies to illustrate this contention. The lesson of the Six-S/ Naam movement of West Africa is that there may be a danger where growth is too dependent on external sources of funds, leading to excessive bureaucratization. On the other hand, the chief success story highlighted here is the Grameen Bank of Bangladesh, an umbrella organization which has raised funds from outside sources to funnel into the activities of local groups. The third example – of development groups in Thailand – highlights what can happen when there is no coordinating group: development action groups remain localized and ineffective in pursuit of development goals.

Six-S/Naam Movement (West Africa)

Until 1995, the Six-S/Naam movement of West Africa was commonly regarded as a good example of a successful Third World development action group (Stiefel and Wolfe 1994: 201; Hintjens 1996: 604). In Africa the harshness of the economic environment, coupled in many cases with the advancing disintegration of the state's administration, has prompted the poor to invent new forms of association, cooperation and organization, often based on fresh interpretations of traditional communitarian values. Naam groups in Burkina Faso, later evolving into the Six-S organization, are traditional bodies of mutual cooperation and community work which developed, largely as a result of serious drought in the 1970s and 1980s, into more proactive development-oriented action groups. Through Six-S, the Naam concept expanded to several countries in the region (Rahman 1988). Until the recent collapse of the Six-S, groups were engaged in collective work, in the pooling of labour and other resources and in collective credit schemes. They proved to be extremely vigorous, adapting in a flexible way to the realities and constraints of development in West Africa, becoming a 'formidable asset to the poor majorities' (Stiefel and Wolfe 1994: 202). On the other hand, attempts to coordinate such successful participatory local action groups into larger, putatively more powerful movements raised new problems and contradictions. To see what these are it is necessary to give an account of the rise and fall of the Six-S movement.

Six-S was founded in 1972 by Bernard Lédéa Ouédraogo, born in 1930 in Upper Volta (since 1984, Burkina Faso) (Ekins 1992: 112). After a career in education and the civil service, Ouédraogo left his job in 1966, apparently frustrated at the lack of success he was encountering in trying to organize the 'official' village groups instituted by the government (Pradervand 1989: 36). All the local farmers were concerned with, according to Ouédraogo, was 'to take advantage of the donkeys, bullocks, carts, hoes . . . [made] available to them. But there was nothing else behind this demeaning form of assistance, no vision, no global conception of development or of the rural world, no doctrine or philosophy' (Ouédraogo, quoted in Pradervand 1989: 36). Ouédraogo was alarmed that there had been no preceding effort at consciousness raising, along the lines of the educationist Paulo Friere's pioneering efforts in Brazil in the 1960s. In order to stimulate community involvement in development, Ouédraogo and some of his co-workers asked themselves whether there was anything in the traditional village organization of society that would serve as a model for development activities. They discovered that the Naam groups – traditional village bodies composed of young people undertaking various communal activities – had the most highly developed cooperative characteristics. As a result, Ouédraogo and his colleagues tried to work with the Naam structures.

Initially, the growth and progress of the Naam groups, made up predominantly of the young and women, were naturally circumscribed by the slow rate of mobilization of their members' own few resources. In 1976, in order to try to circumvent the funding problem, Ouédraogo, aided by the French development expert Bernard Lecomte, founded Se Servir de la Saison Sèche en Savane et du Sahel – Six-S, or the Association for Self-help during the Dry Season in the Savannnahs and the Sahel. Its chief aim was to gain access to foreign funding. In other words, Six-S was the coordinating NGO, aiming to increase the size of the corporate impact of the Naam groups without sacrificing their local orientation. It also strived to overcome the serious problem of dry season unemployment in the Yatenga area of Burkina Faso where the Naam concept began.

Over the next few years the Naam groups prospered. By 1987 there were nearly 3,000, with about 400,000 members, that is, an average of over 130 people per group (Fisher 1993: 201). Naam groups built on tradition, rather than trying to replace it, training and motivating members from *within* the local community, rather than relying on outside experts (Ekins 1992: 114). In short, Naam groups were notable both for their cooperative ethic and for high levels of popular participation, attributes at the root of many successful developmental initiatives since the 1960s (Pradervand 1989: 39–40). Using a mix of locally derived and international funding, the Naam groups involved themselves in a wide range of social, economic, environmental and cultural activities: growing food; tree planting; building dwellings, warehouses, cereal stores, dams and wells; small-scale local manufacture of basic consumer goods; and trading of locally produced agricultural goods in exchange for others not produced locally.

The structure of Six-S grew into a federation of peasant organizations in a number of countries in the Sahelian region, including Burkina Faso, Senegal, Benin, Mali, Togo, Guinea-Bissau and the Gambia. By the late 1980s, Six-S's income was over 700 million local francs ($2.7 million) a year. A General Assembly composed of the groups' representatives decided strategy. Financial disbursements – loans – were controlled by the groups themselves rather than by outside experts. Money did not go to specific projects but was spent at the discretion of the recipient groups, once they had shown themselves to be both responsible and creative. That trust was generated by this system is clear from the impressive rate of repayment of loans. For example, in Burkina Faso Naam groups repaid 60 million local francs in 1986–7 ($230,000), compared to just 1.3 million local francs ($5,000) six years earlier, indicating a rapid increase in economic activity.

Yet by the early 1990s Six-S was in trouble. It had become too large and unwieldy. In addition, its expansion had 'led to such rapid growth that the movement was diverted from its original aims, becoming both over-funded and politicised' (Hintjens 1996: 606). Yet, according to Hintjens, the legacy of community dynamism has not been wasted: many of the individual groups, she claims, did not vanish when Six-S collapsed in mid-1995 (1996: 606). It is not clear, however, how the absence of a coordinating group will affect their activities, although it seems reasonable to expect that it will be more difficult than hitherto to tap into international funding.

The experiences of Six-S/Naam illustrates both constructive as well as less positive elements of local developmental groups in West Africa. There is the wholly welcome development of community organization, based on local preferences, devoted to an array of locally determined goals. The original philosophy of the Six-S/Naam movement was to do away with foreign funding once local groups were in a position to be self-funding. But the allure of international funds was too great: Six-S was increasingly regarded as a permanent 'milch cow' by many members; the goal of self-sufficiency was side-tracked and that of securing foreign funding became progressively more important. On the other hand, it is clear that the state in impoverished Burkina Faso was unable to provide the wherewithal to encourage local groups to continue. In the future, they will need to rely on both local and transnational organization to pursue their developmental goals. Whether they will achieve success remains to be seen.

Grameen Bank (Bangladesh)

The second example of a large development movement with a network of local groups is the Grameen Bank of Bangladesh. Grameen exists principally to make loans; it is a 'development bank' (Ekins 1992: 122). One of the most important initiatives of the Six-S/Naam movement was the ability to provide credit to the poor, the very people who need it most but who often find it impossible to obtain from normal banking channels. The Grameen Bank, founded in 1976 by an economics professor at Chittagong University, Muhammad Yunus, also shares this concern with the provision of credit. For Yunus it is the key to success for local development efforts. The bank coordinates thousands of autonomous borrowers' groups, aiming (1) to extend banking facilities to the poor, (2) to deliver them from the clutches of money-lenders, (3) to create opportunities for self-employment among the unemployed and underemployed, and (4) to bring the poor into an organization which they could both understand and operate themselves, and where mutual support helps to build social, political and economic strength.

By 1980, 25 branches of the bank were operating in about 300 villages. Three years later there were 86 branches in 1,250 villages, extending loans of 195 million Taka ($5.4 million) to nearly 60,000 borrowers. In 1989, Grameen began a four-year expansion programme at a cost of $125 million. The aim was to create a network of 1,000 branches with national coverage, serving more than 1 million landless poor. Up to 80 per cent were expected to be women. By 1990, there were 754 branches of the bank in more than 18,500 villages[1] in over half of the country's districts. By this time there were about 800,000 borrowers with mostly small loans totalling $5.6 million each month (an average of a loan of $7 dollars a month) for 400 economic activities of different kinds.

Grameen also makes loans available for housing purposes, paid back weekly over 10–15 years. By the early 1990s, nearly 100,000 houses had been built, and over $3 million lent for this purpose.

Fisher observes that 'although Grameen's administrative costs are high and cross-subsidized by interest rate earnings from depositing concessionary loans with other banks, the benefits have been enormous for the people most difficult to reach' (1993: 202). Less than 5 per cent of loans are granted to people with more than half an acre of land. Put another way, about 95 per cent of loans are targeted to people who are most in need of the money but who are highly unlikely to be able to gain loans from the official banks because their credit rating is often non-existent. Incomes of borrowers' groups are more than 40 per cent higher than those of comparable groups in non-Grameen Bank villages, and 28 per cent higher than non-members of the bank in the same villages. Of 975 loans surveyed, only 0.5 per cent were more than a year overdue; in other words, only five loans were overdue out of nearly 1,000 granted. 'Many groups have organised their own additional projects such as vegetable gardens or schools' (1993: 202).

Grameen focuses on the landless poor – more than half of the country's population – and is especially anxious to help the poorest of the poor: women. Females make up 90 per cent of the bank's borrowers. In some villages with all-women Grameen groups men are not accepted as members. Suspicion of males in this respect is a result of the fear many women have that should men become involved they would try to control the group. The issue of social justice is an important one in the Grameen philosophy. Before loans are granted, potential recipients must attend an intensive course of training and group discussions. Groups are encouraged to accept a 16-point programe for social justice, group solidarity and women's emancipation (Ekins 1992: 122–3).

The benefits brought by Grameen to its borrowers are remarkable: loan recipients don't starve; their houses are more likely than before to withstand the rigours of Bangladesh's annual monsoon; borrowers are probably able to afford a second set of clothes; by collective effort, some groups have constructed schools and are able to pay teachers to educate their children; as a result of the bank's philosophy, borrowers are strongly encouraged to work together collectively; and they in turn are able to see the concrete results of coperative effort.

The Grameen Bank model has spread to other countries in Asia, Africa and Latin America. In Malaysia, the Amanah Ikhtiar Malaysia, in deference to Islamic values, does not charge interest on its loans; instead it charges a fixed management fee. The Malawi Mudzi Fund had organized over 500 borrowers groups by the early 1990s. Other places where Grameen-inspired banks operate include the Philippines, Guinea, Chile and Peru (Fisher 1993: 203). In conclusion, the Grameen philosophy not only aids development at the community level but is also instrumental in helping to create viable groups with socioeconomic goals which may eventually emerge as a coordinated voice in Bangladeshi civil society.

Development Participation in Rural Thailand

Both Six-S/Naam and the Grameen Bank are examples of what can be achieved by collective effort and a locally relevant development philosophy which the poor perceive as relevant to their needs and expectations. Rural Thailand presents quite a different picture, and is a good example of how a lack of cooperative effort can stymie development at community level. Lacking constructive visionaries like Bernard Lédéa Ouédraogo or Muhammad Yunus, there are 'practically no visible organised participatory efforts of the rural poor that go beyond small-scale local actions' in Thailand (Stiefel and Wolfe 1994: 65). This is in spite of what is for many poor people a rapidly deteriorating situation, the result of the profound economic changes that have taken place over the last 25 years in the rural areas as Thailand swiftly modernized. Between 1980 and 1993 the country industrialized at a rate of about 10 per cent a year, while average annual GNP growth per capita was 6.4 per cent (World Bank, 1995: 163, 165, tables 1 and 2).

A result of the fast changing economic environment was that a previously relatively homogeneous peasantry with a fairly secure subsistence base producing mainly rice for the market was fundamentally transformed. It was changed by the introduction of new export crops such as sugar, maize, cassava, tobacco, jute and pineapple, and by a new articulation with world markets, notably through the establishment of transnational agribusiness corporations (Stiefel and Wolfe 1994: 65–6). While this benefited a few substantially, it led to a crisis of livelihood for the great majority of rural dwellers. Indebtedness and shortages of cultivable land exacerbated the situation. The majority of rural farmers, as a result, experienced increased insecurity, greater dependence, increased relative disadvantage and, for some, absolute misery (Samudavanija 1993).

Officially instituted cooperatives and farmers' groups in Thailand, in practice primarily concerned with the provision of credit, have in fact been largely ineffective in resolving the livelihood problems of the rural poor, who, like their counterparts in Bangladesh and West Africa, are usually excluded from access to institutional credit. This contrasts tellingly with both the Grameen Bank and the Six-S/Naam movement, where access to low-cost credit was crucial to their expansion. A second contrast is that in Thailand most forms of officially sponsored development and community organizations are very often managed by and to the benefit of a small minority at both village and subdistrict level. In other words, official rural development programmes in Thailand 'do not benefit the poor except when social structures permit it and/or when the poor are mobilized to appropriate and retain a share of the benefits' (Stiefel and Wolfe 1994: 67; Samudavanija 1993: 289–90).

This is not to suggest that Thailand is devoid of autonomous and participatory development organizations set up by the rural poor. There are credit unions and savings groups; rice, fertilizer and buffalo 'banks'; medical savings schemes; and cooperative production and marketing groups. Yet they are nearly always small-scale and localized, often unable to establish horizontal links with similar efforts elsewhere. As Turton notes, many such efforts are merely 'strategies for short-term survival . . . ways to avoid even more desperate and socially harmful options, such as recourse to beggary, prostitution, the selling of children to Bangkok sweat-shops, crime and drug addiction, or migration to city slums to work as rag-pickers and scavengers' (Turton 1987: 76). The point is that the rural poor in Thailand are unlikely collectively to improve their often poor developmental position without a dynamic coordinating organization, perhaps along the lines of the Grameen Bank. The inability to organize collectively in pursuit of development also suggests that the emergence of a civil society capable of taking on both the ruling elite and its military allies is not imminent.

Structural Adjustment: Social Costs of Economic Reform

Yet Thailand is widely recognized as an economic success story, unlike the majority of Third World countries, which are not. Many have been unable to cope with a swiftly changing global economy; the result has been serious budgetary imbalances and reductions in the ability to satisfy many citizens' developmental aspirations. Non-oil producers in particular suffered from the impact of the 1970s oil price rises, when the global price of oil increased fivefold. For many, unsustainable levels of international indebtedness resulted. This was one of the most important factors leading many Third World countries to seek the assistance of the International Monetary Fund (IMF) and the World Bank. The outcome of the reforms promoted by the Fund and the Bank has generally been mixed. On the one hand, in many countries macroeconomic shortfalls have been improved; on the other, in many places the cost has been borne disproportionately by the poor. The importance of this for the action groups has already been noted: the impact of structural adjustment, often simultaneous with democratic reforms, has encouraged many to try to improve their socioeconomic positions. Below I shall describe the differing outcomes in three countries: Mexico, Algeria and Ghana.

The IMF, the World Bank and structural adjustment

International indebtedness is the main lever used by the Bank and the Fund to encourage seriously indebted Third World countries to liberalize their economies. Strong pressure to reform has also been exerted by many Western aid donors on Third World governments with balance of payments difficulties. Economic liberalization has aimed for a reduction in the economic role of the state. International loans have traditionally involved stabilization (the IMF) and adjustment (the World Bank), involving currency devaluation, privatization, cuts in public expenditure, slimming bureaucracies, reducing subsidies and promoting exports. The purpose of these packages was not to reduce the power of the state, or confined to generating 'surplus' cash so that debt could be serviced (Mosley et al. 1991a: 45–51; George 1993: 63). Such programmes were often objectively necessary given the scale of economic collapse beforehand. They may have caused quite high levels of unemployment and hence inequality – but that was not their aim. The IMF believed that economic stabilization would lead to a situation where an adjusting country's economy would become largely self-regulating via more open competition between private businesses. The public sector would contract, aiming to provide sufficient services to enable private business to conduct its affairs efficiently and to protect society's weakest members.

The IMF makes the adoption of debt rescheduling programmes conditional on the introduction of various measures, urging debtor governments to take action in five broad areas. *Trade barriers* are to be drastically lowered, exposing local producers to foreign competition. *Subsidies and price controls* must be reduced with the aim of withdrawing them completely, so as to remove 'distortions' in local prices for goods and services. By withdrawing controls on capital movements the aim is to restructure national *financial systems. State-owned enterprises must be privatized;* private foreign investment is encouraged by removing controls on the remittance of profits. Finally, *state economic intervention* is to be minimized, as well as the provision of most social services, henceforward left to the private sector (Mosley et al. 1991a: 66).

The World Bank works closely with the IMF, but is also a powerful economic factor in its own right (1991a: 34–8). By the early 1990s the bank had total outstanding loans of $89 billion, 6 per cent of total Third World debt, giving it considerable clout with debtor governments. In that year the net flow of funds from the Bank to the Third World was nearly $6 billion in ordinary loans and more than $3.5 billion in 'soft' – that is, low interest – loans.

The dependence on the IMF, the World Bank and major Western countries for the design of economic reform packages and the resources needed to implement them is seen by some as a novel form of neo-colonialism (George 1993). It is argued that Western leverage converts into intensive economic policy conditionality and policy changes in return for borrowed resources. Others maintain that given the extent of economic collapse beforehand, such reforms were the only way to stimulate macroeconomic turnarounds (Mosley et al. 1991a). The unanticipated problem, however, was that the authority of many adjusting governments was linked to the way that they dealt with the social consequences of adjustment. Demands for democracy came at the same time as attempts at adjustment: each probably helped to stimulate the other, although it is very difficult to isolate the effects stemming from SAPs from those emanating from other causes, such as the uneven distribution of wealth in society and the effects of domestic class structures.

Four main conclusions emerge from the definitive two-volume study by Mosley, Harrigan and Toye of the impact of SAPs on nine Third World countries – Turkey, the Philippines, Thailand, Ghana, Malawi, Kenya, Jamaica, Guyana and Ecuador. First, the implementation of SAPs under World Bank guidance was nearly always favourable to export growth and the external account. Second, the influence of SAPs on aggregate investment was nearly always negative. Third, the influence of SAPs on national income and on external financial flows was, on balance, neutral. Fourth, choosing their words very carefully, they note that 'living standards of the poor have evidently fallen in many developing countries, including those which have undergone structural adjustment' during the 1980s. This outcome was, at least in part, in response to two developments: the result of cuts in public expenditure, such as the withdrawal of food subsidies, championed by both the Bank and the Fund; and the impact of price reforms advocated by the Bank alone (1991a: 301–2).

In conclusion, the international financial institutions' prescription for Third World economic reform involved reducing the economic role of the state and reforming the structure of the economy, with a stress on liberalizing markets, increasing competition and building strong linkages to the world economy via increases in exports. The result, it was hoped, would be increased development and prosperity in countries which had pursued misguided strategies of economic growth for too long. At the same time, economic reform was to be underpinned, by 'new globalized capital markets and a reborn world trading order, so that the gap between the world's rich and poor [would] not continue to widen' (Callaghy 1993: 161).

The view was that indebted Third World economies were to be opened to external capital investment before loans could be granted. States were to retain control over their currencies and their non-economic policies only in so far as both were compatible with the free flow of money and goods. Such attempts to compel Third World countries to adjust to economic liberalism were, however, made without embedding the policies in the realities of domestic state–society relations. In their efforts to cope with the Third World debt crisis, Western states and actors attempted to apply the 'monoeconomics' of the dominant neoclassical orthodoxy about development to countries dependent on the IMF and the World Bank. Despite the doubtless good intentions of the Bank and the Fund, the result of sometimes insensitively applied conditionality was to force many Third World countries to adjust to full orthodox liberalism without allowing the pace or thrust of liberalization to be tempered by the peculiarities of local state–society relations. Global economic conditions were such that governments that tried to use deflationary policies to deal with economic crises were not able to rise out of recession, while the poor endured economic hardships and social upheaval.

Failed Adjustment: Social Consequences in Mexico, Ghana and Algeria

Efforts to cope with burgeoning debt crises led to the widespread application of economic liberalization in the Third World. Outcomes were mixed, but the social consequence was that in adjusting countries the poor nearly always suffered drops in living standards (Gayama

1993; Knippers Black 1993; Philip 1993; Andreas 1995; Haynes 1995b). Per capita incomes generally declined for all except the rich; for the poorest people the drop was frequently severe. Many people in formal employment lost their jobs and were forced to seek much more precarious and ill-paid work in the informal sector. A large number also suffered from the cuts in public services. Governments understandably wanted to rationalize general subsidies to make them less of a drain on the public purse, so they eliminated many benefits in nutrition, health, education and transport. Yet in doing so they unintentionally undermined the livelihoods not only of the poor but also of many middle-class people. Some sectors or regions were hit harder than others: sometimes adjusting 'governments removed subsidies that had supported particularly vulnerable sectors of the economy, notably agriculture, or that sustained remote regions – and thus created extended pockets of acute depression' (UNRISD 1995: 42). What was not expected was that the 'social impact [might] itself frustrate the desired economic effect' (1995: 42). In short there was a range of social effects, from urban unrest, riots and violence, to efforts by ordinary people – often through action groups – to seek to augment the state's efforts in the provision of social and welfare goods by organizing community initiatives.

The main point is that attempts at structural adjustment often had two unintended consequences: they did not resolve the prior developmental failures, largely because those were much more serious than previously imagined; and they tended to increase inequality and hence, along with democratic openings, promote and allow the expression of dissent in ways that had not been there before. Regarding Latin America, for example, Whitehead (1993: 318) notes 'the acute social inequality, insecurity and loss of welfare' which characterized simultaneous democratization and economic adjustment in the 1980s. The result was widespread 'popular frustration [and] desperation [which] can be expected to destabilize any institutional order'. Brown (1990) recounts how many poor Egyptians developed a number of techniques to resist the state during structural adjustment, while Bayart describes popular modes of political action in sub-Saharan Africa and the way they limited and relativized the state's domain, contributing to its economic failure (Bayart 1983: 102).

Unsurprisingly, the authority of adjusting governments was at least partially linked to how they dealt with the social effects of SAPs. This was far from what the IMF believed would be the outcome of adjustment: a recipient country's economy would become largely self-regulating as a result of more open competition between private businesses. In the 1960s and 1970s, adjusting governments had been able to justify SAP-induced sacrifices to their citizens by arguing – often correctly – that they would only be temporary and that the resulting economic upturn would benefit society generally. By the 1980s, however, the situation had changed for the worse. Global economic conditions were such that governments using deflationary policies to deal with economic crises were not for the most part able to bring their economies out of recession. Sometimes action groups took the opportunity to expand their field of concerns to seek wider – reformist – goals. Case studies from Mexico, Ghana and Algeria show the variable social results of attempts at structural adjustment.

Mexico

Between 1980 and 1993, Mexico's average annual growth rate in GNP per capita was −0.5 per cent. When the country's economic crisis emerged in the early 1990s, it was characterized by a huge trade deficit, an overvalued peso followed by devaluation, extensive foreign currency borrowing, a drop in financial market confidence, sudden hikes in interest rates, a deepening recession, a sharp rise in unemployment, an austerity budget and a sharp rise in VAT and fuel prices (Haynes 1996b: ch. 4). Following the institution of a SAP, more than 800,000 people lost their jobs between December 1994 and July 1995, while many of those fortunate enough to be still in work saw their living standards plunge. The result was not only a wave of strikes, hunger riots and demonstrations (Scott 1995a), but also the emergence of the Zapatista movement in Chiapas state from among the indigenous Indians. The latter are among the weakest economic groups in Mexico. So deep are the socioeconomic divisions in Mexican society, that Paul Rogers, Professor of Peace Studies at Bradford University, is quoted as arguing that there exists in the country a 'pre-revolutionary' situation (Vidal 1996). The Zapatista uprising in January 1994 exemplifies the probably widespread demand among the poor in the country for radical change. Zapatista leaders argue that the capitalist model is not working in Mexico: the free market does not deliver a just society. I shall examine the origins and aims of the Zapatista movement more extensively in chapter 4.

Ghana

If Mexico was in a pre-revolutionary situation in the mid-1990s, Ghana was at that time more than a decade into its own 'revolution'. Proclaiming a social and political reorientation on coming to power on 31 December 1981, Flight-Lieutenant Jerry Rawlings shocked many observers by adopting a SAP in 1983. Over the next decade Ghana received more than $9 billion in foreign loans, principally from the IMF and World Bank. Between 1984 and 1991 the economy grew by an average of 5 per cent annually, while population growth was about 2.6 per cent per annum (Haynes 1995b). Resulting real growth of 2.4 per cent a year was one of the best records in sub-Saharan Africa at the time. Yet many – perhaps most – ordinary Ghanaians found that macroeconomic success was not reflected in increases in their purchasing power. By 1993 the minimum day's wage of 460 cedis ($0.33) could buy, for example, one bottle of beer. With petrol at 1,600 cedis a gallon a minimum-waged worker earning 12,420 cedis a month could buy 7.76 gallons of petrol with his or her monthly salary – and *nothing else*. The World Bank argued that real wage levels would need to be held down *even further* to make African economies competitive with the low-cost, relatively high-skill economies of South-East and East Asia. Yet after the precipitous decline in Ghana's real wage levels during adjustment in the 1980s and early 1990s, further falls were probably not socially or politically possible (1995b: 111). Ghana needed economic growth rates of around 10 per cent a year *for a generation* to drag its fast-growing population of about 17 million people out of poverty; a comparatively good performance of 2.5 per cent a year is nowhere near good enough.

Ghana's structural adjustment, in contrast to that of Mexico's, is widely regarded as a macroeconomic success. One important societal group – poor women – organized themselves into a national development network under the auspices and patronage of the president's wife. Unlike the Zapatistas, the women did not threaten the state. Instead the government was able to pass some of its development responsibilities to ordinary women.

31 December Women's Movement   Ghana's labour force comprises more than 6 million people; more than 50 per cent are women. About half of them work in agriculture, producing foodstuffs both for subsistence and the market. Most women in this sector are self-employed. As Tsikata notes, 'problems such as access to, and the high cost of, land, credit and technology result in low levels of productivity' and hence income (1989: 75). Women outside the agricultural sector engaged or employed in the manufacturing and service industries, such as trading, nursing, teaching, secretarial and clerical duties, also face problems since the vast majority are neither organized nor unionized. In sum, it is fair to say that women in Ghana, like women all over the Third

World, face a specific form of oppression arising from their economic dependence and their inferior position in all areas of life, in spite of their important contributions to society.

The 31 December Women's Movement (DWM) was founded in May 1982 by a small group of women keen to ensure that females benefited from the Rawlings revolution (Haynes 1993b). The movement is run by a three-member national executive, and its work is funded by local membership fees and foreign nongovernmental organizations rather than from official government sources. Its aim is to improve the developmental and socioeconomic position of women. In 1984 the founding executive was able to persuade Nana Konadu Agyeman Rawlings, the wife of the President, to become head of the movement. Mrs Rawlings's interest in women's development had been kindled by a visit to Cuba in 1983, where she had been very impressed with the achievements of the national women's organization, which had spearheaded a general improvement in conditions for females in the country (Shillington 1992: 153).

Following its inauguration, DWM began to organize in the main urban centres, aiming to improve women's literacy, to undertake economic ventures, to provide social services and educational programmes and to lobby for the abolition of discriminatory laws. The national organization has also been involved in arranging workshops on food processing and conservation, and has undertaken educational campaigns on matters including personal hygiene, family planning, health and nutrition (Tsikata 1989: 86). In short, the DWM is concerned with a variety of broadly developmental goals.

By 1987 the movement had grown to become a nationwide entity with branches in the country's ten regions. Membership had grown fivefold from an estimated 50,000 in 1983 to about 250,000 four years later (1989: 85). By 1991 there were 750,000 registered members, with an associate membership probably twice that size. The movement was able to organize branches in the rural areas because, as Shillington describes, they used the established network of traditional society. In every town and tiny village there is a prominent woman who is the accepted source of advice for women's marital, family or social problems (Shillington 1992: 154). DWM representatives went to each of these notables to explain the movement's objectives and ideals. If they were persuaded of the movement's value, they would call the women of the community for group discussion. In this way a new branch of the movement would begin. Sometimes, women 'chiefs' were not convinced of the movement's aims; if this happened it would be very difficult to establish a branch in a village.

Most branches have two main priorities: the health and welfare of their members, and making money. In the mid-1980s the movement's leaders declared that the construction of child daycare centres was an important priority. Branches were encouraged to build or take over buildings for this purpose. Several centres were soon established in Accra and the other main cities. By 1991 the movement had financed 500 daycare centres throughout the country. Success in developing such social facilities helped to attract capital from international agencies for tasks such as the eradication of guinea-worm and for digging wells (1992: 155).

Most of the branches are also involved in schemes to make money to enhance the economic position of their members. The aim is for individual branches to become self-sufficient economic units. One of the first, located at Burma Camp, Accra, the main barracks of the Ghana armed forces, was awarded contracts to supply bread and kenkey (fermented corn dough balls) to the armed forces in 1983. Others make bread, soap or pottery for sale; many also farm cassava, poultry and pigs. Money raised is either invested in further income-generating projects, or is used to pay for various social schemes, such as a daycare centre or the digging of wells.

Critics of the movement argue that it is little more than an arm of government, viewing Mrs Rawlings's active role in the movement as politically motivated (Tsikata 1989: 86). Mikell argues that DWM has difficulty in making 'the type of connection to the rural social structure that will make a viable and enduring development organization' because 'the individualistic and/or overtly political principles' it embodies 'are not in sync with the rural worldview' (1991: 96). On the other hand, even critics might find it hard to deny that the movement has become an effective pressure group in ways that have benefited very many women in Ghana, no matter what their social or economic background. For example, in 1985 it was combined pressure from the DWM, the National Council for Women in Development and the Ghana branch of the Federation of International Women Lawyers which pushed the government into enacting a series of laws affecting the lives of all Ghana's women. The new laws covered a number of fields, including family accountability, intestate succession, administration of estates and customary marriage and divorce. Taken together, they were an important step towards assuring the women of Ghana equality of treatment before the law and in helping the economic position of working women during structural adjustment.

In sum, the success of the DWM as a developmental organization for Ghana's poor women is exemplified by the fact that it has become one of the leading voices in the country's embryonic civil society, championing working women. Those who criticize the movement because of the involvement of the President's wife miss the point that in a traditional society like Ghana's it is absolutely crucial to have the support of important figures in order to achieve collective goals. The fact that the DWM receives funds from foreign NGOs suggests that its important developmental role is increasingly being recognized abroad.

Algeria

In contrast to Ghana, Algeria's women are not organized in their own development organizations. Like Ghana, Algeria has been involved in a SAP for several years. Broadly social results have been the same in the two countries. In Algeria, Bromley notes, the SAP failed to lift a stagnant economy, producing 'growing problems of food security ... rising levels of urbanization and large numbers of unemployed and underemployed youth' (1993: 403). The result has been serious political instability since the late 1980s, encouraging support for the radical Front Islamique de Salut (FIS), as I shall explain in chapter 7. The rigours of the country's SAP helped to stiffen the resolve of Islamists seeking to overthrow the military government; between 1992 and 1996 civil war led to the deaths of about 60,000 people (Haynes 1995c).

An April 1994 IMF agreement with Algeria was predicated upon a 40 per cent devaluation of the country's currency, the dinar; it was denounced by the FIS as a gross example of governmental subservience to foreign pressure. Devaluation was to meet international conditions for tackling the debt crisis, that is, the IMF would try to reschedule Algeria's $26 billion foreign debt if the government would agree to extensive economic reforms. The state owed more than $9 billion in interest to foreign banks and the goverments of France, Belgium, Spain, Japan and the USA; yet its expected income for 1994 was only $8 billion. Western governments, especially France's, were extremely concerned to support the military-backed regime to prevent the Islamists from grabbing power. They feared 'the spread of [Islamic] fundamentalism throughout North Africa' (Gumbel 1994).

But why are the Islamists widely supported? A declining economic and developmental position for many, especially the young and unemployed, is at least partially responsible for the stimulation of Islamist opposition not only in Algeria but more widely throughout the Middle East and North Africa (Bangura 1994: 22; Vaughan 1995). Islamist groups benefit from developmental downturns, as we shall see in chapter 7, especially thriving in the urban centres where growing poverty, youth unemployment and a lowered sense of expectations are endemic (Ibrahim 1991; Williams and Falola 1995).

Conclusion

I have shown how declining economic performances helped to stimulate action groups in a number of Third World countries. I examined development initiatives in West Africa, Bangladesh and Thailand, concluding that success is dependent on the extent to which local, autonomous action groups are coordinated by a dynamic umbrella organization. During the 1980s, however, many Third World countries adopted structural adjustment programmes, often – unintentionally – hitting the poor and powerless rather hard. SAPs had mixed outcomes. Often they managed to stabilize a deteriorating macroeconomic position. On the other hand, they were not a panacea for long-term developmental failures. Macroeconomic stability was often bought at a high price – that is, reductions in living standards for many already poor people. When the latter manage to organize themselves for development goals, as women in Ghana and the poor in Bangladesh have done, it is helpful for local groups to be coordinated by national-level organizations, especially if they can attract foreign funding. However, as the account of West Africa's Six-S/Naam groups indicates, foreign funding is by no means a panacea on its own. The organization became overbureaucratized and overcentralized, growing ever more dependent on foreign assistance. The result was its collapse in 1995.

The chapter also suggested that in at least one case – that of the 31 December Women's Movement of Ghana – poor working women were instrumental in persuading government to allow wider reforms to improve women's well-being. The point is that the conditions of the SAP allowed the DWM to grow from being a 'mere' development group to one with an important voice in the country's embryonic civil society. In both Mexico and Algeria, on the other hand, the hardships associated with structural adjustment were important factors in the emergence of important opposition groups the Zapatistas and the Islamists respectively. The Zapatistas, as we shall see in chapter 4, managed to deliver a stinging critique of society which touched on political and social issues as well as economic conditions. They especially criticized the government for its failure to develop a democratic system which would be truly representative. Something similar happened in

Algeria – both developmental and democratic failures helped to stimulate the Islamists, whose goals were nothing less than a transformation of society along religious lines.

Thus macroeconomic decline and SAPs – along with demands for democracy – helped to focus dissatisfaction with the status quo, encouraging many action groups to organize; and while SAPs hurt the poor and vulnerable, their responses were variable – in part dependent on available avenues to draw attention to their grievances.

4
Democracy and
Indigenous Peoples

Demands for democracy were, like macroeconomic decline and SAPs, an important stimulus to action groups and civil society in the Third World. Until recently the great majority of Third World governments were undemocratic. The transition to formally democratic systems in Latin America and parts of Asia and sub-Saharan Africa was the outcome of both international and domestic pressures.

Regarding the former, during the Cold War it seemed to be sufficient for many authoritarian governments to call themselves 'anti-communist' to receive the support of the West and hence boost survival chances. In the 1980s, however, the international climate changed. Ronald Reagan, then the US President, addressed the British Parliament in 1982 and declared that he was anxious to set in motion a 'Crusade for Democracy'. By this time, both democracy and human rights were much in favour in the West and, as Michael Moore notes (1995: 422), were 'advancing steadily' in the Third World. In short, it is widely accepted that international pressure helped to convince many non-democratic Third World governments to allow competitive elections (Huntington 1991; Bratton 1994a; Pridham 1994; Moore 1995).

The second factor leading to democratic transitions was pressure from domestic civil societies. Taking a cue from the democratic transformations in Eastern Europe in the late 1980s, Third World democrats were encouraged to pressurize their governments towards political reforms. Over the next few years dozens of non-democratic systems gave way to formal democracies, that is, the mass of the people had the opportunity to choose their government at regular intervals. Yet the inauguration of formal democracies did not lead to substantive democracy, that is, where the subordinate – indigenous peoples, the poor, women, the young, religious and ethnic minorities – are able to put their concerns squarely on to the political agenda. In other words, the creation of formally democratic systems, while welcome, is insufficient on its own to shift the balance of power in the favour of subordinate groups. As a result, many have eschewed the institutionalized political parties, preferring instead to pursue their aspirations via their action groups.

The chapter begins by describing and accounting for what Huntington (1991) calls the 'third wave of democracy'[1] in the Third World. Following that I examine the differences between 'formal', 'facade' and 'substantive' democracy, arguing that in the absence of the latter it is rational for subordinate groups to seek other ways of expressing their grievances and seeking ways to ameliorate them. Next, I offer case studies of indigenous peoples in Brazil and Mexico, who – unable to exploit their formally democratic systems to pursue their goals of political and socioeconomic reforms – chose the vehicle of action groups to pursue their aspirations.

The Third Wave of Democracy

Global factors

Until recently, very few – less than 10 per cent – of governments in the Third World were democratically elected. Instead, the 'political terrain was marked . . . predominantly by autonomous, heavily armed authoritarian states' (Potter 1993: 362); 'military governments, one-party regimes and personal dictatorships' were especially common (Pinkney 1993: 1).

Dozens of Third World countries have recently experienced democratic elections, some for the first time in decades. By 1996 all 23 Latin American countries were formally democratic, while seven (of 20) previously authoritarian countries in Asia – Bangladesh, Mongolia, Nepal, Pakistan, the Philippines, South Korea and Taiwan – were also democracies (Potter 1993: 362). In sub-Saharan Africa there were growing numbers of elected regimes: more than half of the region's 48 countries held contested elections during 1989–96 (Wiseman 1995). Only in the Middle East was there little apparent democratic movement, although there were some encouraging signs: in Lebanon, democracy was reintroduced after 20 years; Jordan held reasonably 'free and fair' elections in 1994; and some Palestinians experienced tentative moves towards autonomy in Israel's Occupied Territories.

While it is impossible to overlook the contribution of domestic pro-democracy groups to democratization, it is equally unwise to disregard the role of external factors, not only in the Third World, but also elsewhere during recent times. The end of authoritarian rule in Greece, Spain and Portugal in the mid-1970s, coupled with the impetus provided by the Helsinki Conference on Security and Cooperation in Europe in 1975, focused international attention on democracy and human rights. From Southern Europe the democratizing trend spread to Latin America in the early 1980s, then to Asia's authoritarian states and the Soviet Union and its satellites, before reaching Africa in the second half of the decade.

The Helsinki Agreement was a factor in the emergence of pro-democracy groups in Eastern Europe which eventually contributed to the overthrow of the communist regimes. Collectively, the demonstration effect provided by developments in Southern and Eastern Europe served as a catalyst for the later generation of calls for enhanced human rights and, by extension, greater democracy in the Third World. In Huntington's view the advance of democracy in the Third World was stimulated by a combination of domestic and global developments.

In relation to the latter, of particular importance was the collapse of communist rule in Eastern Europe, putting non-democratic governments in the Third World under intense pressure to reform and encouraging aspiring democrats. Chilton (1995) argues that the unexpected – and sudden – political demise of the Soviet Union and the communist systems of its Warsaw Pact allies was highly influential in galvanizing aspiring democrats in the Third World. However, the Gorbachev reforms in the Soviet Union should not be seen in isolation; rather, they helped reinforce a growing belief in the efficacy both of liberal democracy and of free-market paradigms. Then there was the 'demonstration effect' of the fall of the Berlin Wall in 1989 – watched by hundreds of millions of people on tens of millions of television screens throughout the world. In sum, the demise of the communist counterhegemonic challenge to liberal democracy and capitalism was instrumental in undermining the claimed benefits of centralized, one-party rule: social and political stability and economic planning to smooth out the cyclical hiccups of capitalism (Fukuyama 1992; Rueschemeyer et al. 1992: 294–6).

Second, in addition to the demonstration effect provided by events in Eastern Europe, there was international pressure of a more focused kind from Western governments and international governmental organizations, especially the European Union, the North Atlantic Treaty Organization, the International Monetary Fund, the World Bank and the Council on Security and Co-operation in Europe (Pridham 1994). Third, factors resulting from globalization – the spread of market forces, the communications revolution and the demonstration effects of successful pro-democracy movements elsewhere – were also collectively important in helping to create a global climate where democracy was perceived as a normal human aspiration.

Randall argues that the penetrative capacity of international communications was influential in stimulating the democratization trend in the Third World (1993: 644). The increase in numbers of those able to see television programmes is not, on its own, inherently politically significant. But it is important to see growing television access as a facet of a wider communications revolution which encompasses, *inter alia*, the Internet, portable radios, fax machines and e-mail. Their collective impact is to facilitate the transmission of information within and between countries which cannot easily be controlled even by 'strong' states, even if they manage to dominate local mass media (M. Scott 1990; Reeves 1993: 124; Randall 1993; Theodoulou 1994; *Africa Confidential* 1996; Woollacott 1996).

In sum, the chances of a global democratic offensive after the Cold War appeared to be good. Three developments were particularly important: the fall of the Berlin Wall and the demise of communist rule in Eastern Europe; diplomatic and economic pressure by Western governments and international governmental organizations; and the creation of a democratic 'climate' underpinned by the communications revolution. The result was that many pro-democracy groups in the Third World – via civil society – were encouraged to make redoubled efforts to persuade their governments to allow democratic elections.

Domestic factors

Arguably there is no topic in contemporary politics more important than the character and chances of civil society. Even though the concept is rather vague, it is easy to recognize societies where civil society is strong or weak. When an effective civil society is present there will be strong and autonomous social groups able, Hall argues, to balance excessive assertions of power (1993: 282). In particular, strong political parties are necessary to represent ordinary citizens, to ensure the adoption of better policies and to mediate political conflict. But what happens if political parties are unable or unwilling to represent certain sections of society? What can the unrepresented do about it?

It is not necessarily the case that recent elections in the Third World have served to usher in democratic systems whereby all sections of society are fully represented. What has generally occurred is that 'formal' democracy – characterized by the inauguration and survival of reasonably 'free, pluralistic, and democratic institutions in national life' (Levine 1984: 117) has been inaugurated. However, this is *not* the same as 'substantive' democracy – that is, a 'deeper' democracy empowering weak groups. What are the barriers to substantive democracy in the Third World? Which groups are excluded?

In most Third World countries today 'politics' reflects competition or collaboration among politically and economically powerful elites. Whether regimes are characterized as leftist or rightist authoritarian or as oligarchic democracies – that is, dominated by a small exclusive class – the point is that power monopolies at the apex traditionally form the political superstructure in most Third World countries. Organski (1965) identifies such a power monopoly as a 'syncratic alliance', that is, a concord uniting traditional agrarian interests – too strong to be destroyed – with a modernizing industrial elite. In exchange for obtaining the political support of agrarian interests, powerful urban sectors agree not to disturb the often semifeudal conditions of the countryside. In short, *even with formal democracy*, class structures in many Third World countries remain largely traditional, with the impact of industrialization being in the main accommodated to traditional patterns of dominance and subordination.

In Latin America and parts of Asia, large landowners represent the rural side of the coalition. For example, a succession of democratically elected Indian governments since independence in 1947, despite socialist rhetoric, failed to break with powerful rural elites. Although the former ruling families were formally shorn of their traditional powers after independence from British colonial rule, they very often managed to use their continued social standing to 'pursue the democratic route to power as a very successful alternative' (Calvert and Calvert 1996: 111). Although Organski's description may be less relevant to Africa, support from those with wealth and power is nevertheless almost always more important to political decision-makers than support from other classes (Bayart 1993). In short, while the bases of power of countries in the Third World differ, elites usually control both the basis of economic wealth and the direction of political development.

Such power monopolies make it difficult for broad-based national political parties to develop. Many postcolonial political systems have managed to develop a range of political capacities to enhance their longevity. These include, according to Almond and Powell (1966), the ability to discourage or repress peasant discontent, a distributive capacity to improve the welfare of favoured groups of urban workers, an extractive capacity to obtain resources from rural areas through patron–client networks, and an ability to distract attention by massive public works or military adventurism. These capacities enabled governments in many Third World countries to survive, sometimes for decades.

Syncratic coalitions are not restricted to perennially non-democratic regimes. Often they also define a pattern of political power in countries that regularly alternate between military and civilian rule. Or they may be a means of maintaining the power of the upper classes, as in Colombia, Argentina or the Philippines, even when formally democratic (Rueschemeyer et al. 1992: 174–5; Gills and Rocamara 1993). Dictatorial regimes may be overthrown without necessarily defeating narrowly based monopolies. Thus oligarchical or syncratic democracies may have the outward characteristics of competitive constitutional regimes – that is, opposition groups are free to organize – yet power monopolies remain politically dominant.

Formal, Substantive and Facade Democracy

It does not follow, then, that to usher in a representative democratic system it is sufficient to achieve regular, 'free and fair' elections alone. Yet it is at least a start, a road increasing numbers of countries are taking. Between 1972 and 1994 – broadly the era of the third wave of democracy – the number of countries with 'democratic political systems' increased from 44 to 107. Put another way, the proportion of democracies grew from less than a quarter to nearly 60 per cent of the world's 185 countries in two decades (Shin 1994: 136). Many of them were in the Third World. But having 'free and fair' elections says absolutely nothing about the quality or purpose of the rule which follows. Broadly, there are two kinds of 'democracy' extant in the Third World: 'formal' and 'facade' democracy (Garreton 1991; Potter 1993; Whitehead 1993). Currently, no regimes in the Third World have developed what I call 'substantive' democracy.

Formal democracy

'Formal' democracy is underpinned by regular, 'free and fair', competitive elections based on universal adult suffrage. It is characterized, normally, by the exclusion of excessive use of force by the state against society, theoretically by the accountability of rulers to the ruled through the ballot box, and by reasonable adhesion to the rule of law. There are sufficient civil and political liberties to ensure electoral competition.

The core of formal democracy is that there are meaningful rules and regulations determining the conduct and content of elections, while governments must rule with concern for the process of law. Above all, then, formal democracy encompasses the idea of *choice*; that unpopular governments can be ousted by societal decisions in regular polls. The problem, however, is that many states run systems meeting the criteria of formal democracy while at the same time their governments have never been defeated at the polls. I illustrate this point by reference to Malaysia and Zimbabwe.

Potter identifies Malaysia as having been an 'enduring democracy' since independence from Britain in 1957 because there are regular elections (1993: 361). Jesudason argues that, because the incumbent regime has never been beaten in an election in four decades, Malaysia is no more than a 'statist democracy', that is, the state's key role 'in structuring politics and social life' ensures that it appears to many people that the governing regime is the *only* one possible (1995: 336). Case (1993) prefers to describe the political system in Malaysia as a 'semi-democracy'; Ahmad (1989) calls it a 'quasi-democracy'. Semantic distinctions are, however, beside the point: Malaysia can neither be 'considered as *fully* democratic nor *definitely* authoritarian' (Jesudason 1995: 336, emphases added). The ruling party, the United Malays National Organisation (UNMO), has found ways to manipulate electoral mechanisms and to maintain a firm hold on power. The position UNMO has achieved is called by J. Scott 'limited hegemony' (that is, a form of statist democracy): people believe that any other alternative to the ruling party 'is not realistic . . . the realm of . . . idle dreams' (1990: 74).

Like Malaysia, Zimbabwe is also *formally* democratic. Despite economic travails the ruling Zimbabwe African National Union-Popular Front (ZANU-PF) achieved 82 per cent of the vote in the 1995 elections – winning 147 of the 150 seats – on a respectable turnout of 57 per cent (Sylvester 1995: 403). Like UNMO, ZANU-PF has the power to shape the political rules to its advantage in several ways. First, both parties retain control of the mass media. In Malaysia most of the main newpapers, as well as the radio and television stations, are owned either by the government or by UMNO-affiliated companies or individuals, while in Zimbabwe there are 'relatively few party-autonomous public institutions to aggregate and articulate dissent to official power' (1995: 408). Second, both parties unceasingly trumpet the fact that they are the bodies which brought their countries to independence from British colonial rule. Third, both UMNO and ZANU-PF deal with organized opposition in the same way: buy it off, coopt it or, if the first two fail, crush it (Jesudason 1995; Sylvester 1995).

The result is that while both Malaysia and Zimbabwe are formal democracies, in each the ruling party has developed a firm hold on power to the extent that most people probably find it hard to conceive of rule by another party. In both countries, the national leaders – Mugabe (Zimbabwe) and Mahathir (Malaysia) – have the apparent status of indispensability; their parties have positions of such dominance that the party has become the Party (J. Scott 1990: 74). However, in both Malaysia and Zimbabwe there nevertheless exists what J. Scott (1990) calls 'fugitive opposition', involving forms of resistance offstage rather than centre stage; and it is not necessarily less viable for being in the shadows. Subordinate groups – including women, young people and ethnic and religious minorities – seek ways of escaping the party's and the state's bid for total dominance (von der Mehden 1989; Sylvester 1995).

Facade democracy

'Facade' democracies are common in the Third World. They have the *outward appearance* of democracy with hardly *any* of the substance. In the past they were very common in Latin America, the result of elections said to be 'for the English to look at' (Portuguese: 'para os ingleses ver') (Whitehead 1993: 316). In Africa, Bayart describes how something similar – 'fig leaf' elections – often leads to 'facade' democracies (1993: xii–xiii), in, *inter alia*, Togo, Burkina Faso and, arguably, Cameroon. Facade democracies are also common in the Middle East. For example, presidents Saddam Hussein (Iraq), Hafez al-Assad (Syria), Hosni Mubarak (Egypt) and Muammar Gadafy (Libya) won presidential elections in 1995 with at least 94 per cent of the popular vote. Needless to say, in each of these cases the ruling regimes do not have real democratic pretensions.

Many regimes with only very flimsy democratic credentials were strongly encouraged by the West to preserve their political systems as a bulwark against communism. In effect, the argument is that there was an alliance between domestic and international class actors championing a strictly limited form of democracy in the Third World (Gills et al. 1993). Until the late 1980s, although liberal democracy was the preferred condition, there was little evidence to suggest that Western governments regarded issues such as free and fair elections or civil and individual rights as primary conditions for economic support or military or diplomatic protection. Neither did the World Bank or IMF show a serious commitment to promote democratic government, although as primarily economic institutions there was no real reason why they should. Leftwich (1993) argues that in many cases – Argentina, Brazil, Greece, Nicaragua, the Philippines and Greece – it was seen as much more conducive to Western interests for there to be an authoritarian government of the right than a representative government critical of Western policies.

Where democratic institutions and processes were encouraged, it was at 'low intensity', as for example with the facade democracies of Guatemala or Kuwait. In these countries elected elites worked closely with supporting military agencies, often armed by Western governments. In such conditions, socially progressive or reformist movements were unable to make much headway. Often they were regarded as disloyal opposition, a danger to continued Western support (Gills et al. 1993). As a result, human rights violations coexisted with Western aid programmes, trade links or military pacts. Democratic transition was inevitably impeded. During the late 1970s and early 1980s a period of low intensity democracy sprang from the growing confidence of the Carter and Reagan administrations that capitalism was winning the war – especially the global economic struggle – against communism. By the mid-1980s the way was open for a 'Crusade for Democracy', the term used by Ronald Reagan in his address to the British Parliament in 1982. What 'low intensity democracy' amounted to, it is argued by sceptics, was that democratic transition might be limited to forms of government that could best apply structural adjustment and accommodate social and political results that formed 'a toxic cocktail of absolute decline' (Gills and Rocamara 1992: 506).

Gills, Rocamara and Wilson (1993) argue that recent democratic change in the Third World was controlled by Western governments, especially the USA, and local conservative elites with a vested interest in limiting the extent of political changes. In other words, this is a theory of democratization which highlights both the limited significance of democracy in many Third World contexts, and the role of external actors. The outcome – 'low intensity democracy' – is not much more in most cases, they argue, than a democratic veneer overlaying an otherwise unreformed political structure. Power stays in the same hands as before with only the illusion of greater democratization. It satisfies Western governments' – allegedly insincere – concerns for *deeper* democratization. The idea is that external forces dictate and control the process of political change in the Third World for their own aims connected to continued economic control. There is, however, only limited evidence for the 'low intensity democracy' argument. First, the collapse of communism has removed the need for strategic advantage, which in turn has led to guarded US support for pro-democracy movements in Haiti, South Korea, Taiwan and Angola. Second, the 'low intensity democracy' argument tends to overestimate the extent of Western – and especially American – influence on domestic political developments in the Third World. The West was quite unable to influence the direction of political change in Somalia, Nigeria and Uganda, among others; on the other hand, such influence was apparently decisive in Haiti, Ghana and Tanzania.

The fact is that Western governments have two, not necessarily congruous aims in the Third World: they may well wish to see the development of democracy as a more or less abstract 'good', connected to the embedding of 'good' government; on the other hand, they may prefer *non*-democratic governments under some circumstances. For example, in Latin America in the 1960s and 1970s, successive US governments were decidedly ambivalent about the prospect of social democratic governments coming to power, even by the ballot box as in Brazil and Chile (Pinkney 1993: 79). In the early 1990s the World Bank argued that non-democratic government 'in polarized societies' is more conducive for economic stability in the Third World (Haynes 1995a: 112). More generally, *stability* in the Third World (sociopolitical, and hence economic) – an essential component of global economic growth – is apparently desirable for the 'Big Three' international economic actors: the USA, the European Union and Japan (Bayart 1993: x–xii). While democracy in the Third World may be *morally* desirable, probably of greatest importance is a return to a fully functioning, fully profitable international economic system, with the great majority of Third World countries playing their traditional role of suppliers of raw materials and consumers of Western manufactured goods. For this, *stable* regimes such as China's – rather than *democratic* governments are essential. This is not to argue that external actors can – for long – impose political systems on unwilling countries. Democracy rarely develops without the active involvement of a coalition of self-interested and self-aware class forces acting together to ensure that democratic change endures. In fact, 'external imposition of any kind of regime is difficult, and particularly so of democratic rule. Short-term external intervention can tip the balance in favor of democratization only if the internal balances of class power and the state–society constellation are favorable' (Rueschemeyer et al. 1992: 279; Morales 1994).

There is a relatively clear link between class development and democratic consolidation which augurs badly for the new democracies of Africa and Asia where such class forces are underdeveloped. Everything else being equal, those who have the most to gain from democracy, that is the middle and subordinate classes, 'will be its most reliable promoters and defenders' (Rueschemeyer et al. 1992: 57–8). When these classes are weak, so too is democracy. The groups with most to lose – traditional power holders, the military and, if they exist as in Latin America, big landowners – will seek to resist its introduction or at least will endeavour to reduce its impact on their fortunes by striving to control the democratization process for their own ends.

In sum, the prospects for the consolidation of first formal and then substantive democracy are only auspicious when those classes which have historically pushed for economic and political liberalization – the private sector bourgeoisie and the middle classes – and for democratization – the working class – are both strong enough and, in the case of the first, numerically large enough to force the state to inaugurate and then deepen democracy. Democracy *cannot* be granted by the manoeuvres of political elites alone; for democracy to be meaningful it must involve a lessening of an unequal distribution of power, empowerment of subordinate classes through the vote, popular representation and increased citizens' participation in the collective political concerns of society.

Substantive democracy

Substantive democracy extends the idea of democracy beyond formal mechanisms. It intensifies the concept to include a real stress on individual freedoms and the representation of interests via elected public forums and group participation. It is a deepening of democracy whereby all citizens have easy access to the governmental process and a say in collective decision-making. There are effective channels of accountability for public officials. Substantive democracy is concerned with the development of equity and justice, civil liberties and human rights: in short, 'genuine participation in rule by the majority of citizens' (Potter 1993: 356). Three developments would characterize a shift from formal to substantive democracy: unequivocal and uninterrupted imposition of civilian control over the armed forces; the extension of a range of human and civil rights to the vast majority of citizens; and effective channels of mass participation so the powerless – the poor, minority ethnic and religious groups, women and young people – have a real say in the direction of the nation (Garreton 1991: 106). The lack of examples of Third World countries – or for that matter, some would argue, almost *any* countries – with substantive democracy helps to explain why groups lacking political power form action groups to seek objectives linked to enhanced empowerment (Migdal 1988: 14).

In conclusion, a realistic assessment of democracy in the Third World in the late 1990s would be to perceive the types of extant systems on a spectrum marked 'maximalist' (substantive) at one end and 'minimalist' (facade) at the other. Some democratic systems are well towards the minimalist end, many others somewhere in the middle, a very few nearer a maximalist position. In assessing the prospects for democracy in the Third World, as well as appraising those democracies already in existence, it is necessary, as Clapham and Wiseman observe, to take an 'unromantic and pragmatic view as to what type of system might be consolidated': the idea that all Third World states will 'create perfectly functioning democracies which will survive indefinitely is too improbable to warrant serious consideration' (1995: 220).

What is perhaps beyond dispute is that in many Third World countries there has been at least a *measure* of democratization in recent times. In recent elections, some non-democratic regimes were ousted via the ballot box, and some incumbent governments retained power by winning a majority. Elsewhere, those in power simply refused to allow elections at all: after all, 40 per cent of regimes in the Third World, some 50 countries, concentrated in the Middle East and Africa, are currently devoid of most democratic credentials. Far from being a straightforward process, the introduction and consolidation of substantive democracy is tied up politically with a number of issues, including that of the ruling elite's solidarity and its control over society, the nature of a country's political culture, the strength and effectiveness of civil society and the impact of external pressures on domestic political arrangements. The importance of these issues is shown below in case studies of indigenous peoples' action groups in Brazil and Mexico, which sought to target the inadequacies of the prevailing political and economic arrangements by pursuit of programmes of activities undertaken outside of the confines of institutional politics.

Indigenous Peoples in Brazil and Mexico: the Consequences of Formal Democracy

About 4 per cent of the world's population – roughly 300 million people in 70 countries – are often described as 'indigenous peoples'. They are found in a number of Asian countries, including Indonesia, Malaysia and India, yet it is in Latin America that the highest proportion vis-à-vis non-indigenous peoples is to be found. It is estimated that Indians in Latin America comprise about 70 per cent of the population of Bolivia, 45 per cent in Peru, 40 per cent in Ecuador, 30 per cent in Mexico and just 1.5 per cent in Brazil (Calvert and Calvert 1996: 246; World Bank 1995: 162, table 1). Very often indigenous peoples are noticeably worse off than the rest of the population, with low life expectancy and high infant mortality. Their concerns extend from protection and defence of their natural environments, an issue examined in chapter 5, to socioeconomic and democratic rights. The main catalyst for the emergence of indigenous peoples' action groups was macroeconomic decline and the return of formal democracy to Latin America in the 1980s.

While the term is in common use, in fact there is no objective definition of indigenous peoples, since human beings have moved around the planet from the earliest times. Where such groups do clearly exist, they have the following characteristics: a deep, even mystical, relationship with their land; a common culture, language and ancestry; a belief that they are the original inhabitants of their land (Calvert and Calvert 1996: 246). A simple definition would propose that indigenous peoples survive whenever traditional, sustainable lifestyles endure in opposition to the encroaching power of the modern state. This confrontation sometimes brings indigenous peoples to global attention; perhaps most strikingly in recent times with the Zapatista uprising in Chiapas state, southern Mexico, from 1994 and the contemporaneous mobilization of the Indians of Brazil. Both groups seek major improvements in their socioeconomic and political positions.

Brazil's Indians

In recent years the plight of the Indians of Brazil has caught the world's attention. During 1992 the publicity which the British rock singer Sting gave to the cause of the Yanomani, who live in northern Brazil and southern Venezuela, was an important reason why the federal government granted secure title to nearly 100,000 sq km of ancestral lands. Another catalyst for concern was the publicity surrounding the Earth Summit, held in 1992 in Rio di Janeiro. Yet, while the Yanomani now have reserved land protected by governmental decree, it is doubtful whether the invasion of outsiders – for timber, farming land and minerals – will be easily halted.

Part of the problem, many Indian leaders feel, is that the country's political system is not flexible enough to allow the concerns of Indians to become an important issue on the national agenda. Quite simply the desires of bands of scattered Indians are normally not enough to make a serious impression on the minds of the political elite based in far away Rio or São Paulo. What can the Indians do about this? One response has been to join together to form action groups to press the Indians' claims for land and the reversal of the tide of immigrants who see farming opportunities in apparently 'empty' land.

Since the European colonization of Brazil began 500 years ago, the number of indigenous people has declined from around 5–6 million to no more than 250,000, a fall of more than 95 per cent. Those remaining are divided into more than 120 tribes living in isolated forest areas. Brazil's swift industrial growth – 9.4 per cent a year during 1970–80, 0.7 per cent in 1980–93 (World Bank 1995: 165, table 2) – means, however, that such isolated areas are becoming fewer and fewer. As noted above in the case of the Yanomani, the state response to protect indigenous people has been via the creation of 'reserves'. By 1990, 27 million hectares had been set aside for this purpose, yet they were not, for the most part, physically delineated. The consequence was that loggers, large companies, ranchers and miners did not seem to be deterred from entering – and colonizing – Indian lands. The result was that conflict between the Indians and outsiders became increasingly common. In Brazil's Amazonia state, for example, a large population relies on the forest and its products for survival. According to Allegretti (1990), there are some 200,000 Indians in the state relying on forest products for survival, including oils, fruits and fibre. Additionally, around 1.3 million non-Indians harvest forest products, especially rubber, combining this with subsistence agriculture and fishing.

During the period of military rule (1964–85) there was an increasing concentration of land in the hands of a few large owners in Brazil. Many undertake large-scale cattle-ranching and are extremely well connected to the political elite (Diegues 1992: 21). The result is that government often turns a blind eye to the acquisition of land by well-heeled farmers. Because cattle require pasture rather than forests, the result is increasing deforestation. Both the Indians and the rubber tappers suffer. Not only are the rubber tapping areas being reduced, but deforestation is also affecting the availability of fish and game, the Indians' traditional sources of protein. Many rivers are also polluted by mercury, used by itinerant gold prospectors to flush gold particles from river sediment.

The return of Brazil to democracy in 1985 was a catalyst for Indians to organize themselves. After 20 years of military government, characterized both by a desire for swift industrialization and an apparent neglect of the rights of indigenous peoples, a civilian president, Collor, took power in 1990. While trumpeting plans to reshape Brazil's political and economic system, he was forced to resign at the end of 1992 following charges of corruption. Collor's departure meant the end of his plan to reform Brazil's political system (Cammack et al. 1993: 120).

In the past, many Indians seemed to accept rather passively the taking over of their land by outside groups or, at least, only reacted sporadically and hence ineffectively. Recently, however, their resistance began to become more organized. In the early 1980s the Tikuna Indians created a General Council of the Tikuna Tribe, formed by 68 community leaders. Later, following the return of democracy, the União dos Povos Indigenas (IPU: Indigenous People's Union) was created. It had an important role in the defence of Indian interests. In 1986 the IPU joined with the Rubber Tappers National Council to create the Alliance of Forest People. The aim was not just physical defence of the forest but also more generally to lobby for forest people's interests. Some successes were achieved: a few Indian tribes ·- notably the Caiapos - began to receive a share of the money generated by mining activities on their lands (Diegues 1992: 26). In sum, the return of democracy coupled with macroeconomic pressures stimulated Indians and their rubber tapper allies to pursue their socioeconomic and political interests through a number of action groups.

The National Council of Rubber Tappers   In Brazil 10 per cent of the population controls more than 50 per cent of the national income and the majority of the best arable land; as a result, the latter is in increasingly short supply for the country's fast growing population of over 160 million. Because of their political clout, big landowners are able to confiscate forested land, clearing it to grow crops like soya beans or to provide grazing for cattle. Large profits are realized when the resulting produce is exported (Rueschemeyer et al. 1992: 174–5; Cammack et al. 1993: 38).

The National Council of Rubber Tappers (NCRT) campaigns for the defence of the forests where members gain their livelihoods, against logging companies, corrupt government officials and land speculators. The council's main initiative, Projeto Seringueiro, attempts to inform those that work and live in Brazil's forests, particularly rubber tappers and Indians, that it is necessary to identify closely with the forests where they work and live, so that they will understand the necessity of defending them from felling. Its purpose is to 'encourage the rubber tappers to identify more closely with the forest, to understand it, to learn more about it and defend it' (Breyman 1993: 129). Chico Mendes, the NCRT's first leader, murdered in 1988, underlined the importance of education for the NCRT's endeavours: he noted that 'the strengthening of our movement has coincided with the development of the education programme . . . all our advances, the fight against the destruction of the forest, the organizing of the cooperative and the strengthening of the union, were all possible thanks to the education programme' (quoted in Breyman 1993: 129).

The NCRT endeavours to build a coalition between Indian groups and the mostly *mestizo* (mixed race) rubber tappers. The alliance seeks a variety of goals, of which preventing tree felling is only one. The Indians also demand the right to govern themselves, using their own laws, traditions and institutions.

In conclusion, Indian and allied groups in Brazil campaign and lobby for defence of the forest, land redistribution, economic opportunities and civic rights via their action groups. So far, however, while helping to raise the issue of the protection of the forests of Brazil to become an international issue, the NCRT-Indian campaign has not yet managed to curtail the forests' destruction or to initiate greater rights for the indigenous inhabitants. Part of the reason is that Brazil's political system – despite the reintroduction of democracy – is not responsive enough to the demands of marginal groups.

The Indians of Mexico

The Ejército Zapatista de Liberación Nacional (the Zapatistas)   While the struggles of Indians and rubber tappers in Brazil were encouraged by the return of democracy to Brazil, indigenous peoples in Mexico are faced with a different set of problems, as one of their leaders suggests:

> We have nothing, absolutely nothing – not decent shelter, nor land, nor work, nor health, nor food nor education. We do not have the right to choose freely and democratically our officials. We have neither peace nor justice . . . Today we say enough. (Zapatista rebel, January 1994, quoted in Vidal 1996)

Following a civil war, Mexico has been ruled by the Institutional Revolutionary Party (PRI) without a break since the overthrow of the dictator (*caudillo*) Porfirio Díaz in 1911. Since then all governments have claimed to employ democratic forms of constitutionalism and elections, while emphasizing democratic values in public education (Pendle 1976: 198). After reviewing a substantial literature, however, Booth and Seligson (1993: 110–11) characterize Mexico as an authoritarian political system. In 1988 there was a large vote against the PRI in presidential elections (1993: 131). On the other hand, between 1988 and 1991 the PRI managed to improve its position in regional elections. One commentator remarked that Mexico looked set to remain a single-party state (Hall 1993: 284).

Many Mexicans seem to have become increasingly disillusioned with the PRI-dominated system because freedom to protest, dissent and work for change is limited. However, few expected the armed uprising by about 4,000 Indians of the Ejército Zapatista de Liberación Nacional (EZLN) movement – the Zapatistas[2] – in Chiapas state on 1 January 1994. People familiar with the remote region were astonished by the scale of the rebellion and the Indians' remarkably sophisticated organization evidently built over several years (Harvey 1995: 39).

The Zapatista uprising probably represents a watershed in modern Mexican history. The goal of the Zapatistas differed from those of earlier guerrilla movements in both Mexico and Latin America in that they did not aspire to seize state power or lead the masses in social revolution (Gott 1973). The government asserted that the rebellion was led by 'a bunch of white intellectuals with links to radical groups', claiming EZLN's predecessor was the banned urban guerrilla movement, the National Liberation Force, active in the 1970s. There is no evidence, however, to back the government's claim that the EZLN was dominated by intellectual *agents provocateurs* bent on violent revolution (Gunson 1996). Instead, popular support for the EZLN – focused on the Tzeltal, Tzotzil, Zoque, Chol and Tojolobal Indians in the Altos and Selva regions of Chiapas – grew as a result of popular initiatives, coordinated by the region's progressive Catholic Church, which had brought Indians and their supporters together in a series of meetings and conferences over the last 20 years (Harvey 1995: 57).

The Zapatistas called on all Mexicans, not just indigenous peoples, to participate in their broad movement for 'jobs, land, housing, food, health, education, independence, freedom, democracy, justice and peace' (1995: 39). The aim was to defeat the ruling PRI, to shift the balance of social forces in favour of popular and democratic interests, to make the government more accountable and to achieve popular representation for all Mexicans, especially those of the indigenous population. But what caused the rebellion? First, it was the absence of avenues for democratic change. The movement called on the legislative and judicial branches of government to depose the president, Carlos Salinas de Gortari, and to install a transitional government to organize fair elections. Second, there was the state's failure to promote success-fully cultural and ideological integration under PRI leadership, an in-ability to 'subdue or neutralize the powerful myths or symbols of ethnic identity' held by the country's indigenous inhabitants, the Indi-ans (Camilleri and Falk 1992: 204). Third, there were several economic and developmental reasons. Developmental indicators are generally poor in Chiapas, which is overwhelmingly rural and dependent on rain-fed agriculture for its livelihood: there is a shortage of adequate land for farming, and only half of the inhabitants have access to elec-tricity, a third to clean drinking water. Only 10 per cent of the state's roads are paved (Harvey 1995: 41–2). Attempts to modernize the economy, including rural land reforms and reducing the guaranteed prices for coffee beans – the main crop – had a negative impact on many *campesinos* (small farmers), particularly in the Selva and Altos regions (1995: 45, 50–3). The EZLN demanded the redistribution of land to the landless. Further, the EZLN regarded the inauguration of the North American Free Trade Agreement (NAFTA) on 1 January 1994 as a 'death certificate for the Indian peoples of Mexico, who are dispens-able' for the Salinas regime (quoted in Harvey 1995: 39). The Zapatistas believed that NAFTA would impoverish Indian farmers, unable to compete with the large agricultural combines of the USA.

Despite the lack of achievement of any of its goals, it seems unlikely that the EZLN will simply fade away. The Zapatistas' rebellion amounts to a demand for a new order in Mexico whereby all Mexicans – including indigenous peoples – will have the ability to make the most of their developmental chances. In short, it is an uprising against the political and economic realities of a country whose authoritarian politi-cal system has denied for three-quarters of a century opportunities for ordinary people to have a say in the running of their affairs. The significance of the Zapatistas is not, however, simply that subordinate peoples believe that they have been forced to take up arms against an unresponsive government. It is also that they set in motion a potentially important process of democratization under the auspices of the Na-tional Democratic Convention (NDC), an umbrella organization of pro-democracy groups (Harvey 1995: 63). The emergence of the NDC and the raising of its voice in civil society probably encouraged more vocal demands than ever before for a thoroughgoing reform of Mexico's political and economic systems. Yet the August 1994 presidential election saw the PRI's candidate, Ernesto Zedillo, gain power in a relatively clean poll (1995: 64). The result of the election for the governorship of Chiapas in the same month also bolstered the PRI's position: its candidate, Eduardo Robledo Rincón, won with just over 50 per cent of the vote; two opposition candidates managed 43 per cent of the vote between them, claiming that there were serious irregularities in the ballot. The EZLN issued a statement condemning the alleged electoral fraud, calling on Robledo not to assume office in order to avoid a potential 'blood bath' (1995: 65). Despite the threat, Robledo acceded to office, while at the national level the government agreed to talk with the EZLN about their grievances. Negotiations between the Zapatistas and the government during the next three years failed to achieve agreement between the two sides, while the government took the opportunity of locking up and torturing Zapatistas and their supporters (Gunson 1996).

Conclusion

Global trends recently facilitated the introduction of formal democratic systems in more than half of the world's countries, including many in the Third World. While some social groups benefited, many others did not. There were two main sets of pressures – global and domestic – which facilitated the shift from authoritarian to formally democratic systems. Interest groups in civil society – trade unions, students, churches, the media and professional organizations – tended to be in the forefront of demands for democratic changes. I argued, however, that the vast majority of systems which resulted were formal democracies, that even where regular elections are held there are few – if any – real opportunities for power to change hands away from a relatively small elite group. In other words, the chances are very limited for those at the bottom of the socioeconomic pile to improve their lot in a formally democratic system. Instead, it is often rational for such subordinate groups to seek alternative means of expressing their grievances and to seek other ways to ameliorate them. To illustrate this argument, I described the efforts of indigenous peoples in Brazil and Mexico who – unable to exploit their formally democratic systems in pursuit of political and socioeconomic reforms which would benefit them – instead chose the vehicle of action groups to pursue their aspirations. They sought, on the one hand, to pursue group demands via their organizations. In the short term, the indigenous peoples of Brazil and Mexico were unable to achieve their goals. On the other hand, the significance of their organizations is that they managed to place their demands on the national political agenda. In both Brazil and Mexico, civil societies were enriched by the creation and consolidation of national organizations – respectively the Indigenous People's Union and the National Democratic Convention – to focus and pursue indigenous people's democratic demands.

But a pursuit of democratic change is by no means the only aspiration for many people in the Third World. For some, immediate socio-economic goals may take precedence. In chapters 5–7, I examine action groups organizing around three main aspirations: environmental protection, women's rights, and the creation of an Islamic state. What they have in common is that they organize subordinate people in pursuit of objectives which formally democratic systems are unable to deliver. But they may be even more significant: a new input into civil societies, injecting the demands of the have nots on to national agendas – often for the first time.

5
Environmental Protection

Power ... is Brazilian rubber tappers struggling to preserve the forests upon which their livelihoods depend. Power is Indian peasants resisting hydroelectric projects that will flood their land. . . . Around the world, ecology movements are demanding and creating the power to shape their own environments.

S. Breyman, 'Knowledge as power'

The state's claim to defend threatened resources and its exclusive right to the legitimate use of violence combines to facilitate its apparatus-building and attempts at social control. State threats or use of violence in the name of resource control helps them to control people, especially unruly regional groups, marginal groups, or minority groups who challenge its authority.

N. L. Peluso, 'Coercing conservation'

In chapters 3 and 4, I examined two important stimuli for action group formation: on the one hand, macroeconomic decline and structural adjustment programmes, on the other, demands for democracy. It emerged that Third World action groups are (1) concerned with strategies for defence of livelihood and/or identity; (2) important elements in emerging civil societies. Political space has opened up, encouraging groups to pursue their goals via a variety of methods, including lobbying, campaigning and sometimes direct action. Groups concerned with environmental protection are common. Table 2.1 indicated their objectives, organizational levels, perception of the state, role in political process, membership profile and the tactics they adopt to achieve their goals.

It would be simplistic to claim that environmental action groups always want to protect their local ecology while nasty business interests wish to destroy it. On the other hand, most environmental action groups are notable for the fact that they realize that if their local environment is seriously degraded or destroyed, then it is they who will lose out. The issue may simply be one of *who* has the 'right' to destroy the natural environment – local people or outside interests? The central point is that environmental protection is always highly political, an issue made plain in the quotations above. Breyman points out that environmental action groups see their goals in relation to their members' subordinate position, while Peluso notes that the state may use violence against such groups if it deems it necessary to assure its control of valuable resources, such as oil, forests, minerals or hydroelectric power.

I focus on environmental action groups in India, Malaysia, Indonesia, Cambodia, Kenya, Nigeria and French Polynesia, for reasons detailed shortly. They are concerned with the consequences of deforestation; large hydroelectric dams; oil extraction; and nuclear weapons tests. All were founded over the last 25 years, that is, since the 1972 Stockholm United Nations Conference on the Human Environment established environmental protection on the global agenda. Since then 'tens of thousands' of environmental action groups have emerged in the Third World (Fisher 1993: 209). Most are located in Latin America or Asia. There are few in sub-Saharan Africa, hardly any in the Middle East. Such a distribution is not unexpected given the comparative development of civil societies in these regions.

Despite their vast numbers, it is possible to generalize to an extent about them. First, they aim to mobilize local people in defence of the local environment against outside interests, whether the state or big business. Second, environmental action groups are usually rurally based. Third, women usually form the core of their memberships. Fourth, while some of the groups have a narrow conservation focus, many others have wider socioeconomic and political concerns. Fifth, environmental action groups are more likely to succeed in their goals when they can exploit democratic and legal avenues. Sixth, it helps to enlist important foreign allies, such as Greenpeace International, athough this does not ensure success. Finally, environmental action groups often do not win their struggles: failures outweigh successes.

In the case studies below, there are no – even partial – successes recorded for environmental action groups in Kenya, Nigeria or Cambodia. These are all countries without either developed civil societies or effective democratic structures. On the other hand, those from more democratic countries with more effective civil societies – India and arguably Malaysia – have recorded successes. For success, it is necessary to have a facilitating political environment, an umbrella organization of some kind to to coordinate local groups' endeavours and often the enlisting of outside help to strengthen local campaigns.

The structure of the chapter is as follows. First, I outline the background to the emergence of environmental action groups. Second, I present case studies supporting the argument that they are likely to have success in democratic environments. Third, I argue that environmental action groups are important elements of emerging civil societies in the Third World and that protection of the natural environment is a new – and crucial – dimension in state–society relations.

From Stockholm to Rio: Two Decades of Politicization of the Natural Environment

The 1972 Stockholm Conference focused world attention on the necessity of protecting the natural environment to ensure the sustainability of life on earth. During the 1980s the message was reinforced by a series of environmental disasters, including the 1984 Bhopal disaster in India, when an explosion at a factory producing toxic chemicals killed more than 4,000 people (Rettie 1994), and a near-meltdown of the nuclear reactor at Chernobyl in 1986. Further threats were the destruction of some of Europe's forests by acid rain; growing holes in the ozone layer and increases in skin cancers; pollution of the seas and overfishing; and global warming, which endangers the very existence of certain low-lying and island countries.

The 1980s were dubbed the 'decade of the discovery of the environment' (Hadjor 1993: 105). The issue of the relationship between people's social and economic demands and the natural environment began, for the first time, to be discussed in a scientific way. A tangible sign of growing global concern was the Earth Summit sponsored by the United Nations and held in Rio di Janeiro in 1992. More than a hundred heads of state and 30,000 bureaucrats and representatives of nongovernmental organizations met to discuss 24 *million* pages of preparatory documents and to make wide-ranging decisions regarding the future of the global environment.

The Earth Summit was called in order to confront two of the world's most pressing, interlinked problems: environmental degradation, and poverty and underdevelopment. There was a widespread hope that the relaxation of Cold War tensions juxtaposed with a new awareness of environmental matters would be a conducive background to real progress. The conclusion of the Earth Summit was marked by the signing by representatives of all the countries present of a document known as 'Agenda 21', trumpeted as 'a plan of action to save the planet'. Agenda 21 was a compromise between the advocates of environmental conservation (most Western states) and advocates of more or less unbridled growth with scant regard for the environment (many Third World governments). It was an aspirational response to public concern, rather than a document encompassing concrete measures.

Despite high hopes, however, the immediate outcome of the Summit was less than many environmentalists expected. Governmental representatives from Western industrialized countries sought to proclaim fine principles of wide-ranging environmental concern, yet without agreeing to do anything very concrete to make them come to fruition. Many Third World governments, on the other hand, expressed ambivalent feelings about environmental protection, arguing that the West's industrial development had only come about through the exploitation of their local environments as well as those of their colonies, and simultaneously asserting that there was no good reason why *they* should be denied the ability to 'catch up' industrially. If the West developed by exploiting the natural environment, why, they ask, should the Third World be any different? Many Third World governments are additionally irritated by the West's attempts to lay down universal environmental standards. Annoyance also centres on what is perceived as the industrial democracies' sudden concern with protection of the environment following years of practices which, many Third World governments feel, have contributed far more to the degradation of the natural environment than does deforestation, the main environmental 'sin' in the Third World.

Economic growth and increased consumption are, of course, highly important to governments everywhere; those in the Third World are no exception. 'Too great' protection of the environment is, as a result, sometimes perceived as a luxury only rich Western governments, under pressure from a relatively wealthy, middle-class electorate, can afford to entertain (Sethi 1993; Huus 1994; Jayasankaran 1994; Rettie 1994; Miller 1995: 43–6). The consequence is that the environmental concern of many Third World groups is perceived as evidence of their 'anti-development', 'anti-nation' or 'anti-people' bias. Besides, so the argument goes, the West cannot have it *both* ways: on the one hand it professes to deplore environmentally harmful policies in the Third World, while, on the other, Western governments urge Third World governments to 'open up' their economies to foreign investment and to develop exports of agricultural products which may lead to greater rather than less environmental degradation and destruction (Miller 1995).

State–Society Relations: the Environmental Dimension

When focusing on the domestic rather than the global dimensions of environmental protection, it seems that there is very often a clear difference in environmental perceptions between environmental action groups and the state. While many Third World countries lack economic flexibility as a result of a subservient position in the international economic system, this is by no means the only factor determining governmental environment policies. They are also influenced by a variety of domestic factors, including the nature of the local political structure and the distribution of wealth and income in the society.

Agricultural pricing policies, investment incentives, tax provisions, credit and land concessions are usually designed to further elite interests. The political elite is very likely to include rich people with interests in a variety of environmentally destructive industries such as commercial logging, mineral and oil exploitation, plantation cropping and large-scale irrigated farming. In addition, the costs and benefits of development projects are nearly always distributed to the advantage of the 'haves' at the expense of the 'have nots'. Relatively powerless, usually rural peoples – especially if they belong to national minorities – will nearly always suffer the socioeconomic and environmental costs of development schemes, sometimes losing their homes, farms and fishing grounds; rarely will they be compensated by the state for their losses (Miller 1995: 42).

What this amounts to is that environmental issues are often highly political, involving, on the one hand, the state and its allies and, on the other, those with little political power. Measures to protect the environment will be likely to attract the commitment of state officials and policy-makers in the Third World if they are likely to benefit personally. This can be seen in relation to the conservation of elephants in Africa. For example, the governments of Kenya and Zambia only began to support a global ban on trade in ivory when their countries' own herds had declined to an alarming degree. It is perhaps unnecessary to mention that those who had benefited most from the ivory trade were senior figures in the state, especially politicians and military personnel (Ellis 1994: 62). The utility to such people of implementing a global ban on the ivory trade was that elephant stocks could then recover, allowing a later resumption – whether legal or illicit – of the trade. Such regimes will seek to grab the moral ideology of global conservation to justify state systems of resource extraction and production which nearly always benefit a few at the expense of the rest of society.

The extraction of valuable resources is of course a revenue-generating strategy embraced by very many Third World governments. They always claim to allocate rights to extract resources for the 'greater good of society'. But what this amounts to is that they have a vested interest in preserving or gaining jurisdiction over valuable resources. Governments often interpret the value of resources in relation to three factors: the world market price of the product, the strategies by which they will be exploited, and the allocation of resulting monetary benefits from their use or non-use. The last two will be the most important in stimulating state–society conflict (Peluso 1993: 52). When the state's view of what is the correct procedure and weight of the distribution of the benefits fails to meet the expectation of local communities, the result may well be conflict.

Action Groups and the Natural Environment

Environmental action groups in the Third World often attract members of subordinate groups – especially young people and women – who share a perception that the status quo is inimicable to their interests (Fals Borda 1992: 311; Bayart 1993: 112). Put another way, the striking increase in Third World environmental groups not only signals serious trends in ecosystem decline but also an accompanying 'social stress that results from and feeds into that decline' (Princen and Finger 1994: 10). In short, environmental issues in the Third World are very often closely linked to wider issues of economic and sociopolitical power. This is because many environmental activists probably feel that key decisions affecting their lives and environments are beyond their control. Many seem to tie human rights to environmental rights, arguing that the natural environment cannot be protected without sustaining its human communities. For example, the Coordinating Council for Human Rights (CCHR) in Bangladesh coordinates a growing network of human rights and environmental groups, now totalling more than 120. The CCHR has instituted machinery for providing legal aid to local communities threatened by unwelcome environmental developments, especially the consequences of deforestation (Fisher 1993: 31, 105, 148).

The social consequences of deforestation in the Third World

Deforestation is one of the most important catalysts to the formation of environmental action groups in the Third World.[1] The term 'deforestation' refers to a massive, often irreversible destruction of forests. Tropical moist forests, usually referred to as 'rain' forests, cover an area of 1.5 billion hectares globally. Two-thirds are in Latin America, with the rest divided between sub-Saharan Africa and East and South-East Asia. Rain-forests are the 'richest ecosystems in biomass and biodiversity on land', yet in the 1990s alone around 20 million hectares were destroyed *each year* (Thomas et al. 1994: 62). At current rates of destruction, there will be *no* rain-forests left in 75 years time.

Millions of hectacres of tropical rain-forest are destroyed each year for a variety of reasons. In Brazil, for example, 167 million cubic metres of rain-forest were destroyed in 1987. Over three-quarters (128 million m^3) were burnt to create farming land. Less than 1 million m^3 of timber was exported. In contrast, Malaysia produced 42 million m^3 of timber in 1987; 36 million m^3 (88 per cent) was for export. Table 5.1 shows the contrast between the two countries. Whether largely for farming, as in Brazil, or mostly for export, as in Malaysia, deforestation has negative consequences at local, regional and global levels. Locally, it threatens or destroys the lifestyles of forest-dwelling peoples; regionally it provokes the leaching and erosion of soils, flash-flooding and desertification; and globally it leads to reduced biomass stocks and species diversity, altered patterns of rainfall, and long-term climate change.

Table 5.1 Production of tropical timber in Brazil and Malaysia, 1987 (million m^3)

	Non-fuelwood	Non-fuelwood exports	Fuelwood	Total
Brazil	39	0.8	128	167
Malaysia	36	27	6	42

Source: Thomas et al. 1994: 62.

Once environmental action groups begin to campaign against deforestation they will find themselves up against not only the state but also large farmers and business interests. The ability of anti-deforestation groups – and of environmental action groups more widely – to succeed in their objectives depends on two main factors: it is crucial that groups do not remain autonomous but link together into a regional or national alliance; and a campaign seems more likely to succeed if the alliance can pursue its goals through democratic and legal channels. In other words, the effectiveness of environmental endeavours is partially dependent on the political circumstances which prevail. Next I offer a series of case studies to illustrate these contentions, from (1) India, where both democracy and a strong civil society exist; (2) Malaysia and Indonesia, where neither democracy nor civil society are strong, but where there are signs that both may be improving; and (3) Kenya, Nigeria, Cambodia and French Polynesia, where both civil society and democracy are undeveloped.

India

The Chipko movement

India's forests, covering about one-tenth of the land area, are an essential resource for the livelihoods of rural and indigenous peoples, providing food, fuel and fodder (Sethi 1993: 124). The Chipko movement is the result of hundreds of decentralized and locally autonomous initiatives, often led by women. Their slogan – 'ecology is permanent economy' – epitomizes the movement's chief concern: to save forest resources from commercial exploitation by outside contractors. 'In effect the Chipko people are working a socio-economic revolution by winning control of their forest resources from the hands of a distant bureaucracy which is concerned with selling the forest for making urban-oriented products' (United Nations Environment Programme, quoted by Ekins 1992: 144).

The Chipko movement is that rare thing among Third World environmental groups: a success. It was founded in 1973 in Uttar Pradesh to stop tree-felling. Over the next five years it spread to many other districts of the Himalayas (Sethi 1993: 127). The name of the movement comes from a local word meaning 'embrace': people – usually women, the bedrock of the movement – have stopped the felling of trees by standing between them and the loggers, literally embracing them. Chipko protests in Uttar Pradesh achieved a major victory in 1980 with a 15-year ban on green felling in the Himalayan forests of the state, although it is not clear whether the ban has been renewed. During the 1980s the movement spread through India, to Himachal Pradesh in the north, Karnataka in the south, Rajasthan in the west, and Bihar in the east. 'In addition, the movement stopped clear felling in the

Western Ghats and the Vindhyas and generated pressure for a natural resource policy more sensitive to people's needs and ecological requirements' (Ekins 1992: 143).

The Chipko movement is an example of how non-violent resistance and struggle by thousands of ordinary people, without the guidance and control of any centralized apparatus, recognized leadership or full-time cadre, can succeed under certain circumstances. More generally, Chipko helped to shift attention to the centrality of renewable resources – soil, air, water, trees – at a time of swift industrialization in India. Chipko is a voice from the margins of Indian civil society, and it managed to demonstrate 'that the crucial environmental conflicts are not just city-based [such as pollution] or related to the depletion of non-renewable resources useful for industry, but arise directly from the philosophical premises embedded in the modern Western and capitalist vision' (Sethi 1993: 127).

The Narmada Valley Project

A second successful Indian example of an environmental campaign is the stopping of the Narmada Valley Project (NVP), a huge hydroelectric dam and irrigation project involving over 3,000 major and minor dams. The Narmada is India's largest western-flowing river, and its fifth largest overall, with a length of 1,312 kilometres. More than 20 million people – including many minority tribal peoples – live in its basins, using it as an important economic and ecological resource. According to the World Bank, however, the Narmada river 'is one of [India's] least used – water utilisation is currently about 4 per cent and tons of water effectively are wasted every day when it could be put to use for the benefit of the region' (quoted in Ekins 1992: 89). The NVP was perceived as the solution to this alleged under-use. It was to comprise two very large dams – the Sardar Sarovar Project (SSP) and the Narmada Sagar Project (NSP) and 28 small dams and 3,000 other water projects. The planned benefits included irrigation of 2.27 million hectares of land in Madhya Pradesh, Gujarat and Rajasthan states, pisciculture, drinking water and electric power. The two main dams would also be designed to moderate floods. The World Bank agreed a $450 million loan for SSP and was considering support for NSP when its backing for the entire project came to an end in 1994 (Tran 1994).

Until recently, big dams had been widely regarded in India as prestige symbols of industrialization and development. India's first post-independence Prime Minister, Nehru, called large dams the new 'temples' of modernizing India (Ekins 1992: 88). Large-scale dams were planned to supply, via hydroelectricity, an adequate supply of cheap electricity for industrialization. Because of this benefit they were thought to justify huge capital investments and the forced removal of local people from designated land.

The successful anti-NVP campaign exemplifies the way large dams now often encounter 'dwindling acceptance and militant resistance' in the Third World (Stiefel and Wolfe 1994: 180). The importance of the Narmada issue is that it struck directly at one of the fundamental development tenets: big is beautiful. It also shows that ordinary people – if they organize – may defeat both state and business interests. Despite the expected benefits, a vociferous campaign against the NVP developed once it became clear that the dams would entail massive displacement of local people. The campaign originated initially not as anti-dam *per se*, but as groups of activists aiming to ensure that the environment would be protected and that people displaced by the dams would be properly financially compensated. Soon, however, the separate groups joined together in common cause against the dams, forming what Ekins describes as 'one of the most powerful social movements ever to emerge in post-independence India' (1992: 90). Anti-dam activists – including about 1 million potential 'oustees' from more than 150,000 families, as well as voluntary social groups and local and foreign environmentalist groups – were pitted against an opposing coalition made up of the state governments of Madhya Pradesh, Gujarat and Rajasthan states, the World Bank and big local landowners. The latter saw a potential in the scheme for a major boost to irrigation and the supply of electrical power, local construction firms foresaw a bonanza, while many ordinary citizens believed that the benefits of the scheme would lead to an all-round growth in prosperity 'through flood control, increased drinking-water supply, new jobs through a spurt in industry and allied activities' (Sethi 1993: 133).

Struggles at several levels – grassroots, provincial, national and global – focused not only on the pros and cons of the NVP itself but also more widely to include the benefits and disbenefits of large 'development' projects more generally. The anti-NVP campaign won because it managed to build a powerful anti-dam coalition, involving an alliance of local peasant, women's, youth and environmental groups and transnational groups, including Greenpeace International, Friends of the Earth and the US-based Environmental Defense Fund. The anti-dam campaign forced the World Bank – because of adverse publicity – to withdraw its funding in 1994. As a result, it appears that the project has been put on hold, and perhaps quietly sidelined in the absence of alternative funding. As Lori Udall of the Washington-based International Rivers Network explained, the cancellation 'sends a strong signal to international donors that large dams are risky, expensive and destructive investments and that they should support smaller, more flexible projects' (Vidal 1995a).

Two conclusions emerge from the accounts of the Chipko movement and the Narmada anti-dam campaign. The first is that it takes not only a high degree of popular organization and mobilization to gain success but also a responsive government prepared to react favourably to such efforts. Second, it may also help to have external allies, although this in itself is no guarantee of success. When such conditions are absent it is very difficult for environmental action groups to achieve similar successes. In the next two case studies – those of environmental action groups in Malaysia and Indonesia – partial success has been achieved because they have managed to build powerful local coalitions which have been able to exploit legal avenues to challenge the government. It may even be that their partial successes reflect something altogether more significant: the gradual emergence of civil societies which may begin to pressurize their governments to democratize meaningfully.

Malaysia and Indonesia

Sahabat Alam Malaysia

As with the 1994 uprising in Chiapas, Mexico, indigenous peoples are leading the fight for the survival of Malaysia's forests, demanding both land and social reforms (Calvert and Calvert 1996: 246–7). Conflicts in Malaysia between local people and tree fellers are indicative of the conflicting interests involved in the exploitation and conservation of forest resources. The use by subsistence-based people of forest resources for their survival is often in conflict with their use for industrial or cash-crop purposes.

Conflict in Sarawak, Malaysia, is between loggers and the indigenous people over tree felling. By the 1980s tree cutting was proceeding at a rate fast enough for Sarawak and its neighbour, Sabah, to provide almost 40 per cent of the world's total logs for industrial use. The scale of logging is systematically destroying the culture and livelihood of the area's indigenous peoples, the Pelabit, Kayan and Penan peoples. Conflict over the issue erupted in the mid-1980s when local people blockaded logging camps and physically fought the loggers, albeit without success (Ekins 1992: 144). Gradually, however, their efforts began to be coordinated by Malaysia's Friends of the Earth organization, Sahabat Alam Malaysia (SAM) which, by pressurizing the government, was able to gain concessions regarding excessive tree felling (Cohen 1994).

SAM was founded in 1978 by S. Mohamed Idris, a businessman, now the organization's president. Over the next two decades it grew into an environmental network coordinating over a hundred member groups, helping victims of deforestation, overfishing and industrial pollution (Fisher 1993: 110). It publishes a monthly newsletter in two languages, a bimonthly environmental news digest and numerous single publications (Ekins 1992: 145). Over time it has emerged as an important voice in the country's gradually emerging civil society.

Wanana Lingkungan Hidap Indonesia

Indonesia, like Malaysia, is one of the world's fastest growing economies. The former had an average annual growth rate of GNP per capita of 4.2 per cent between 1980 and 1993, the latter 3.5 per cent (World Bank 1995: 162, table 1). The most potent pro-conservation voice in Indonesia is that of Wanana Lingkungan Hidap Indonesia (WALHI), the Indonesian Forum on the Environment. It was formed by 79 groups in 1980, rising to 320 a year later. By 1992, WALHI had over 500 members (Princen and Finger 1994: 2). WALHI has 'board members from local business and from multinationals such as IBM' (Fisher 1993: 176). Its founder, Erna Witoelar, expresses WALHI's philosophy thus: 'I like to think of a network of diverse groups as a tropical rain forest. The more diverse the tropical forest is, the greater its survival rate' (1993: 139). Like Malaysia, the growth of an important environmental lobby in Indonesia – bringing together, *inter alia*, local and foreign business interests – suggests that as civil society emerges in the country, it will have an increasing voice in development decisions.

In October 1994, WALHI began a court case against the government to spark an inquiry into the government's Reforestation Fund. The lawsuit has helped to focus attention on various environmental concerns, receiving unprecedented attention from government ministers, the private business sector and the national press. The suit challenged President Suharto's decision to funnel $185 million from the Reforestation Fund allegedly into the coffers of the nation's aircraft industry. According to WALHI, the decision violated the government's commitment to refurbish Indonesia's vanishing rain-forests (Cohen 1994: 44). The government's defence lawyers maintained that WALHI had no legal standing to bring the suit, as the 'non-government organisation does not represent the interests of the general public', while, in addition, 'the reforestation issue should be aired in parliament, not in the courts' (Cohen 1994: 44). A confidential Asian Development Bank report commissioned by the Ministry of Forestry pointed out that just 16 per cent of the reforestation funds was spent in the four years to March 1993: 'Direct funding of natural forest rehabilitation and conservation activity formed only 3 per cent of allocated funding' (1994: 44). In other words, less than *half of 1 per cent* of funds allocated for reforestation in Indonesia was actually spent on that purpose between 1989 and 1993! The report noted delicately that 'there is evidence of considerable and increasing flexibility on how funds are spent', although no details were given. Cohen notes that 'reforestation levies, collected from concessionaires as an alternative form of rent capture, have always been disbursed at the discretion of the president.' In addition, 'many plantations have been situated in logged-over forest, prompting the clear-cutting of remaining trees so as to create a homogeneous forest suitable for Indonesia's rapidly-expanding pulp and paper industry' (1994: 44). Nevertheless, the conservation message championed by WALHI appears to be gradually getting through: Indonesia's forestry minister, Djamaloedin Soeryohadikoesoemo, announced in late 1994 that Indonesia would reduce its timber output by 30 per cent between 1995 and 1999 in the interests of sustainable development. Djamaloedin also expressed interest in 'pilot projects in community forestry, now in operation in Kalimantan and other areas (allowing) villagers more responsibility in protecting resources' (1994: 46).[2]

In conclusion, the importance of SAM and WALHI is that they are forcing government to clean up its environmental act as a result of unprecedented attention from business and the media. This contrasts with the situation in a variety of other Third World countries and regions – such as Cambodia, Nigeria, Kenya and French Polynesia – where the weakness of civil society is reflected in the inability of environmental action groups to take ecological issues seriously.

Cambodia, Kenya, French Polynesia and Nigeria

Logging in Cambodia: the lack of action group response

Whereas deforestation in Malaysia and Indonesia is met by coordinated resistance from both local people and national organizations, there is little sign of a synchronized response to the plight of the forests

in South-East Asia. This is the region with the greatest range of standing forests under threat, yet uncontrolled logging is not strongly challenged by local people. This is no doubt the result of a lack of
democracy and weak civil societies: national environmental action
groups do not exist. As in Brazil and Malaysia, uncontrolled logging is
a highly lucrative activity which many governments in South-East Asia
encourage. A consequence is that by the early 1990s there was severe
damage to forests in the region. The Philippines was almost stripped of
forest, Cambodia was subject to uncontrolled, rapidly escalating logging, while the fast shrinking forests of Myanmar (Burma), Indonesia
and Thailand were being logged on a massive scale.

In Cambodia forests are destroyed with the collusion of the government, Thai border authorities and the guerrilla movement, the Khmer
Rouge. Forest cover in Cambodia has been reduced by half in 20 years
– from 74 per cent in 1974 to 30–5 per cent by the mid-1990s. A London-
based NGO, Global Witness, claimed in March 1995 that Cambodia's
logging ban, imposed two months earlier, was a 'mockery' (Global
Witness 1995). Trucks were passing through border checkpoints
manned by Khmer Rouge and Cambodian government troops. The
guerrillas were allegedly making millions of dollars a month from
levies on the timber. The ecological, social and economic results were
clear: deforestation was damaging the country's natural irrigation system, leading to flooding, drought and failures of the rice harvest. The
Cambodian government's March 1995 assurance in Paris to the International Committee on the Rehabiliation and Reconstruction of Cambodia that measures had been taken to halt deforestation was described
by Global Witness as a 'complete whitewash' (Ezard 1995). In the
absence of effective local environmental action groups, it was very easy
for both the government and the Khmer Rouge to encourage the destruction of the country's forests to the point that environmental disaster threatens to strike the country sooner rather than later.

The Green Belt movement (Kenya)

It might be argued that the situation in Cambodia has been formed by
two decades of civil war, so that it is not reasonable to expect environmental action groups to have power. Yet if we turn attention to Kenya,
independent for over 30 years and without civil strife during that time,
we find that it has not managed to produce an effective civil society or
successful environmental action groups. The absence of an effective
environmental lobby is due to the government's skill in crushing dis-

sent, as well as the fact that society is seriously divided along ethnic and religious lines.

For 15 years until its abolition in 1992, the Green Belt movement had been devoted to tree planting and general conservation issues, its membership predominantly made up of women. Led by Wangari Maathai, Professor of Anatomy at Nairobi University, Green Belt had begun under the auspices of the state-sponsored National Council of Kenyan Women (NCKW) (Fisher 1993: 102–3; Ekins 1992: 151) The NCKW organized the Green Belt movement to assist women in solving environmental problems and to teach them to distinguish between problems like desertification and symptoms like famine. By the early 1990s, Green Belt had organized more than 80,000 women and half a million schoolchildren to plant and nurture more than a thousand tree nurseries. At that time over 10 million trees had been planted; their survival rate was an impressive 70–80 per cent. By this time, Green Belt had succeeded in building an international position for itself, attracting international funding for its conservation efforts (Fisher 1993: 102–3, 175). During the 1980s, Green Belt had been supported by the government. Like the *harambee* development movement (see chapter 2), Green Belt was seen to be providing a highly important national service – in this case, tree planting – aiding the country's anti-desertification efforts.

The relationship turned sour in 1989. Green Belt generally and Maathai in particular were attacked by the government because of their opposition to the construction of a 'world media centre' in Nairobi, planned to be the tallest building in Africa with a giant sculpture of Kenya's president, Daniel arap Moi, in pride of place. The project was to be in one of the few public parks in the city, removing one of the few green spaces in an increasingly built up environment and depriving local people of open space. Because Maathai mobilized domestic and international pressure against the plan, 'she was vilified and placed under virtual house arrest . . . In November 1990, [she] was prevented from returning to Kenya after a trip to the USA' (Ekins 1992: 151–2). Following her expulsion, opposition to the project collapsed, and so did Green Belt itself.

The Maathai story is a good example of the connection between human rights abuse, 'prestige project' development and unsustainability of environmentally destructive policies practised in the name of development in the Third World. In Kenya, civil society is in a very embryonic state. There was little coordinated support for Green Belt in 1990, despite this being a time of demands for democracy in the country. This may have been in part because Green Belt was perceived by many men to be run by educated women – a class viewed with suspicion by many male Kenyans.

Nuclear testing at Mururoa atoll: the catalyst for Tahiti's cultural revolution

This next case study recounts the struggle of Tahitian groups against French nuclear testing. The Tahitians' objective was both environmental and political. Their campaign not only sought to stop nuclear testing but was also directed against the French colonial presence. The anti-France struggle focused the attention of the main groups in Tahiti's emerging civil society particularly Hiti Tau, an environmental, development, women's, youth and cultural umbrella group, Tavini Huira-atira, the pro-independence party, and the Atia I Mua labour union – on nuclear testing, a symbolic issue focusing attention on independence (Rood et al. 1995: 17; Vidal 1995b).

The decision by the French government to detonate eight – later reduced to six – nuclear explosions at Mururoa atoll in late 1995 and early 1996 was followed by a wave of global condemnation (Ghazi 1995). On Bastille Day, 14 July 1995, French products were boycotted and the country's embassy compounds around the world were stormed by Greenpeace protestors. Anti-nuclear protestors staged raids on the offices of French companies in Sydney, Australia, while in Adelaide a wrecked Renault car covered with 5,000 signatures was taken to the parliament building. In Suva, Fiji, 2,500 protestors marched on the French embassy and presented a 50,000-signature petition. In Cambodia Buddhist monks and nuns marked Bastille Day with a demonstration outside the French embassy; Green Party activists in Germany demonstrated outside the French embassy in Bonn; and in Prague, capital of the Czech republic, anti-nuclear demonstrators collected signatures against the nuclear tests, protests which were also signed by many of the (French) troops guarding France's embassy (Zinn and Bowcott 1995). Despite these protests, however, the government of Jacques Chirac stood firm: the French detonated the first nuclear explosion at Mururoa atoll in September, and others followed.

The tests did more than stimulate global anger; they also encouraged the Tahiti independence movement, Tavini Huira-atira, to greater efforts. The point is that while global environmentalists saw the tests as contrary to the 1990s spirit of conservation, many Tahitians saw them as an example of French arrogance, a further indication that the colonial power cared little for the views of its 'subjects' in French Polynesia.

There is a long history of nuclear tests in French Polynesia. During the Cold War the islands of the South Pacific were linked directly to the grand strategies of some Western countries. The remoteness of some atolls and the strategic location of others made them attractive sites for nuclear weapons testing. British and American nuclear tests were conducted in the South Pacific in the 1950s and, following the Partial Test-Ban Treaty of 1963, France established its Centre d'Expériments du Pacifique, carrying out 41 atmospheric tests at Mururoa atoll over the next decade before announcing a 20-year moratorium on further testing (Fry 1993: 228, 237).

Nuclear tests were disastrous for many local communities: the Chamoro people of Guam as well as the Tinian and Marshall Islanders were ejected from their homes, while the Bikini Islanders suffered the effects of radioactivity: 'all people in the region potentially suffer from the fallout of the 163 atmospheric tests conducted . . . before 1975' (1993: 228). Despite such problems, the Cold War was used as justification by the United States and France to continue testing, thus severely constraining the ability of the islanders to gain autonomy or independence (Danielsson and Danielsson 1986).

For South Pacific societies, the Cold War was influential in two further ways: first, it moulded the way in which regional security was conceptualized; and second, it helped to foster a regional pan-nationalism. As Fry notes, while this originally affected 'only relations among states, it increasingly affected social and political forces within them' (1993: 234). In both American-controlled Palau and the French possession of New Caledonia, Cold War imperatives were used to justify opposition to moves for self-determination. Later, campaigns for greater autonomy and independence gained in strength, stimulated by perceptions that the end of the Cold War would lead to less bargaining power and a more stringent economic climate for the South Pacific as attention was focused elsewhere (Callick 1991). It was clear, however, that the traditional Cold War justification for French involvement in the Pacific was not the only reason for the country's interest in the region. While French Polynesia retained its importance as a nuclear testing site, the remaining colonial possessions, including Tahiti, gave the French a presence in a region which contains important countries like Australia and New Zealand (Woollacott 1995).

Until the recent upheavals, France was successful in containing dissent by the assiduous use of money, spending close to $2 billion dollars annually on its possessions in the South Pacific (*The Economist* 1995b). In French Polynesia per capita GDP in 1993 was estimated by the World Bank as in the 'high income' category, that is, greater than $8,626 per annum. It was four times that of independent Fiji ($2,130) and many times greater than other independent island states in the region: Tonga ($1,530), Vanuatu ($1,230), Western Samoa ($950) and Solomon Islands ($740) (World Bank 1995: table 1a, p. 228). A report commissioned by the Tahitian government on the economics of the island noted that Tahiti 'lives off a French military arsenal'. The economy is 'both prosperous and protected, without the worry of international competition' (*The Economist* 1995a).

French Pacific policy is to retain its role in the region, despite the withdrawal by the other erstwhile colonial powers, Britain, Germany, the Netherlands and Portugal. The French government maintains that its Pacific possessions are an integral part of France and that '[a] Tahitian has the same citizen's rights as a Parisian' (1995a). Nearly 40 years ago, the people of France's Pacific possessions – French Caledonia, Wallis and Futuna, and New Caledonia – were asked if they wanted independence, which would have meant a complete cessation of French aid. Referenda resulted in a wish by each territory to remain a part of the French 'family'. By the 1980s, however, it was clear that the mood was changing: in New Caledonia a vociferous pro-independence movement clashed with the governing administration, but France persuaded the native Kanaks to put off a decision about independence until 1998, promising in the interim to channel generous aid to the island (Fry 1993: 234).

A background of growing anti-French feeling underpinned the 1995 riots in Tahiti. The island particularly benefits as a supply base for Mururoa atoll, 1,400 km to the south-east. Many Tahitians work there, mostly in menial jobs, although many earn salaries allegedly in excess of $40,000 dollars a year (*The Economist* 1995a). These jobs are of course highly valued in Tahiti itself, where unemployment is high: between 25 and 40 per cent of the young are without work (Vidal 1995b). Every year about 1,000 young people cannot find jobs when they leave school; the young provide many of the cadres for the pro-independence movement. The shanty town of Faaa, three miles from the capital Papeete, is a collection of 'battered thatched huts and fetid beer halls clogged with jobless Polynesian youths'; as George Pittman, a pastor of a local evangelical church, commented, the youths 'are aggressive, not like before . . . They are very angry and confused. I hear them shouting and screaming. This is the most dangerous bomb for us, not the atom bomb' (Higson 1995). Thus the riots grew from an explosion of anger, especially by the young, to become a broader-based demonstration of anti-French feeling. Vaihere Bordes, leader of a women's group, claimed that 'everyone here is united against France and the nuclear testing [yet] local government does not listen' (Vidal 1995b).

The French decision to resume nuclear testing at Mururoa atoll was the catalyst for an eruption of anger against the French colonial presence. For three days in September 1995, coinciding with the first nuclear test, demonstrators took to the streets, destroying, burning and looting. By the end, Tahiti's capital Papeete was badly damaged. The Chirac government could not understand the Tahitians' reaction, perceiving it akin to that of a pet animal biting the hand that feeds it.

Calls for social justice and an end to environmental destruction in French Polynesia were part of the same demand: key decisions affecting people's lives must be brought back under their control. It was the exclusion from decision-making that fuelled popular resentment. As Bordes asserted: 'France has said for years that if we allow the bombs then we can have work. It's political colonisation, but its worse; it's colonialism of the mind' (Vidal 1995b).

The point is that Tahitians felt divorced both from their culture and from the ability to decide their own futures. Denied self-determination, many Tahitans, especially the young and unemployed, were no longer prepared meekly to submit to the dictates of France. Having attempted to persuade the French for two months by peaceful demonstrations and petitions, it was perhaps understandable that protests would turn violent if the French disregarded both local and global calls for restraint. 'The French have treated us as rubbish, as rats,' declared Roti Make, a social worker, 'and now you see what happens' (1995b).

The Tahitian outburst should also be seen against the background of global demonstrations against the decision to resume nuclear testing. Tahitians were well aware of this because with access to television and radio they were able to see the worldwide protests at first hand. As Bordes noted, 'Minds have changed. If you go back just 30 years our parents didn't realise what nuclear power meant. In 1966 we didn't have radio, TV or an airport. Now we're in contact with the world, and we see the catastrophe' (1995b). Tahitians also perceived, no doubt, that their own anti-French demonstrations would have the eye of the world and that the anti-colonial campaign would, as a result, be galvanized.

In conclusion, the outburst of anti-French feeling in Tahiti united unemployed young people, women, labour activists, and the pro-independence movement behind the goal of autonomy or independence. Tahiti, in common with many other Polynesian islands, exhibits a dangerous demography, with an overly youthful population, and a clear division between haves and have nots, overlapping with racial differences. New Caledonia is due to hold a referendum on the question of independence in 1998; the Papeete riots of September 1995 may well lead to a similar ballot in Tahiti. It may well be that the decision to resume testing at Mururoa atoll will be seen in the future both as the first step in France's withdrawal from the Pacific and also that of French Polynesians to rediscover their culture and pride.

Environmental degradation in Ogoniland, Nigeria

Half a million Ogoni people – 0.5 per cent of Nigeria's population – live on the Niger delta in the province of Rivers State in the south-east of the country. The Ogoni are by tradition farmers and fishers; in the past, they produced food not only for local people but also for much of Rivers State. Large quantities of oil were discovered in Ogoniland in the late 1950s, the first major find in Nigeria. Since then, oil has come to dominate both the Nigerian economy and the Ogoni people's lives. Yet, despite repeated promises from the federal government, local people have enjoyed only very limited benefits from their oil. As Naanen remarks, what has happened instead is that 'the patterns of power distribution between central government and the component units, on the one hand, and between the various ethnic groups, on the other, have politically emasculated the Ogoni people, causing them to lose control of their resources and their environment' (1995: 46–7).

From an environmental point of view, perhaps most disastrous has been a succession of oil spills from ruptured pipelines which were driven – above ground – through farms and villages. Ogonis have had to live with the continuous noise and pollution of numerous gas flares burning. Ogoniland has two of Nigeria's four oil refineries, the country's only major fertilizer plant, a large petrochemical factory and the fourth largest ocean port in the country – all located within a few kilometres of each other (Osaghae 1995: 330). The impact of industrialization and oil exploitation is especially serious because of the high population density in the area – 500,000 Ogoni crammed into 404 square miles, that is, 1,238 people per square mile – coupled with the fact that the vast majority depend on farming and fishing for their livelihoods. Both the Nigerian government and Shell are not over-anxious to publicize the Ogonis' plight: an attempt by the Unrepresented Nations and Peoples Organisation (UNPO), an international non-governmental organization, to send a fact-finding mission to

Ogoniland was frustrated by the Nigerian government. A visa to the area was also denied to representatives of Britain's 'Body Shop' company (Body Shop nd).

The poor environmental conditions, the lack of development in the area and the unwillingness of the government to listen to the Ogoni demands were the catalysts driving the Ogonis to rebel during 1990–3. The trigger for the revolt came in October 1990 when villagers at Umuechen in Ogoniland attacked Shell production workers. Shell, active in the area since 1958, called in the Mobile Police (known locally as 'kill-and-go'), who shot 80 villagers dead and burned down around 500 houses, some with the inhabitants trapped inside (*Africa Confidential* 1995).

The uprising was led and coordinated by the Movement for the Survival of the Ogoni People (MOSOP), which was run by a steering committee drawn from various community groups, including those of women, young people – organised in the National Youth Council of Ogoni People (NYCOP) – and professional groups. MOSOP was led, until his execution in November 1995, by the writer Ken Saro-Wiwa. Not all Ogoni support MOSOP's aims; there is strong opposition from some Ogoni traditional leaders, who are, as a result, accused of being state agents. Anti-MOSOP individuals suffered: their houses and other property were destroyed by members of NYCOP (Osaghae 1995: 334). Part of the reason for the anti-MOSOP stance of many traditional leaders was because the broadly based community group threatened to diminish their power by encouraging previously subordinate groups, such as young people and women, to challenge them. It is clear, however, that the great majority of the Ogoni were sympathetic to MOSOP: a banned march involving 300,000 black-wearing Ogoni took place on 4 January 1996 to commemorate 'Ogoni Day' and to mourn the death of Saro-Wiwa and his eight comrades. Six of the marchers were killed by federal soldiers (Duodu 1996).

Attempts to organize and mobilize the Ogoni people had begun seven years before, in 1989. In 1992 Ken Saro-Wiwa presented the Ogoni case before the United Nations Commission on Human Rights in Geneva. According to Naanen, this 'marked an important turning point in bolstering people's confidence', leading directly to demonstrations in January 1993, involving 300,000 Ogoni, and to a subsequent apparance by an Ogoni delegation at the UN Human Rights Conference in Vienna in August of that year (1995: 69). From this time, environmental and human rights organizations, including UNPO, the World Rain Forest Action Group, Amnesty International, the Body Shop and Greenpeace, helped to publicize the Ogoni plight. Pressure was also brought to bear on both Shell and the Nigerian government by the British Parliamentary Human Rights Group. The government's response had elements of both 'carrot and stick'. The government of General Babangida (1985–93) encouraged dialogue with MOSOP while nevertheless jailing Saro-Wiwa and several other Ogoni leaders on what many regarded as trumped-up charges. In early 1995, Saro-Wiwa received $30,000 from the Goldman foundation, an American organization, in 'recognition of his struggle for human and environmental justice' (*Africa Confidential* 1995).

The recent struggle against the federal government and the oil companies is but the most recent manifestation of the Ogonis' desire for control over their own affairs. It had taken until 1908 for the British to subdue them initially. During the colonial era the Ogoni, along with other Delta groups, demanded a separate administrative division. This was finally achieved in 1967, after independence, with the creation of Rivers State (Naanen 1995: 63). In 1974, following allegations of domination by the numerically larger Ijaw people, the Ogoni unsuccessfully petitioned for the creation of a separate Port Harcourt state to be carved out of the Rivers State. Since then the demands for a separate state increasingly dovetailed with a number of other problems: economic decline, oil-based ecological degradation and the undermining of traditional smallholder agriculture and fishing, the mainstays of the Ogoni local economy (Saro-Wiwa 1992).

Ogoni discontent at their position as a powerless national minority was increased by the contribution to Nigeria's economic development of the oil resources on their land – six oilfields producing 200,000 barrels a day by 1972 – while they were denied material benefits, including piped water, electricity, medical facilities and roads (Naanen 1995: 65). The relationship between the Ogoni and the federal government has been described as a 'modified version of "internal colonialism" [helping] to illuminate the relationship between the central Nigerian state and the oil-producing periphery' (1995: 49).

The process of ethnic domination and peripheralization is aided by the presence of multinational oil companies, as well as state-owned enterprises. The oil multinationals added environmental degradation to the Ogonis' list of woes. Oil-based environmental degradation undermined traditional farming and fishing in the oil-producing areas without producing a viable economic alternative (1995: 50). A former minister and first president of MOSOP, Garrick B. Leton, claimed that the Ogoni, content to live in a federation, were not asking for the entire amount brought in by rent and royalties, only an equitable portion. He argued that 'if the land is ours, irrespective of the law put in place by the major ethnic groups, anything that comes out of the land should be ours' (quoted in Osaghae 1995: 327).

While the Ogoni demands were not successful in the short term, there were a number of concrete achievements, especially the raising of national and international awareness about the Ogonis' predicament, while the case has become a *cause célèbre*, a test of the Nigerian government's attitude towards the country's minorities and their demands for control of their lands. The hanging of Saro-Wiwa and eight other Ogoni activists in November 1995 for their alleged encouragement of members of MOSOP to murder four pro-government Ogoni chiefs was met by an international outcry. The death of Saro-Wiwa, the author of over 20 books, an Amnesty International Prisoner of Conscience and a recipient of a prestigious environmental award and the 'alternative Nobel prize', the Right Livelihood Award, was condemned by governments and NGOs around the world, including Greenpeace, International PEN, Amnesty International, Human Rights Watch and UNPO. Following what then British Prime Minister, John Major, called the 'judicial murders' of Saro-Wiwa and his comrades, more than 20 other Ogoni leaders and activists, including Ledum Mitee, MOSOP deputy president, were arrested. They too faced charges to be tried under the same 'fatally flawed' judicial procedure. There was a massive federal troop presence in Ogoniland (Ogoni Community Association UK 1995; Black et al. 1995).

The Ogonis' struggle against central government illustrates two factors in contemporary relations between the state and local minority groups in Africa: the importance of land, and the concern with which states view challenges to their power from putative separatist groups. Saro-Wiwa's execution was not because he led the campaign for environmental justice, but rather because the Ogonis' struggle crystallized for many other minority groups in Nigeria the stranglehold on power which the country's three dominant ethnic groups hold. The country's civil war between 1967 and 1970 had cost millions of dead and hundreds of millions of dollars in damage. Since then the federal government has reacted with great alarm to any manifestations of a desire for autonomy or separatism.

Conclusion

With examples from Asia, Africa and the South Pacific, I have examined a selection of the 10,000 environmental action groups in existence, having a collective membership in the millions. We have seen not only how environmental protection has emerged as an important focus of state–society conflict in the Third World over the last quarter-century, but also how transnational groups are sometimes involved in campaigns.

The struggles of the Ogoni and the Tahitians are good examples of what happens when leaders of minority or marginal ethnic and social organizations feel dissatisfied with the structure of power sharing and resource allocation in their polities. They seek to restructure the configuration of power in a manner more acceptable to them and their followers. Yet the failure of both campaigns to achieve their goals – at least in the short term – underlines how important it is for civil society to be powerful enough to take on the state and achieve its goals in such struggles. Both the Ogonis and the Tahitians were successful in gaining foreign support, but were incapable of putting together a domestic coalition of interest groups of sufficient strength to achieve their goals. The Ogonis found that neighbouring ethnic groups – with some of which they had a history of tension – were encouraged by the state to attack them. In Tahiti the situation was complicated because France is an important employer paying salaries far above the local average. People may well have warmed to the notion of greater autonomy or even independence from colonial rule, yet such aspirations may well have been offset for many by concern at what would happen to their incomes if France departed.

A desire to protect the natural environment is often a factor in wider demands for political and economic reforms. The point however is that environmental campaigns are only likely to succeed under certain conditions. First, it is essential that there are democratic and legal avenues to pursue environmental goals. Second, it is crucial to build a wide-ranging coalition of groups and organizations – perhaps including foreign groups – which can take on the state and its allies, such as large landowners and important business interests. Such a struggle is only likely to be successful in a democratic environment with a strong civil society. Of the countries discussed in this chapter, only India falls into this category. On the other hand, we found when examining the situation in Cambodia, Kenya and Nigeria that a powerful state against an undersupported environmental campaign was highly likely to prevail. However, the accounts of environmental action groups in Malaysia and Indonesia – currently at best semidemocracies with only rather elementary civil societies – none the less suggested that if environmental protection coalitions are of a sufficient size and tenaciousness, then they will successfully challenge the state on a range of environmental issues. A wider point is that in both Malaysia and Indonesia we may be witnessing the emergence of stronger civil societies than hitherto.

A final point is that many Third World environmental action groups challenge both governmental and corporate practices, while frequently advocating sustainable development strategies. Groups like Chipko (India), SAM (Malaysia) and Indonesia's WALHI (see pp. 102–3, 105–7) organize to ensure that people at and near the bottom of the socio-economic pile have the opportunity to participate in shaping their own destinies. They want communities to be consulted on local development projects that affect them. Many Third World citizens are of course poor and, because they lack political and economic power, development policies are imposed. But successful attempts to implement development schemes need to be informed by an understanding of the people who are participating in the development process. If the development is *for* them, it should occur on their terms and incorporate their ideas (Miller 1995: 151).

6
Women and Empowerment

In chapter 2, I divided action groups into development and sociopolitical categories. I noted that this categorical simplification was necessary for analytical purposes. While the first type is primarily concerned with development issues – that is, broadly increasing members' 'quality of life' – the second commits itself to achieving a variety of sociopolitical goals leading to members' increased 'empowerment'. Empowerment means acquiring the awareness and skills necessary to take charge of one's own life chances. It is about facilitating the ability of individuals (and groups) to make their own decisions and, to a greater extent than hitherto, to shape their own destinies. In sum, for increased empowerment, people *must* be able to participate in decision-making. Groups with empowerment goals normally have most success in democratic – or democratizing – societies. This is because they have more of the necessary 'space' to pursue their goals; such space is absent or severely constrained in authoritarian political systems. In the current chapter, then, I will pay particular attention to those in the more favourable political environments of Latin America and India.

At the other end of the continuum are women's development groups, common in sub-Saharan Africa and parts of Asia. As discussed in chapter 2, they are primarily concerned with increasing women's developmental position, often from a very low starting point; many, including the predominantly women's *harambee* groups of Kenya and the 31 December Women's Organization in Ghana, have close links to the state. The point is that almost everywhere in the Third World, women's empowerment is essential to achieve wider female access to decision-making and resources. Yet, equally clearly, prevailing sociocultural conditions very often militate against this happening, espe-cially in much of Africa and the Middle East. At the same time, there are encouraging signs of progress in parts of Latin America and India.

The aim of the current chapter is to describe and assess a representa-tive range of women's empowerment groups, chiefly in Latin America and India, in terms of (1) what they do, and (2) how they do it. Their sociopolitical significance is not that they threaten the stability of the state; rather, their importance is related to the extent that they empower women in men-dominated societies.

The first section describes the socioeconomic and political position of women in the Third World, to make it clear why greater empowerment is sought. I describe how economic malaise serves to reduce still further the position of many poor women. Although concern with human rights has been a feature of the global scene for 50 years, the position of most women in the Third World – the Indian state of Kerala and Cuba, in the Caribbean, are notable exceptions – lags behind that of most men, even the poor. This is not to claim, incidentally, that the position of the latter is anything but bad. After that I assess the impact of economic decline on the formation of women's groups. Finally, I examine a range of women's groups in Latin America and India to find out what they have in common and to what extent they contribute to the growth of their civil societies.

The Socioeconomic Position of Women in the Third World

The socioeconomic position of women and girls in the Third World is reflected in an array of development statistics. In very many of the countries, females score unsatisfactorily compared to males in every conventional measure of development, including literacy, school enrol-ment, clinic attendance, rates of pay, access to land, availability of credit, and political office holding at all levels (UNDP 1996: 138–43, tables 2 and 3).

Females, making up around 50 per cent of the world's population, do an estimated two-thirds of the world's work. Yet they earn only 10 per cent of global income and own less than 1 per cent of the world's property. This implies that much of their work is unpaid, often con-nected with familial duties, such as bearing and rearing children, clean-ing and maintaining househlds, caring for the aged and the sick, tending animals and fetching water and fuel for domestic use. In addition to these domestic chores, many women do work, often poorly paid, outside the home (Ekins 1992: 73). Of the 1 billion people in the world who are illiterate, two-thirds are female, while over 60 per cent of those deprived of primary education – 81 million out of 130 million people – are girls. In sum, as James Grant, Executive Director of UNICEF explains: 'Employment rights, social security rights, legal rights, property rights, and even civil and political liberties are all likely to depend on the one, cruel chromosome distinguishing human male from female' (quoted in Brittain 1994). In other words, *all* indices of modernization that promote widespread, self-perpetuating change in society – the spread of modern education, increases in literacy, urbanization, prolonged economic growth and so on – favour men over women apparently regardless of individual countries' cultures.

Yet, while such is certainly the position of women in the vast majority of Third World countries, the position is notably better in the Indian state of Kerala and the Caribbean country of Cuba. Kerala provides a model of incremental but comprehensive poverty alleviation under democratic and decentralized rule. Cuba furnishes an alternative method of women's empowerment: there a highly centralized state has, since the inception of the communist regime in 1959, worked assiduously to improve the socioeconomic position of women. This is reflected in a variety of developmental statistics. For instance, infant mortality per 1,000 live births is 14, comparing well with some of Cuba's neighbours at higher levels of development: 20 in Trinidad and Tobago, 30 in Argentina, 59 in Brazil, 37 in Mexico, 34 in Venezuela. The same picture of an effort to improve women's well-being is reflected in Cuba's literacy statistics: 93 per cent of Cuba's women can read, compared to 80 per cent in Brazil, 21 per cent in Peru, 53 per cent in Guatemala and 29 per cent in Honduras (Thomas et al. 1994: 74–5). However, Cuba is a relatively well-known women's 'success story'; that of Kerala is less often highlighted, and as a result, I shall focus on it.

Women and development in Kerala

Kerala's governments have been putting the poor – including women – first for decades. This is not necessarily because the state's politicians and bureaucrats care more about the plight of women than their counterparts elsewhere in India. The point is that they have been forced by popular opinion to distribute resources according to where society believes they are most needed.This has come about because Kerala is a highly democratic and literate state where many people are keenly aware of the divisiveness caused by disparities of wealth and power in society.

Kerala, located in the south-west of India, has a population of over 30 million in an area the size of Switzerland (41,000 sq km; population 7.1 million) (World Bank 1995: 162–3, table 1). Because state policy has favoured a general alleviation of poverty, the position of the poor – and especially poor women has improved greatly over the last 40 years. This is reflected in an array of statistics. Kerala's adult literacy rate at over 90 per cent is nearly twice that of India's (52 per cent); its people live on average to the age of 72, compared to India's national rate of 61 years; its birth-rate is a third lower than India's generally, while the death-rate of infants – 27 per 1,000 – is one-third of the Indian average (1995: 162–3, table 1). Overall, inequalities between the sexes 'are less pronounced than in any other [Indian] state' (Durning 1989: 64).

Such results have been possible because the poor are well organized and vocal; governments, concerned for their longevity, are, of necessity, committed to help them. In short, a political culture has emerged in Kerala geared towards the improvement of the position of have-nots in the society. Nearly all of Kerala's villages have access to basic health, education and transportation services at a level unknown elsewhere in India; schools and clinics are spread throughout the state; ubiquitous 'fair price shops' sell basic goods at low prices. In a recent survey, Kerala ranked first in provision of basic services among India's states in 15 out of 20 categories (1989: 63). Safe water supplies and family planning services are available to a large majority of the population, while comprehensive – and successfully implemented – land reform programmes have redistributed land to 1.5 million landless people.

It is important to understand that the position of women in Kerala is not typical of that of India more generally. Calvert and Calvert claim that in India 'since 1911 there has been a steady decline in the ratio of women to men . . . There are now 929 women to every 1,000 men' (1996: 242). This is not due to some mysterious biological reason: it is the result of the killing of baby girls. This perhaps more than anything else hints at the position of females in Indian society – Kerala excepted. The main practical problem is the rising costs of dowries: girls are a very expensive liability for parents; to have one can – and often does – mean future financial ruin. Dowries were made illegal 30 years ago by decree of the federal government; nevertheless, the custom flourishes. The trend is towards larger and larger sums of money payable from the parents of the bride to that of the bridegroom on marriage. If the agreed price is not paid, the woman may well be returned to her parents. Some women are badly treated for not bringing in larger dowries; on extreme occasions, bride-burning is the outcome – the bride will be set on fire by paraffin or kerosene to simulate an accidental fire in the cooking area. According to official figures, 2,500 women were killed in this way in 1991, although the figure may be much higher (1996: 244).

While such deliberate cruelty is unusual, more common is the impact of cultural norms promoting inequality. It is this sense of traditional cultural normality which India's women's empowerment groups seek to change. There is a ready-made model: that of Kerala. The state's overall developmental record shows what can be achieved through mobilization and organization. Achievements come under six main headings:

1 *Increased literacy* facilitating wider access to written sources of information. For women this leads to improved health and smaller families.
2 *Secure land rights* allowing the impoverished – including women – to increase their income and hence economic security.
3 *Increased local control over common resources* helping to break the cycle of economic-ecological degradation.
5 *Greater access to credit* enabling poor men and women to buy essential livestock and tools.
5 *Clean drinking water and community-based health care* protecting adult lives from debilitating diseases and saving deaths among children. A beneficial consequence is that parents have smaller families.
6 *Cheap, efficient family planning* offering women the chance to control their own fertility effectively, enabling them to space births at healthy intervals, in turn improving their own health. (Durning 1989: 64–5)

The example of women's empowerment in Kerala suggests that it is of crucial importance to have a responsive government as well as an electorate educated and concerned enough to vote for politicians who will seek to ameliorate poor people's development positions. Because of the overall success in achieving regimes committed to poverty amelioration, there is less need in Kerala than in many other places for single-issue action groups to pursue the aspirations of the subordinated.

Women and Structural Adjustment

If structural adjustment packages normally incorporated some of the measures adopted in Kerala, they might well help the poor more than they usually do. They might enable larger numbers of poor people to generate more income for themselves – in turn aiding national development. Or structural adjustment might alternatively focus on removing economic distortions and inefficiencies which primarily benefit the rich. As noted earlier, however, because structural adjustment packages need to be drawn up quickly in reponse to crisis, they tend to go for the most immediately effective solutions to budgetary imbalances: for example, removing subsidies to the poor, such as those on basic foodstuffs, without touching invisible subsidies to the rich, such as industrial subsidies. Thus structural adjustment is nearly always serious for the poor. Given that women are very often the poorest of the poor, then it is not surprising that poor women are often among the hardest hit during structural adjustment.

The combined effects of structural adjustment, economic crisis and poverty propel millions of Third World women into poorly paid work. Economic upheavals have led to a phenomenon known as the 'feminization of poverty' – that is, when females suffer disproportionately compared to males. The numerous ways in which women absorb the fall-out from economic crisis amount to what feminist economists have called the 'gender-related costs of invisible adjustment' (Marchand 1995). This is reflected in relation to work and to health and welfare programmes.

Work

During structural adjustment wages are routinely squeezed by governmental policy (ILO 1994: 108). Women, already receiving proportionately lower wages than men across the Third World, find that as a result of falling wages they can afford fewer processed foods than before (UNRISD 1995: 28). Since they are unlikely to have a refrigerator, they must spend more time shopping for small quantities of cheaper items. They may also be forced by economic pressures to try to grow more of their own food. A study in Java found that during economic downturns women spend more time than before growing vegetables on family plots, both for home consumption and for outside sale. Female work burdens pass to daughters: a study in Ecuador found that when mothers work outside the home, daughters must spend more time on domestic work at the expense of their education (Sparr 1994: 26).

Some assume, however, that because women are increasingly represented in the industrial workforce in the Third World it means that their socioeconomic position generally is improving. Kamrava, for example, asserts that in the Third World 'traditional values such as the importance of motherhood, the inadmissibility of women earning money, and other primordial core symbols are [being] eroded as the general social and economic [position] of women is somewhat ameliorated through industrialization' (Kamrava 1993: 115). Others claim, however, that the position of females may actually be declining *despite* increasing industrialization (Marchand 1995). Moreover, 'women's access to paid work is constrained both by discrimination and sex segregation in the workplace and by the assumption that women are "naturally" responsible for all or most of the unpaid work of the household' (Okin 1994: 13)

Working women in East and South-East Asia The participation of women in the paid workforce is higher in some Third World regions than others. Women amount to about 40 per cent of the workforce in East Asia, a figure comparable to that of some Western countries, 35 per cent in South-East Asia and 29 per cent in Latin America (Thomas et al. 1994). Women in East and South-East Asia make up a larger proportion of factory workers – more than 25 per cent – than anywhere else in the world. Yet high involvement of women in the industrial sector does not seem to have impacted greatly on their political activity. The main reason for this is that East Asian societies are often strongly influenced by patriarchal Confucian traditions of family organization and control. Daughters do not inherit; they are under their father's control until marriage and their husband's after it; after wedlock women move into their spouse's familial home; community and family decision-making is heavily male orientated. As a result of such social conditions, daughters may leave school around the age of 11, going out to work soon after. Up to three-quarters of their earnings are handed over to the family, often for boys' education. They may work for a decade in a factory before marriage, as fathers are reluctant to lose their earning power. In Taiwan in the mid-1980s nearly a quarter of the workforce was made up of females aged between 15 and 29 years, with a large proportion employed in manufacturing.

In conclusion, women are not necessarily liberated by joining the paid workforce; they are rarely free agents within the labour market, but 'resources mobilized by the family' for perhaps 15 years between leaving primary school and their marriage (Cammack et al.: 221). The result is that despite, or perhaps because of, a high level of involvement in the labour force, females in East Asia have not been in the forefront of demands for change in family or gender relations.

Working women in sub-Saharan Africa Sub-Saharan Africa is a region with a relatively small proportion of women employed for wages. Many females are restrained from developing their full potential by restricted employment opportunities. For example, fewer than 10 per cent of lawyers, engineers and medical doctors in Kenya are female, while in Nigeria only about 6 per cent of academic staff are women. Generally, as Parpart observes, opportunities for wage labour are few; even when they do arise women are usually paid less and are promoted slower than their male counterparts (1988: 217). Informal economic activities are, however, widely open to women. Many make a resounding success of trading; yet even then it is men who usually own the larger, more profitable shops. In an attempt to get round the often small scale of their trading activities and the fact that banks are rarely willing to extend credit, women in a number of countries have established their own minibanks: women have developed their own credit organizations in, *inter alia*, Nigeria, Kenya and Ghana (Fisher 1993: 40).

Health and welfare programmes

A further gender-related cost of economic decline and adjustment is often a reduction in health care for females. A 1994 Oxfam report, *Paying for Health*, suggests, for example, that Zimbabwe's attempt at structural adjustment, which *inter alia* led to steep increases in user fees for medical services, resulted in a near 2.5 times increase in maternal deaths between 1989 and 1991. In addition, death-rates among women doubled between 1991 and 1992 in the capital Harare (quoted in Brittain 1994: 12).

Structural adjustment also often affects women's access to welfare programmes. They are likely to suffer from cuts in public services: as health services deteriorate, they are called upon to look after sick relatives, and when education cuts reduce school hours, they must spend more time supervising children (UNRISD 1995: 147). When social safety net programmes are introduced to provide employment opportunities to those worst affected by structural adjustment, women tend to receive far fewer work chances than men. In Bolivia, for example, only 1 per cent employed in social programmes were women. India had a better record: 16 per cent of such workers were females, while in Honduras 'only' three-quarters of such 'social jobs' were held by men (1995: 53).

In conclusion, while the effects of economic crisis and structural adjustment in the Third World have led to increased poverty for the poor, women have been particularly badly hit. This is manifested in three ways: they must work harder both in the home and outside to try to maintain income levels; they experience declining levels of health care and welfare; and they often receive fewer benefits than men from job creation schemes.

A 1994 United Nations Development Programme (UNDP) proposal to help resolve the situation focused on the creation of a 'global compact' of donor countries to raise levels of aid from 7 per cent to 20 per cent in the key areas of education, health and women's development. Recipient countries would be asked to double their social spending to '20 per cent of their budgets by cutting their military expenditure and their spending on prestige projects' (Brittain 1994). The $30–40 billion which the scheme would have raised, UNDP calculated, could have had a dramatic impact on world poverty and on the position of females within a decade. The scheme was however deemed unacceptable by both the putative donors and recipient governments. There were two main problems: first, donor countries were unwilling to commit new money to the extent required; second, very few Third World governments were inclined to alter current spending patterns to the benefit of women.

Given that the cards seem to be stacked against women in the Third World, there seems to be little chance that either international organizations or their governments possess the financial ability or political will to work assiduously for an improvement in the socioeconomic position of women. It seems that it is far more important for rulers to maintain their hold on power by placating the military and other important (male) groups than to be overly concerned with raising the position and prosperity of women, a course of action with few net political 'payoffs'. So what can women do about it? They have two broad choices: suffer in silence or try to do something about it. If the latter course of action is chosen, a further preference must be selected: do women try to change things by conventional means such as trying to elect a more sympathetic government or joining political parties to influence things – or do they go it alone, via their own action groups?

Women's Empowerment Groups: the Relative Importance of 'Practical' and 'Strategic' Concerns

There are two broad kinds of women's empowerment groups in the Third World. First, there are Western-style *feminist* groups, rather elitist and restricted in significance, with memberships made up primarily of 'Westernized, middle-class, university-educated women who . . . defy the classification of passive, voiceless and tradition-bound' Third World women (Marchand 1995: 61). Second, by far the most common, are the *feminine* groups concerned with an array of material concerns: from consumption issues to questions of sociopolitical status. Feminist groups pursue what are known as 'strategic' objectives, while feminine groups seek so-called 'practical' goals (Molyneux 1985; Jaquette 1989; Alvarez 1990; Safa 1990). According to Alvarez,

> feminist organizations [in Latin America] focus on issues *specific* to the female condition (i.e. reproductive rights), feminine groups mobilize women around gender-related issues and concerns. The cost of living, for example, is one such issue. . . . Women . . . may organize to protest the rising cost of living because inflation undermines their ability to adequately feed, clothe, and house their families. (1990: 25)

Waylen (1993) notes that the 'unitary category of "woman" undifferentiated by class, race or nationality' is not at all helpful intellectually in seeking to analyse the sociopolitical impact of women's groups. One way of seeking to deal with the problem is to divide women's groups between those which conceptualize their chief concerns around 'practical' gender interests, such as economic survival, and those involved in 'strategic' gender interests associated with feminist objectives. It is important to note, however, that such categories are more for analytical convenience than anything else; in practice, there is much blurring between categories. Nevertheless, there may be fairly clearly defined social divisions between those involved with the practical concerns of the feminine organizations and those belonging to the feminist groups. On the other hand, urban working-class women's organizations may well not only address 'bread and butter' survival issues, but also concern themselves with issues like domestic violence and reproductive rights, interests they share with feminist groups (Waylen 1993: 574).

However, the feminine–feminist dichotomy is not only a heuristic device; it is also employed by Third World women themselves to denote the class position of activists. Middle-class, educated women involved in 'women's issues' would classify themselves as feminists, while poorer, less educated women reject the 'feminist' label (Alvarez 1990; Marchand 1995). Yet, as Safa (1990) points out, an initial involvement in 'practical' interests often leads on to a concern with more 'strategic' questions. Fisher asserts that the 'distinction between feminist and [feminine] organizations is beginning to blur in some countries, as middle- and lower-class women define their common interests' (1993: 103). Perhaps the best way is not to try to dichotomize the types of group, but rather to see them on a continuum with a large middle area where concerns are both practical *and* strategic (Marchand 1995: 64). The benefit of concentrating on the middle ground is that it allows us to overcome the private/public dichotomy whereby 'practical' concerns are relegated to the *private* sphere and 'strategic' issues to the *public* realm of politics.

Usually when gender is discussed as a political issue, definitions of what is 'political' are based on this kind of public/private division. Women tend to be designated as upholders of the private foundation of the political world of men (Pateman 1988). Yet one of the main catalysts for the emergence of the women's movement in the West – with the slogan: 'the personal is the political' – was dissatisfaction with the outcome of democratic politics in terms of the (lack of) progress in bettering the position of females. The aim of the women's movement was – and for many activists still is – to build a more active, *participatory* democracy at both institutional and personal levels. To achieve these aims it would be necessary both to organize to fight the prevailing political order and to change interpersonal relations between men and women (Phillips 1992).

Women's empowerment in the Third World

Like Western feminists, it appears that many Third World women are dissatisfied with a position of subordination; millions have joined action groups for empowerment. Fisher (1993: 40) claims that women's groups – both development and empowerment oriented – are probably the most rapidly proliferating types of action groups in the Third World.

Some idea of the numbers of women's groups in existence may be gauged from the fact that the New York based International Women's Tribune Center (IWTC) is the contact and referral office for over 6,000 women's groups in over 160 countries, an average of nearly 40 in each. In addition, there are probably additionally *tens of thousands* of women's groups in the Third World *not* registered with the IWTC (1993: 40). Durning (1989: 28) reports that in rural Brazil the recent growth of women's groups has been 'explosive', yet virtually none of these organizations would be registered with the IWTC. In Zimbabwe, Sylvester (1995: 409) declares that women's organizations 'flourish in a climate in which all the main political forces in the country have, at some point in their histories, been masculinised'. However, as Geisler (1995: 46) makes clear, the general inability of women in southern Africa to make their mark in politics – because of men's discrimination – propels them towards the NGO sector. There, she claims, 'women's groups and funding from international donors abound'. The point is that women's groups flourish in many Third World regions in part because men refuse to let women take a full role, whether in running the state or playing a leading role in civil society.

None the less, in the case studies that follow we see how women in Argentina, Brazil and India have used democratic space to pursue their interests. The case studies suggest that attempts to improve women's socioeconomic position usually start from a concern with so-called 'women's projects' – that is, enhancing housekeeping skills, handicraft production or microenterprise development. Over time, however, women's groups often to come to a realization that a general ameliora-tion of their members' socioeconomic and political position depends on changing the prevailing power structure in society in order to have an effect on, *inter alia*, infant mortality rates and environmental protection. These initiatives involve educating women to defend and then improve their overall societal position.

Latin America

The recent history of Latin America has been characterized by a distinc-tive process of modernization which, proceeding from export-led de-velopment to limited industrialization, has had a marked effect on the status of women. Until recently, the lack of political participation by women was in line with a pattern of subordination underpinned by the influence of traditional Catholic ideas on female subservience.[1] Over the last few years, however, a combination of social responses to eco-nomic crisis, widespread challenges to dictatorial rule, the dissemina-tion of feminist ideas and a decline in the social power of the Catholic Church has resulted in a pronounced shift in the nature and scope of women's political organization. Women often do not find it easy to make headway in the institutionalized political parties, having great difficulty in converting influence into institutional representation dur-ing periods of democracy (Safa 1990; Waylen 1993: 574).

Women's groups in Latin America represent an innovative form of politics, recasting both political agendas and political action (Slater 1985; Jelin 1990; Redclift 1988). During military rule the inhibition of conventional political activity served to increase women's activities in the private domain, enabling them to gain greater visibility and prominence. As Waylen puts it, 'One effect of the suppression of organisations such as trade unions and political parties was to move the locus of much political activity . . . from institutional to community-based activities where women have greater opportunities to participate' (1993: 576). A second consequence was that because many male activists were killed or imprisoned, it was often women who kept parties going – in secret – when they were banned. Third, the period of military rule aided the emergence of feminist movements, galvanized by the realization that authoritarian power relations were present not only in the public sphere but in the household and family as well.

Developments during military rule – that is, increases in female participation in community-based activities, greater women's involvement in political parties, and the growth of feminism – empowered women in both the private and the public spheres, despite the absence of democracy. When democracy was reintroduced in the 1980s and conventional party politics reestablished, women's groups were faced with a clear choice: continue autonomously, or merge with the political parties. If they continued to operate outside the conventional party political arena, they could retain their independence but at the price of risking political marginalization in the new democratic era; if they worked within the new institutions and parties, they risked being coopted and losing their autonomy. While it is not necessarily clear that mergers of once-independent groups necessarily result in cooptation, it is certainly the case that the choice appeared to be a fairly stark one. Many women's groups chose merger and, it is argued, they were then very often 'marginalised within party structures without any meaningful power and influence' (1993: 578). The marginalization of women within the parties suggests that the low participation of women in the national politics of many Latin American countries is a result of the way in which political parties are structured and the fact that women are not taken seriously in this regard.

Latin America's redemocratization did not destroy the networks of women's groups which grew up during the period of dictatorship. Rather, there are now two systems of political activity: on the one hand, there are the male-dominated legislatures and political parties, and on the other, the thousands of women's groups pursuing a range of concerns. One of the most common – and poignant – concerns is the quest for information about the thousands of men who disappeared during military rule. Thousands of women have tried to extract information from reticent authorities about the fate of their loved ones. In short, women are crucial to human rights protests throughout Latin America. Probably the most famous is Las Madres de Plaza de Mayo in Argentina. Others include the Mutual Support Group in Guatemala, the Group of Relatives of the Detained-Disappeared in Chile, and the Mothers and Relatives of Those Tried by Military Justice in Uruguay (Radcliffe and Westwood 1993a: 16–17). Such groups combine a concern with human rights with that of justice. I examine Argentina's Las Madres de Plaza de Mayo to highlight how members' initial demands for information concerning their missing loved ones grew into a wider demand for women's sociopolitical justice.

Las Madres de Plaza de Mayo (Argentina)

Las Madres de Plaza de Mayo (the Mothers of the Plaza de Mayo) was formed in April 1977 by the wife of a diplomat and the spouse of a factory worker (Navarro 1989: 241). It was a response to the policy of abducting and killing individuals during the period of military dictatorship which had begun a year earlier (Feijoo and Gogna 1990: 87). The euphemistically named 'process of national reorganization' (*proceso*) inaugurated by the junta leader Jorge Rafael Viedla had led to intense repression during which an estimated 9,000 people died – at the hands of the state's security services. Many were young, nearly 70 per cent being between the ages of 16 and 30 years (Elshtain 1995: 548–9).

Initially, the Mothers comprised 14 women aged between 40 and 60 years, parents of some of the people who had disappeared. Gaining no information from the authorities regarding their children's whereabouts, they took to demonstrating in front of the main government building in Buenos Aires in the Plaza de Mayo. By July 1977 the group had grown in size to about 150 women. In October of that year they handed in a 24,000-signature petition to the authorities demanding an investigation into the disappearances of their children and the freeing of the thousands of prisoners detained without trial. The police dispersed the Mothers delivering the petition with tear gas and fired live rounds in the air; about 300 were briefly detained while identity papers were checked (Feijoo and Gogna 1990: 87). For the Mothers, their treatment at the hands of the state simply for asking for information regarding the whereabouts of their sons and husbands 'gave political form and shape to their protest, linking them to an international network of associations and watchdog societies', including Amnesty International and Americas Watch (Elshtain 1995: 551).

Demands for information and for the release of their men were maintained by the Mothers during the 1980s. In 1986 an amnesty law was passed which effectively absolved the military of responsibility in relation to the 'disappeared', requiring that prosecution for acts of repression should take place within 60 days of the alleged disappearance. This meant in effect that the military remained above the law; there were very few – if any – prosecutions for human rights violations.

In conclusion, the case of the Mothers is important because what began as a demand for information about disappeared loved ones developed over time into a search for an enhanced sociopolitical role for women. In effect, the Mothers' activities became politicized, leading them to a transformation in their consciousness and a questioning of the female role in society. The Mothers' experience presents a very interesting case from two different perspectives which converge: one is that of a concern with the creation of a political scenario to legitimize the process of democratization and of new ways of conducting politics; the other stresses the gender of the political agents.

Working women's organizations in Brazil

During the period of military rule in Brazil, the vast majority of the population was excluded from institutional politics. As a result, non-institutional politics, in the form of popular movements, became the principal arena for political participation and opposition to military rule. Research has shown that women played a significant role in popular movements in Brazil at this time (Brydon and Chant 1989). The example of the women-dominated *favela* (slum) organizations of Rio di Janeiro and other large cities in Brazil – examined in chapter 2 – illustrates how large numbers of women participated in popular protests concerned primarily with a lack of employment opportunities and the failure of the authorities to provide basic services, especially for the poor.

Increasingly since the early 1970s, Brazil's working women have protested about the lack of basic services, health provision, transport, housing and employment. Such women form the majority within the ranks of the poor, a social group whose socioeconomic experience in Brazilian society is neither reflected nor represented in other forms of political organization (Corcoran-Nantes 1990, 1993). Women have played a major role in the formation and development of popular movements in the country. What seems to have developed is a 'bifurcated political sphere: male/institutional politics and female/non-institutional politics which are identifiable by the nature of political/ gender organisation and action' (Corcoran-Nantes 1993: 138).

Many poor women in Brazil have managed to acquire a wealth of political and organizational experience, the result of three interrelated developments: authoritarian political conditions, the result of more than 20 years of military rule; an economic position declining for many poor people, encouraging organization; and the gradual dismantling of welfare provision, the consequence of structural adjustment (Cammack et al. 1993: 232). Such a pattern of events was not confined to Brazil, but evident first in Chile. There, monetarist policies were applied from the mid-1970s, spreading throughout the region over the next decade. Women often led efforts to develop community-based survival strategies, including craft-making activities, the provision of soup kitchens and the organization of health groups. Many found themselves drawn into political activity through the need to organize to provide such vital services, to lobby for resources from the authorities, or to seek grants and aid from international charitable organizations. Such activities gave rise to distinctive women's movements in many urban communities in Brazil's cities.

São Paulo's Shantytown and Unemployed Movements   The development of political consciousness and group solidarity among working women in Brazil's cities can be illustrated by examining two organizations located in São Paulo, one of the country's largest cities. The movements I have selected for examination are the Shantytown Movement (O Movimento de Favela) and the Unemployed Movement (O Movimento dos Desempregados). Both are significant because working women are strongly represented among their leaders and activists. Through these movements many women have been encouraged to struggle for 'recognition of their roles and rights as workers, residents and citizens' (Corcoran-Nantes 1993: 138).

By the 1980s the number and types of social movements in Brazil had grown as popular protest increased. Both state administrations and the federal government were being pressurized into taking action to ameliorate deteriorating socioeconomic conditions. In São Paulo, action groups mushroomed at this time, stimulated by the increasing social polarization resulting from attempts at structural adjustment and more generally, from economic decline. A sense of exclusion from the benefits of economic growth was acute among those of the poor forced to live alongside the wealthy in the *favelas* (shantytowns), that is, the urban periphery. *Favelas* expanded rapidly, principally the result of rural–urban migration. This development placed enormous pressure on the already limited capacity of public services to provide clean water, electricity, sanitation, transport, housing and healthcare (1993: 141–2).

The Shantytown Movement was founded in 1976 to secure land titles for shantytown dwellers and to seek improvements in basic services and communication infrastructures. The Unemployed Movement was formed in 1983 to try to deal with the problems of mass unemployment in São Paulo, seeking unemployment benefits for those without work. In addition, it helped form workers' cooperatives to build houses. These two organizations are representative of a wide range of movements which mushroomed in the urban periphery of São Paulo in the 1970s and 1980s. One common feature of both is that, increasingly, many activists and leaders are women.

Both the Shantytown Movement and the Unemployed Movement began on a very small scale with meetings taking place in activists' homes. To take the Unemployed Movement first, it experienced swift growth, spreading from São Paulo to other urban areas. Initially women's groups within the movement were encouraged by the men who initially had organizational control of it. The latter wished to remove what they regarded as 'women's issues' from the demands of the movement. Yet the women's groups quickly became an important forum for the discussion of a wide range of issues of relevance to females, including women's political participation, male domestic violence and the sociopolitical and economic role of women in society. They frequently developed into mutual support collectives. Many joined with other women's organizations and feminist groups on demonstrations and political protests concerning issues such as abortion, violence against women, and family planning. Many of the women who organized or participated in these groups went on to be elected local and regional coordinators of Committees of the Unemployed (1993: 147). The point is that the initial impetus to form a group linked to unemployment helped to convince many women that they might achieve a range of social and political goals through collective effort. Over time, women began to assume leadership positions within the Unemployed Movement, leading it to take a greater heed of 'women's problems'. In particular, cooperative work and mutualist schemes were useful for developing solidarity among the women participating in the movement.

Cooperative work was a means of resolving socioeconomic problems over the short or long term (Mainwaring and Viola 1984); such arrangements usually entail the sale of goods or commodities, benefiting those who participate in them. The Unemployed Movement developed a range of cooperative schemes to help deal with members' subsistence problems. They became especially popular during the 1980s as economic liberalization took hold in Brazil. Women were strongly involved in cooperative money-making ventures covering a wide range of small commodity production, including bread and confectionery making, tailoring and craft production. They were all eminently suitable for women's participation because production could be located in or near their homes, using flexible work rota systems and offering highly useful supplementary incomes. Corcoran-Nantes (1993: 151) asserts that many such cooperatives were organized along democratic lines, with group decisions made by the collective.

The second form of collective endeavour known as 'mutualist' schemes involves the provision of services – like clean water or education – which benefit all the local community, not just those who participate in them as cooperatives do. Many mutualist schemes have become an integral part of the political philosophy of local communities; extending members' political commitment to the idea of collectivism outwards (1993: 150). Mutualist schemes are used to resolve a variety of problems within many local communities in São Paulo, including childminding crèches, house construction for the homeless and community refuse collection.

The Shantytown Movement set up many mutualist schemes in the 1980s due to the difficulty of getting general services installed. Between 1983 and 1985, for example, the movement in Vila Sezamo, an area of São Paulo, organised a mutualist scheme for the construction of its headquarters, as well as a centre for local rubbish collection. In both cases, volunteers, predominantly women, undertook the physical work involved, while others donated money, tools and food. The local movement liaised with the local authorities, persuading them to supply a truck each week to a prearranged point at the edge of the *favela*. Local refuse collectors then collected rubbish and deposited it in the truck. The local council also provided placards aiming to prevent dumping, as well as a number of large litter bins in various locations in the area. Members of the local Shantytown group held consciousness-raising meetings about the importance of the scheme for local people's health. The scheme was a success, encouraging the São Paulo's umbrella Shantytown Commission to start other kinds of schemes, including cooperative work projects (1993: 151).

In conclusion, the types of activities developed predominantly by women for women in São Paulo helped to raise female consciousness in relation to a number of socioeconomic and political issues. They helped to stimulate and develop an array of alliances. As women acquired a greater sense of themselves and of gender inequality through their participation in the Unemployment and Shantytown movements, their own organizations emerged in the low-income areas, developed and grew in strength and numbers. In developing a political identity as women of the working poor, they were able to define their relationships more clearly than before.

India

In chapter 2 I examined two of India's successful women's groups, the Self-Employed Workers Association (SEWA) located in Ahmedabad, and the Calcutta-based Socio-Legal Aid, Research and Training Centre (SLARTC). These groups are engaged in different areas of endeavour – SEWA is concerned with organizing a trade union and credit organization for females working in the informal sector, while SLARTC organizes women across north-east India into legal groups to monitor and confront abuses against those who are unable to defend themselves. It is clear, however, that their aspirations are similar: to enhance the societal position of poor women, to empower them to gain an enhanced position in society. A further example of a successful women's group in India is the Working Women's Forum.

The Working Women's Forum

The Working Women's Forum (WWF) was initially concerned with a relatively narrow agenda: credit provision and unionization among working women. Over time, however, it developed into a national organization rather like the Grameen Bank of Bangladesh examined in chapter 3, also organized to provide credit to women workers in the urban informal sector. In contrast to the bank, however, the WWF has also been concerned with getting working women to organize themselves by unionization. Over time, WWF has developed into an organization with both a large membership – in the tens of thousands – and a wide agenda aimed at enhancing the position of poor women generally. It is worth noting that the success of WWF in enhancing the general socioeconomic position of women – in contrast to the Grameen Bank, concerned 'only' with credit provision – reflects the differing democratic environments of India and Bangladesh. Whereas the latter is frequently run by undemocratic military regimes, India has been a democracy for half a century. Political space enables the WWF to expand its activities into overtly sociopolitical areas, whereas the lack of it in Bangladesh may well constrain the Grameen Bank's operations.

The WWF was founded in Madras in 1978 by Jaya Arunachalam, a social worker and prominent member of the Congress (I) Party, who had resigned the year before from the party because she felt that it was quite ineffective in reaching poor women (Fisher 1993: 203). The WWF began as a grassroots union of poor women workers in the informal sector with 800 members. Its growth was swift: by the early 1990s it had grown into a national movement with more than 150,000 workers in four states, Tamil Nadu, Karnataka, Andhra Pradesh and Uttar Pradesh. 'The most astonishing aspect of all this has been the ability of illiterate and extremely poor women to pass on the word and extend their movement to other districts, towns and states in India' (Lecomte 1986: 118). Many local WWF leaders set up groups to raise funds, build up savings, negotiate bank loans and provide for members' welfare needs (Fisher 1993: 203).

Following abortive attempts to forge links with a government-administered loan scheme, the WWF set up its own Working Women's Cooperative Society (WWCS) to issue credit. The only people who can apply for loans are the members of the WWF, women not only marginalized by their informal – and hence insecure – working status, but also by their gender and poverty. Frequently, such people will be at or near the bottom of the social pile, ill-treated and exploited by money-lenders and, if they have them, employers. As Ekins (1992: 119) notes, it is an 'extraordinary achievement for such women to have organised themselves in large numbers effectively to combat this oppression and materially improve their quality of life'.

The success of WWF springs from the way that, like the Six-S movement (described in chapter 3), it embedded itself among its members and drew inspiration from their inputs. The WWF's key organizing characteristics include placing the priorities of poor women first; promoting leadership from below; using clout to get poor women their rights; and only working with the poor (Chambers 1985: 17–18). Jaya Arunachalam was able to use her influence with high-level government officials to achieve some state backing for the pursuit of poor women's rights, while the WWF recruited members from a variety of occupational areas, including traders, embroidery workers, agricultural fieldworkers and fishers.

Credit provision remains the main material service to members. By 1991 more than 100,000 WWF members had received loans totalling 390 million rupees ($16 million). WWF is also active in health care and family welfare. Jointly with the International Labour Organization, the Indian government and the United Nations Family Planning Association, WWF employs 400 poor women in Tamil Nadu to educate their peers about health issues. WWF also organizes child labour rehabilitation centres for working children who would not otherwise receive any education. It organizes mass demonstrations on the problems of its members; its political importance can be measured by the fact that in 1988 the then prime minister of India, Rajiv Ghandi, twice came to Madras to hear the grievances of WWF members. In sum, WWF's objective is much greater than simple provision of credit for poor, working women: it aims to increase consciousness and to raise members' awareness of social and economic injustice while putting political pressure on government to deal with members' pressing concerns.

Conclusion

This chapter has illustrated how the socioeconomic and political position of poor women in the Third World is dependent on a number of factors. I described how the position of women in Kerala is much better than in other areas of India because the state government has been forced to be responsive to an educated and sophisticated electorate which values equality highly. As the discussion of the 'normal' position of poor women in the Third World made clear, such a position is, to say the least, unusual.

The case studies of the chapter highlighted how important it is (1) for working women to organize in pursuit of their socioeconomic goals, and (2) for them to share a desire to work collectively. Argentina's Mothers de Plaza de Mayo began as a group with a narrow aim: discovering what had happened to their husbands and sons after they were picked up by the state's security services. Over time, however, many members began to question the overall position of women in Argentinian society.

As the case studies of Brazil's Shantytown and Unemployed movements made clear, when government is unwilling to legislate to improve the position of poor women – and of the poor more generally – then probably the only realistic choice they have is to organize themselves. The stimulus for both the Unemployed and Shantytown movements was, put simply, poverty and the absence of services supplied by the authorities. For India's WWF and SEWA, on the other hand, the lowly position of many women workers was the stimulus for organization; solidarity was the key to the success of these groups in building networks in the country.

Two conclusions suggest themselves. The first is that such vehicles of women's emancipation do not seriously threaten the state; however, they probably alarm many men who feel that their privileged position is undermined by displays of women's assertiveness and collective strength. The second is that all the women's socioeconomic and political groups examined in this chapter have found it possible to thrive in democratic environments. Very few examples of such women's groups are found in either sub-Saharan Africa or the Middle East. This serves to underline further a point made earlier: action groups with socioeconomic or political aspirations will find that their progress will only be possible in democratic or democratizing environments. This is because governments in such conditions cannot deal in a heavy-handed fashion with such groups even if they would like to.

The paucity of examples of women's empowerment groups from either the Middle East or sub-Saharan Africa should lead us to beware of excessively optimistic conclusions regarding an improvement in the sociopolitical and economic position of poor women throughout the Third World generally. On the other hand, the success of several women's organizations in Latin America and India related here suggests that in some countries progress is being made.

There is a long way to go. The position of women in the Third World generally lags behind men whether looked at socially, economically or politically. It needs to be underlined that the position of the vast majority of women in most Third World societies is almost uniformly worse than that of men – and this is not to assume that women's socioeconomic and political positions in many Western societies is anything to be complacent about. What *is* of particular concern, however, is the structural position of women, that is, where their gender often determines their socioeconomic position.

The importance of a democratic environment and of a relatively developed civil society for the growth of socioeconomic political groups has been repeatedly stressed in the chapters of this book. In the next we turn to an assessment of Islamist action groups – that is, those seeking an Islamic state and society – which at first glance may appear to have little or nothing to do with democratic aspirations. As we shall see, however, the appearance of such groups in the Muslim societies of the Middle East and elsewhere is a particular manifestation of the desire for a greater sociopolitical profile for subordinate groups. In their own way, they help to augment skeletal civil societies.

7
Islamist Action Groups

Since the beginning of Islam over 1,300 years ago, religious critics of the status quo have periodically emerged in opposition to what they perceive as unjust rule. Contemporary Islamists[1] – that is, politically radical Muslims fighting for an Islamic state – are the most recent example, characterizing themselves as the 'just' struggling against the 'unjust'. The dichotomy between 'just' and 'unjust' in the promotion of social change throughout Islamic history parallels the tension in the West between 'state' and 'civil society'. In other words, 'just' and 'unjust', like 'state' and 'civil society', can be regarded as mutually exclusive concepts: strengthening one implies weakening the other. The goal of the 'just' is an Islamically based society; Islamist groups are the vehicle to achieve this end.

To Islamists, liberal democracy is fatally flawed and compromised, a concept of relevance only to secular, Western(ized) societies which, to them, appear unacceptably morally deficient. Islamists strive to achieve the goal of direct democracy under the auspices of Sharia law. According to the concept of *shura* (consultation), the ruler must use his wisdom to settle disputes brought before him by his loyal subjects. Yet *shura* does not imply popular sovereignty – sovereignty is with God alone: 'rather it is a means of obtaining unanimity from the community of believers, which allows for no legitimate minority position' (Dorr 1993: 151–2). Yet despite an unwillingness to accept any sovereignty other than God's, some Islamists accept the need for earthly rulers to seek a mandate, via the ballot box, from their people. For example, Dr Abdeslam Harras, leader of the Moroccan Islamist movement Jama'at al-Da'wa al-Islamiyah, asserts that the ruler of an

Islamic country should be elected by a majority of the people (1993: 152).

While not all Islamists share Dr Harras's belief that rulers must be elected by popular mandate, it seems that the influence of radical Muslims is growing in many of the countries of the Middle East and North Africa. Why should this be? Apart from international factors – such as the humbling defeat of Arab Muslims at the hands of Israeli Jews in the Six-Day War of June 1967 and the success of the Iranian revolution a decade later – there are domestic causes underpinning the rise of the Islamists. These include perceptions of poor government, and growing unemployment and social crisis. While many governments have been content to gain rents from the sale of oil, little has been done to develop democratic polities, plan for the future or reduce unemployment (Gaffney 1994; Owen 1992; Bromley 1994). Normally, such regimes seek to use Islam as a facet of national identity and state power, setting up and sponsoring national Muslim organizations (Bayart 1993: 190). Yet, faced with state power seeking to control or destroy communitarian structures and replace them with the idea of a 'national citizenry', popular – as opposed to state-controlled – Islamic organizations have appeared. Many people, especially the young and the unemployed (often the same people), are highly dissatisfied with the status quo. In effect, this is Muslim civil society, where 'one sees Islam at work' (Coulon 1983: 49).

Many states in the Middle East and North Africa are conscious that their 'secular discourse and secularity is scarcely effective as a [popular] mobilizer' (1983: 50). As Fossaert notes,

> men-in-society are organized in and by the state, but they are also organized in families, in village communities, in provinces, in workplaces, in factories in which the state is not always the proprietor, in trade unions, in parties and in associations and in other ways which the state does not necessarily control. (1978: 149)

For many ordinary people in these regions, popular Islam is their chief expression of community, an 'anti-structure' expressing what Turner (1969) calls 'the powers of the weak' – that is, a countersociety. Manifestations of Muslim community outside of the state's control include a variety of Muslim associations – such as the Hamadiyya Shadhiliyya of urban Egypt – and community mosques throughout the Middle East and North Africa. These are the recruiting grounds for the Islamists. Especially in urban settings, Islamist groups – offering new forms of Muslim solidarity – have widely replaced former social solidarity networks based on kinship structures, clan or age. They offer important ways of affirming the autonomy and the identity of a community by pursuing a range of sociopolitical goals. The state is often extremely wary of them because of their sociopolitical potential – that is, the power to direct and organize the disaffected. In this chapter I focus on a number of such groups from the Middle East and Africa: Algeria's Front Islamique de Salut (Islamic Salvation Front); the Muslim Brotherhood in Egypt; Hamas and al-Jihad in Israel's Occupied Territories, and, *inter alia*, the Yan Izala and Da'wa organizations of Nigeria.

We saw in Chapter 2 that Islamist groups in both Kenya and Tanzania are stimulated by their rulers' efforts to secularize society, in other words, by the latter's determination to mobilize their citizens in 'mass' parties and to crush expressions of religio-ethnic autonomy. In these countries, Islamist groups have appeared because minority peoples believe that they are not getting a fair deal at the hands of the state – that is, their goals are concerned with a range of sociopolitical and economic issues. In this chapter the Islamist groups analysed are not stimulated by ethnic concerns; rather, they wish to see the creation of an Islamic society. Often they are the main expressions of opposition to incumbent governments. Yet creating an Islamic state at home is not their only goal; they also wish to see what they call a Khalafah, a *global* Islamic state. Setting them apart from nationalist or ethnic groups *exclusively* seeking state power, the Islamist groups examined in this chapter have a further aim: they believe it is essential to change the morality and social norms of society by rebutting the values of secularism; in short, by reaffirming and reimposing Muslim values. Because of this dual concern – with capturing state power and imposing Islamic morality – Islamist action groups are not conventional political parties. Instead, they are a category of action group. See table 2.1 on p. 26–7 for a representation of their goals and raisons d'êtres.

Before presenting the case studies, it is perhaps necessary to say a little more about Islamist aspirations and goals, because they are widely misunderstood. It is often argued, for example, that Islamism is merely the negative face of intolerance and anti-modernity, a defensive reversion to primordial beliefs (Shupe 1990: 19). To critics, Islamism implies a rigid, exclusivist, narrow-minded, dogmatic world-view. Its advocates, on the other hand, regard it as a liberating force, focusing on freeing believers from the twin fetters of ignorance and bondage.

A second view perceives Islamism as a significant threat to Western security. It is seen as an aggressive, expansionist ideology masterminded from Tehran by Iran's religious rulers (Huntington 1993). As the *Financial Times* of 27 July 1994 reported, Israel's then prime minister, Yitzhak Rabin, warned against 'extreme Islamic radical terrorist movements, with infrastructure around the world, following the radical teaching of Ayatollah Khomeini, the late Iranian religious leader'. Rabin described the threat as 'Khomeinism without Khomeini', claiming that all 'moderate' Arab governments, Israel and Western states were at risk. The Iranian revolution certainly provides images of fear and hate for many Westerners who feel threatened by the rise of Islamism. The fact is, however, that after 17 years of Islamic government, Iran cannot claim much success abroad or at home. Despite all the talk of exporting revolution, there is not a lot to show. Equally, the sorry state of the economy leaves little to crow about. While the secretive Islamic republic releases few figures on the state of its economy, it seems likely that an annual inflation figure of 17.1 per cent and a 'real earnings per employee annual growth rate' of −6.8 per cent during 1980–92 would be unconducive to a general increase in prosperity (World Bank 1995: 163, table 1; UNDP 1996: 168, table 16). But what Iran *has* been able to do, to a modest extent, is capitalize on the political and economic failures of others. In the process its capacity for trouble-making has been purposely exaggerated, not least by some Middle East leaders, such as Egypt's President Mubarak, who credits Iran as being the mastermind behind many terrorist attacks in his country. However, the fact is that Islamist movements thrive most where there is a partial collapse of the state (Lebanon and Sudan), where economic deprivation and disparities are particularly marked (Algeria and Egypt), and as a result of occupation (Israel's Occupied Territories and Lebanon).

A third perspective, one that I share, maintains that the contemporary political importance of Islamism is best understood as a rational response not only to the failure of many governments in the Middle East and elsewhere in the Muslim world to rule wisely or well – but also to something even more fundamental: the lack of opportunities that opposition groups have to unseat them (Kepel 1994).

Often Muslim countries which do not have democratic political systems feature Islamist groups as important articulators of popular opposition (Roberts 1992). Yet nowhere – so far as it can be judged in the widespread absence of competitive elections – do Islamists have overwhelming popular support. Many Muslim societies are polarized between the growing numbers of 'have nots', often looking to the Islamist groups to champion their interests, and the 'haves' – that is, the much smaller middle and upper classes – desiring more secular, Western-style polities.

Apart from their political role as champions of the dispossessed, Islamist groups also have moral and social concerns. Their rulers, they believe, are performing inadequately and are corrupt. Why is this? The

Islamist answer is that they have strayed from the path of Islam. To remedy matters it is necessary to reinstitute Islamic principles and values. While reflecting particular sets of national circumstances, Islamists – wherever they live – have a variety of shared characteristics. First, they feel their way of life to be under threat from unwelcome Western influences. Second, Islamists seek to reform society in accordance with the tenets of the Quran and the Hadith (the teachings of the Prophet Muhammad) – that is, to change their society's laws, morality and social norms in accordance with Sharia law. It is necessary, Islamists believe, to 'effect a return to the Texts . . . The enemy is not modernity but tradition, or rather in the Muslim context, all that is not in the Tradition of the Prophet. It is really a question of reform' (Roy 1985: 12). Third, Islamists fight governments because the jurisdiction of the latter encompasses areas which they hold to be integral to the building of an appropriate society, including education and employment policies. Fourth, Islamists struggle not only against 'nominal' co-religionists, whom they perceive as lax in their religious duties, but also against members of religions other than Islam.

This is not to suggest that Islamist interpretations are always identical. Because Sharia law, albeit of divine origin, is not a blueprint for running a modern society, contemporary Islamists feel free to use it as an ideological *tabula rasa* which may be either 'left' or 'right' wing. Interpretations on the 'right', which groups like Afghanistan's Taliban exemplify, include hostility to *any* innovations since the time of the Prophet Muhammad some 1,300 years ago; no contacts with the West; a highly restricted social role for women – in effect, they are treated as little more than domestic slaves; only boys to be educated *at all*; and discrimination against non-Muslims. On the other hand, a 'leftist' Islamist programme might embrace attempts to establish a more egalitarian society through redistribution of wealth and land and reform of the Islamic establishment, the *ulama* (Mayer 1993: 111). Both visions – right and left – perceive honest, corruption-free government as a *sine qua non* for other social reforms.

In the case studies that follow, we shall see that the division between 'left' and 'right' wing interpretations of the Islamic state tends to divide Islamist groups in many national settings – they may well fight each other as well as the state. Second, because Islamist groups are nearly always proscribed, many seek funding and encouragement from foreign governments, especially Iran or Saudi Arabia. Often the precise vision of an Islamic state and society will be moulded by what their sponsors perceive as appropriate – broadly, Saudi Arabia's Islamic state pertains to the 'rightist' interpretation, Iran's to the 'leftist'.

Finally, in all cases analysed below, Islamist groups articulate and express the concerns of society's have-nots, especially the young, the unemployed and the alienated; in effect, they often function as important voices in civil society. It is less clear, however, that many women are attracted to Islamist programmes.

Nigeria

Since independence in 1960, Nigeria has experienced nearly three decades of military governments, a short-lived oil boom, and growing religious polarization between the country's 35 million Christians and 45 million Muslims (O'Connell 1989: 196; Williams and Falola 1995). Antipathy between the religious communities was fuelled because many Christians – focused in the south of the country – believe that the predominantly Muslim north enjoys a disproportionate share of political power and economic resources (Ibrahim 1991: 135).

Tension was also exacerbated by the government's secret decision in 1986 to join the 45-member Organisation of Islamic Conference (OIC). Whereas the Nigerian government's motivation for joining the OIC was probably partially financial – aid was expected from Saudi Arabia or Kuwait – many Christians feared that Nigeria's membership would jeopardize the country's status as a secular state. Proponents of membership of the OIC countered that Nigeria was a member of the Commonwealth, a 'Christian' organization because it is led by the British monarch who, legally, must be a Protestant Christian. The outcry forced the government to climb down: in October 1988 it announced that Nigeria would remain a secular state and that membership of the OIC merely reflected the fact that about half of Nigerians are also Muslims. A third issue helping to polarize Muslims and Christians around this time was whether a Sharia court of appeal would be allowed in a future democratic regime. Predictably, many Muslims wanted a federal Sharia court of appeal, while Christians were equally widely opposed to such a move.

These issues – OIC membership, a mooted Sharia court of appeal, and a perception that Muslims had a better deal than Christians – served to fan the flames of religious intolerance in the 1980s. Anti-Christian riots took place in parts of Muslim-dominated northern Nigeria. Churches and mosques were destroyed and over 3,000 people were killed (Maier 1991).

In most democratic societies popular concerns do not normally centre on religious issues. The context of the religious violence in Nigeria was that an authoritarian military government had banned open political debate. With political parties prohibited and with no functioning legislature, anger and frustration among many Nigerians was largely channelled into religious issues. Many ordinary Muslims were turned into Islamic chauvinists. Many Christians feared what appeared to them to be a growing threat from Islamist groups.

Reflecting the inability to express opposition through democratic or civil society channels, a number of Islamist groups have emerged in Nigeria in recent times. Their general aims are three: to diminish the sociopolitical and religious influence of Christianity; to purge Nigeria of traditional Sufi conceptions of Islam; to strive for an Islamic state. Reflecting their concerns, an attempt was made in 1990 at the Centre for Islamic Legal Studies, Ahmadu Bello University, northern Nigeria, to forge an Islamist political programme to achieve such ends. Proposals included federal laws forbidding prostitution, gambling, alcohol sales and consumption; compulsory *zakat* (Islamic 'poor tax'); confiscation of land from business corporations in favour of 'the peasants'; general – yet unspecified – Islamic economic reforms; and Islamicization of higher education courses in 'economics, banking, [and] political science' (Birai 1993: 193–4).

The precise parameters of a putative Islamic state in Nigeria not only involve differing interpretations among local Islamists but are also moulded by the models presented by their foreign backers such as Iran, Libya and Saudi Arabia (Abubakr 1986). Nigeria's federal government has become increasingly fearful of what it sees as foreign-inspired subversion; in the late 1980s, several states including Gongola, Bauchi and Kwara banned open-air religious preaching and Kungiyar yan Shia, an Islamist group inspired by Iran.

Despite such measures, Nigeria's Islamist constituency is probably growing in size and influence, although it is extremely difficult to come up with numbers of 'committed' Islamists. Williams and Falola claim, however, that one of the largest groups, the Muslim Students Society, has five million members (1995: 175). Below I describe four leading Islamist groups: the Yan Izala, Da'wa, the Islamic Movement, and the Muslim Students Society. All seem attractive to the young, especially the reasonably well educated who often cannot find employment commensurate with their qualifications (Birai 1993; Falola and Williams 1995: 173).

Ideologically, the groups are split between followers of Iran – the Islamic Movement and the Muslim Students Society – and followers of Saudi Arabia, the Yan Izala and Da'wa. However, the basic difference between the two sets of groups is not necessarily about ends – an Islamic state is the common goal – but about means to achieve it. Generally, the Iranian-influenced groups believe that an Islamic state must be created as soon as possible by any means necessary, while those cleaving to the Saudi model believe in more gradualist agendas. The latter emphasize that first people's world-views must evolve towards an Islamic interpretation of reality. In other words, Islamic reform must encompass individual's religious behaviour leading to Islamic social change.

The Yan Izala

The Yan Izala (Izalatul-Bid'a wa Iqamat al Sunna: 'Those who reject innovation') was founded in Jos, northern Nigeria, in 1978, by Mallam Ismaila Idris of Bauchi. Initially an anti-Sufi organization, during the 1980s it enjoyed a period of strong expansion on an Islamist platform, spreading to all the main urban areas of northern Nigeria (Kane 1990: 8). The Yan Izala's current leader is Sheikh Abubbakar Mahmud Gumi, a senior religious figure. The group aims to eradicate 'innovation' (*bida*), that is, it seeks to eradicate non-orthodox Islamic ways of life, promoting an interpretation based solely on the Quran and the Sunna. Influenced by the austere Saudi brand of Islam, the Yan Izala is strongly opposed to Iran's revolutionary programme.

Da'wa

Da'wa, founded in the 1970s, is led by Sheikh Aminudeen Abubbacar who is personally close to figures in the governments of both Kuwait and Saudi Arabia. During the 1980s, Abubbacar persuaded such benefactors to finance the construction of his religious centre – a very large modern mosque, a primary school and educational facilities for adult courses – in an exclusive residential area of Kano, northern Nigeria. It is alleged that some individuals associated with Abubbacar's Islamic centre became involved 'in money-lending and frequently attacked Imam Khomeini for being a demagogue' (Kane 1990: 9).

The Islamic Movement

The position of Da'wa and the Yan Izala among Nigeria's Islamists is challenged by two Iranian-influenced groups, Mallam Ibrahim El-Zak

Zaky's Islamic Movement, widely regarded as more radical than the 'gradualist' Yan Izala, and the long-established Muslim Students Society (MSS). Like Da'wa and the Yan Izala, the Islamic Movement rejects the idea of a secular state constitution for Nigeria. But it differs from them not only in regarding Iran's theocratic state favourably but also in believing that an Islamic state must be built in Nigeria by *jihad*, that is, 'holy' war (Birai 1993: 197).

The Muslim Students Society

The MSS was founded in Lagos in 1954 by 14 Muslim students who wished to stop what they saw as the indoctrination of Muslim children into Christianity by missionaries. During the 1970s a 'hardcore extremist leadership' took control, based in the northern universities of Zaria, Kano and Sokoto, allegedly fuelled by Iran's revolution (Williams and Falola 1995: 178). By the 1980s the MSS had grown strongly in both the north and south of Nigeria, with a claimed 5 million members (ibid.: 177).

The MSS wishes to see an Islamic state in Nigeria modelled along Iranian lines (Ibrahim 1991). Its leaders are said to be very close to Iran's government, to distribute Iranian propaganda against Nigeria's secular state, and to have been in the forefront of Muslim–Christian clashes in several Nigerian universities in the 1980s (ibid.: 179; Haynes 1996a: 217).

This brief survey of some of the leading Nigerian Islamist groups has underlined that while all of them want to see an Islamic state in the country, both the means to achieve such a state and the precise models for it differ. While the significance of the groups is probably growing, it would be wong to imply that every Nigerian Muslim supports them. Birai estimates that up to two-thirds of the country's Muslims – some 30 million people – do not belong to, or even sympathize with, an Islamist group (1993: 195). On the other hand, what stimulates the Islamist groups – a fear of Christianization, secularism, and the reality of bad government – no doubt concerns many non-Islamist Muslims. The point is that most Muslims, like other Nigerians, have suffered greatly as a result of their rulers' economic mismanagement and political ineptitude. As a result, it is scarcely surprising that the Islamists' revolutionary programmes have appeal, especially to the dispossessed and the alienated. Stimulated by class polarization as a result of the short-lived 1970s oil boom, Islamist ideals, bolstered by foreign support from oil-rich Middle Eastern governments, became a focus for concerns about wage exploitation, inflation and declining living standards. Such social frustrations combined to produce an explosive situation in parts of Nigeria, a climate exploited by the Islamists. Under such circumstances it is not surprising their support levels have grown. Many no doubt feel cheated by Nigeria's recent, traumatic economic decline: in the 1980s and early 1990s GNP per capita fell by 0.1 per cent a year – a figure made worse by population growth of 3 per cent annually (World Bank 1995: 162, table 1).

Egypt

Over 90 per cent of Egypt's 60 million people are Muslims; many of the remainder are Coptic Christians. Like Nigeria, Egypt has suffered both interreligious conflict and serious economic decline in recent times; the main people affected have been the Islamists. Urban unemployment is a serious problem in Egypt: there are currently more than 3 million unemployed graduates of universities and high schools, thought to be the main source of recruits for radical Islamist movements such as al-Gama'at al-Islamiya (Auda 1993: 385). Also like Nigeria, economic restructuring programmes have involved privatization of state industries, throwing huge numbers of people out of work. It is argued that for many, hardships are more difficult to bear because of the obvious corruption of the government, the bureaucracy and the military elite, and the ostentatious wealth of the *arriviste* middle classes (Gaffney 1994). A further parallel with Nigeria is that the process of division between an increasingly secular, Western-oriented elite and an Islamist opposition is well advanced in Egypt.

The growth of Islamist groups in both countries reflects not only declining economic conditions but also the diminishing legitimacy and authority of their governments. Egypt's Islamists are inspired by the success of the Islamic mojahideen in Afghanistan who managed to rid their country of the 'godless' Russians. It is reckoned that many returnees from the Afghan war play leading roles in Islamist groups not only in Egypt, but also in Algeria, Tunisia and the Gulf countries (Salame 1993: 27). Generally, prescriptions among Egypt's Islamists are akin to those of their Nigerian counterparts: to reject Western values and influence in favour of a reintroduction of Islamic norms and morals. The principal target of the Islamists' action, apart from the Christians, is the state, which has failed, they believe, to strive to eradicate

Western influence. Just as importantly, it has also not delivered on its promises to improve the material well-being of the mass of people or to democratize.

Egypt's Islamists have prospered by providing a variety of welfare measures, including medical facilities and schools, for the urban poor, who by and large do not have access to such goods. According to Voll their popularity is reflected in the fact that hundreds of thousands of Egyptians are involved 'in some way in the Islamic resurgence . . . in some respects, [they] represent the majority of society' (1991: 345). Certainly, many people listen to radical preachers, such as Sheikh Muhammad Sha'rawi and Sheikh 'Abd al-Hamid Kishk, in person or via audio cassettes and video tapes (Gaffney 1994). Ironically, Voll notes, those who constitute the core of the Islamic revolution 'have had the greatest exposure to modern technologies, educational systems, political processes, cultural values and lifestyles'; yet, they can also relate to the experiences of 'ordinary' Egyptians suffering unemployment, poverty and substandard accommodation (1991: 346). Often this will be because they themselves suffer the same conditions. Generally, advocates of the Islamic state in Eypt find a powerful basis for unity in a dissatisfaction with the contemporary character of society where corruption, 'women's liberation', Westernization and a lack of piety among many Muslims are thought to be behind the decline of the country's position in the Arab world.

The Muslim Brotherhood and its offshoots

The most important Islamic movement in Egypt is the Muslim Brotherhood, founded by a teacher, Hasan al-Banna, in 1928. Over the years it grew to encompass tens of thousands of adherents, before emerging as a political party in the early 1980s (M. Deeb 1989: 64). Initially, however, it was just one of a large number of tiny Islamic associations engaged in charity work among the poor of the country's fast growing cities. Mosques, schools and clinics were built by the Brotherhood, providing an Islamic welfare framework through which Muslims could benefit, enhancing the ability to live 'without [much] reference to the western and secular influences around' them (Ayubi 1991: 131). By such means the Brotherhood grew rapidly, its progress also stimulated by the personality of al-Banna, a 'charismatic leader' (Owen 1992: 179). Al-Banna managed to build up a loose structure of self-sustaining local neighbourhood groups, directed nationally by the leadership with access to newspapers and other forms of direct communication, such as radio.

As a result, the Muslim Brotherhood was able to recruit at a rapid rate. During the 1940s it acted much like a conventional political party. Following al-Banna's assassination in 1949, however, it became close to the revolutionary government of Gamal Abdul Nasser, which took power in 1952. But by 1954 relations had soured to the extent that the Brotherhood was proscribed and its new leader, Sayyid Qutb, arrested following an unsuccessful attempt on the life of Nasser. During the next ten years in prison, Qutb produced a reworking of Islamic history. He argued that Egypt was not an Islamic country, but in a state of *jahiliyya* (religious ignorance). Muslims could not live a proper religious life in such circumstances; as a result, what was necessary was an overthrow of the existing political order (Zubaida 1989: 51–3). Qutb was executed in 1966.

Following Sadat's accession to power in 1970, the Brotherhood enjoyed a period of good relations with the government. Building mosques, schools and clinics, it improved its financial position by taking advantage of Sadat's economic liberalization to start profitable Islamic companies and financial institutions. None the less, such entrepreneurial flair was not appreciated by all Brotherhood members. While one strand believed in slowly Islamicizing society by increasing the Brotherhood's influence by a variety of means, including proselytization and strengthening its financial clout, another believed that this gradualist approach was bound to fail. The Takfir wal-Hijra and al-Jihad organizations broke away from the gradualist group, believing that the Islamic state must be fought for: the government would never allow it to happen via gradualist means. Both organizations became important components of a shifting set of religio-political organizations under the general title of al-Gama'at al-Islamiyya – the Islamic Groups – characterized not only by a denial of conventional, ballot box politics, but also by a resort to terrorist tactics to achieve the Islamic state (Owen 1992: 180). Stimulated by the writings of Qutb, such rejectionists argue that these methods are the only possible ones to lead from the *jahiliyya* to a society ruled by Sharia law and consultation (*shura*) between leaders and the people (Auda 1991).

Members of Takfir wal-Hijra have been responsible for a number of political assassinations from the 1970s, while the al-Jihad group not only killed President Sadat in 1981, but also tried to kill two government ministers and the parliamentary speaker in the same period (M. Deeb 1989: 63–4). Five alleged perpetrators of Sadat's murder, including Khalid al Istambuli, who claimed to be the leader, were sentenced to death. In the mid-1980s the state also decided to crack down on al-Jihad. More than 300 of its members were arrested; some were executed for their alleged involvement in the murder of state security forces in the town of Asyut.

From the mid-1980s the Islamic Groups became involved in a de facto civil war with the authorities (Auda 1993), latterly turning their attentions to the Coptic Christian minority, murdering several people. Foreign tourists were also killed (Bromley 1994: 134–5). The aim was threefold: (1) to stymie both foreign investment and the influx of foreign tourists in order to put the state authorities under pressure, leading to (2) conditions ripe for the overthrow of the government, followed by (3) the inauguration of an Islamic state. In all, between 1992 and 1996, more than 900 people are thought to have died in the conflict between state and Islamists.

In conclusion, a division in world-views between secularists and Islamists has developed in Egypt into a conflict between two different conceptions of society and social change. It has spilled over from the religious sphere into the fields of the politics, the economy and social affairs; in the process it has split Egypt's society. Dessouki (1982) notes several areas where Islamic political activism now manifests itself: the reinstitution of Islamic law, the language of politics, religious social symbols, sociopolitical opposition and the economy. What this amounts to is that the Islamists, irrespective of the extent to which they differ in terms of tactics, leaders and, to an extent, the precise vision of an Islamic society, have as their project the religious hegemonization of society involving the displacement of modernizing elites from state power. What is involved, then, is not merely the aim of grabbing power in order to introduce Sharia law for moral goals, but also the comprehensive (re)creation of an Islamic society.

Algeria

Egypt is a country whose rulers have opted for modernization along Western lines. This engenders Islamist opposition. Ayubi argues that Islamist movements 'appear to be more vigorous in countries that have openly discarded some of the symbols of "traditionalism"' (1991: 118). Such countries, he asserts, include Egypt. But this surely misses the point. Ayubi's argument suggests that countries like Egypt should have stronger Islamist lobbies than, for example, Saudi Arabia, whose constitution is an Islamic one. Yet while Saudi Arabia's stability is increasingly challenged by an *Islamist* opposition, modernizing Muslim countries such as Tunisia and Morocco appear to have managed to keep the lid on Islamist dissent. This suggests that it is not so much a question of tradition versus modernization as an issue of how skilled government is in dealing with Islamist demands – that is, defusing them by a variety of means, including (partial or quasi) democratization and real increases in living standards. During 1980–93 Saudi Arabia's per capita GNP fell by 3.6 per cent a year, while Tunisia's grew by 1.2 per cent, as did Morocco's. That of Algeria also declined – by 0.8 per annum – during the same period (World Bank 1995: 161–2, table 1).

It is a combination of declining living standards and a denial of democracy which seems to be behind the growth of the Islamists in Algeria. Following independence from France in 1962, Algeria was governed by the secular National Liberation Front (FLN) for three decades. By the late 1970s, however, an Islamist constituency had begun advocating a complete restructuring of society, including the application of Sharia law to replace Algeria's – French-influenced – civil code. At this time, the Islamists also pushed for reforms based on so-called 'Islamic principles', such as a stricter dress code for women, more religious broadcasts on radio and television, and the banning of the consumption of alcohol in public places. They began to seek such goals by direct action, especially by taking over government-controlled mosques and installing their own preachers. Sometimes bloody clashes resulted. Conflict also broke out on university campuses between Islamists and secularists; there was also harassment of 'inappropriately' dressed women (M.-J. Deeb 1989a: 7). As a result of such turmoil, the state began a systematic clampdown on the Islamists: it arrested their leaders and tried to control the movements of activists. Nevertheless, an Islamist movement, Ahl al-Da'wa, the People of the Call, still managed to survive (Kepel 1994: 45). By the mid-1980s there was a growing Islamist network organized around the themes of anti-Westernization, anti-unemployment, anti-poverty and Arabization. The latter goal was manifested in a campaign against French, the language of the elite even though nearly everyone – except a few – had Arabic as their first language. Islamists were thus able to link religious and cultural issues with the country's growing economic problems.

Economic decline was largely due to a collapse in the price of oil. This one commodity accounts for 98 per cent of Algeria's export proceeds. In 1986 only 25 per cent of the country's food came from local sources, down from 90 per cent in 1969, and the country found it could not feed itself. During 1980–93 the declining economic situation was reflected in a negative annual growth rate of GNP per capita of 0.8 per cent. As in Nigeria, an overreliance on the proceeds of oil sales to buy what the country needed led to economic disaster; as in Nigeria, the Islamists were the beneficiaries. In order to qualify for desperately needed aid from the West, Algeria's rulers had to allow multiparty elections. Under pressure they agreed, apparently not realizing how unpopular they had become among the people; electoral benefits went to Islamists.

The Islamist movement grew swiftly after liberalization of the constitution in February 1989, following food riots the previous October (M.-J. Deeb 1989a: 8). Hitherto both fluid and nebulous, it began to solidify into a variety of distinct organizations, including political parties as well as Islamic groups with religious and sociocultural as well as political objectives. The largest was the Islamic Salvation Front (FIS). In addition, there was Hamas (al-Haraka li-Mujtama' Islami: Movement for an Islamic Society – not linked to the group of the same name in Israel's Occupied Territories) and the MNI (La Mouvement de la Nahda Islamique; the Movement for Islamic Renewal). There were also several smaller groups, such as the Rabitat al-Da'wa al-Islamiyya (League of the Islamic Call) and the Party of Algerian Renewal (Roberts 1991: 133). While differing in their routes to an Islamic state, a common position was that Algeria's problems were caused in no small measure by the downgrading of Islam during three decades of Westernization. They also argued that, as a result, Western conceptions of democracy were inappropriate to Algeria, given its roots in Islam (Roberts 1992).

In June 1990 the FIS emerged as the main political rival to the ruling FLN, taking control of more than 50 per cent of municipalities in local elections, with over 54 per cent of the vote. Until 1991, FIS was financially backed by the Saudi Arabian government; then Iran became its chief foreign funding source. The Iranian government supplied $3 million to help the FIS finance its 1991 electoral campaign, and the FIS victory in December's elections was greeted as a 'triumph of Islam' in Iran's parliament (Tahi 1992: 411).

The FIS, Hamas, MNI and the Party for Algerian Renewal took part in the December 1991 elections, with a second round due in January 1992. The FIS won 188 of the 430 seats in the National Assembly in the first round of voting (nearly 3.26 million of the 6.8 million votes cast, 47.9 per cent). The FIS view was that Algeria should move at once to become an Islamic state on the basis of Sharia law and *shura* to replace Western conceptions of pluralism and representative democracy. At the time of the poll, both of the main leaders of FIS, Abassi Madani and his deputy Ali Belhadj, were in prison.

The second Islamist group, Hamas – unlike its namesake in Israel's Occupied Territories – was a 'gradualist' group, led by Sheikh Mahfoud Nahnah. Rather like Egypt's Muslim Brotherhood, it appealed primarily to more 'moderate' Islamists (Roberts 1991: 136). Like the Muslim Brotherhood, Hamas leaders apparently believed it was necessary to reform society through missionary activity before seeking to create the Islamic state. Hamas saw its own pragmatic stance as an alternative to FIS 'extremism', yet it was able to win only 368,697 votes (2.78 per cent) in the December 1991 poll (Tahi 1991: 407).

The MNI, led by Abdallah Djabalah, was the third Islamist party to fight the elections. It tried to carve itself out a place on the 'left' of the Islamic movement. It was committed to defending the public sector against the privatization measures introduced at the behest of the International Monetary Fund (*Africa Research Bulletin* 1991–2). Its disappointing showing in the December elections (150,093 votes, 1.13 per cent) reflected its inability to make inroads into the FIS's popularity.

Tahi argues that the success of the FIS in the December 1991 elections reflected popular dislike of the incumbent regime as much, if not more, than a desire to see an Islamic state in the country. In any case, although the FIS victory was both comprehensive and unexpected, the party's more than 3.25 million votes needs to be contextualized by reference to the fact that Algeria's electorate was 13.25 million people. In other words, just 24.5 per cent of eligible Algerians chose the FIS in the December elections, compared to the 1.6 million (12 per cent) who chose the ruling FLN. In all, recognizably Islamist parties gained about 52 per cent of the vote in the poll, with the FIS taking the lion's share.

Despite the low turnout, most independent observers have characterized the December elections as amongst the freest ever held in the Arab world. The result, however equivocal in terms of overall popular preferences, *did* come up with a FIS victory. It was virtually certain that the party would have gained enough seats in the second round of voting in January 1992 to secure an overall majority in the National Assembly. Instead, the army stepped in, cancelled the elections and ruled the country behind various frontmen. The overturning of an election result which would have been an expression of the democratic will (however unpalatable that might have been to certain constituencies) was defended by the military on several grounds: that an FIS victory would have been a recipe for Algeria's break-up (because it would have led to demands for secession by the anti-FIS Berber province of Kabylia); that an FIS victory would have led to the withdrawal of crucial international loans; and that the FIS, with a clear-cut electoral victory, would have been unable to restrain the party's radicals who wished to abolish the pluralist constitution. This would have aroused the irreconcilable antagonism of a significant part of public opinion.

These were the army's claimed reasons for intervening to stop the second round of the elections. But it is difficult to separate self-interest from national interest concerns in the army's coup. On the one hand, its cessation of the electoral process was a clear sign of its reluctance to let Algerians choose their government; on the other, the fact that the FIS gained only a quarter of the electorate's votes, while its chief rival, the FLN, achieved only one-eighth, gives some credence to the army's claims that its actions represented the will of Algeria's population as a whole – a plague on the houses of both the FLN and the FIS.

The army forced the FLN's leader, Chadli Benjedid, to resign, replacing him with a five-man collective presidency, the High Committee of State (Haut Comité d'État, HCE), chaired by Mohamed Boudiaf (Roberts 1992: 453). Boudiaf was assassinated in June 1992, not by the FIS but almost certainly either by or at least at the behest of certain senior army figures. They were allegedly alarmed that Boudiaf was setting in train corruption investigations which threatened to implicate them and their associates, a shadowy group popularly known as 'the mafia' (1992: 454).

After the aborted poll, the FIS was banned and thousands of its activists and supporters were incarcerated. An estimated 60,000 people have died in the ensuing civil war. Presidential elections in November 1995 attracted a large turnout despite threats by Islamic militants to kill voters. Results gave a clear victory to the government's candidate for the presidency, Liamine Zeroual. Most Islamic groups, including the banned FIS, boycotted the poll. Following the election, there was a resurgence of violence in Algeria. In early December 1995, 15 people were killed and more than 30 injured in a car bomb explosion in the capital, Algiers. Parliamentary elections in June 1997 resulted in a victory for Zeroual's party.

For the regime to crush the Islamists it will be necessary to induce strong economic growth over a sufficiently long period of time to reduce unemployment and hence improve the quality of life for the mass of Algerians. The problem is that every four years a million more Algerians enter the job market. Currently over 2 million urban unemployed struggle for non-existent jobs. The FIS was able to capitalize on the economic and social crisis of the country in elections in 1990 and 1991 when millions of people voted for the party in protest against high levels of unemployment, housing shortages, corruption and steep price rises in consumer goods. Unless the government can somehow deal with such issues it is highly unlikely that the attraction of the Islamists will diminish appreciably.

Israel's Occupied Territories

Many Muslim Palestinians in Israel's Occupied Territories – the Gaza Strip and the West Bank – have turned to Islamist groups as their vehicle of sociopolitical liberation in recent times. In December 1987 the *intifada* (uprising) erupted, receiving wide support from many Palestinians, particularly the young. A mix of political, economic and social factors were central to the *intifada* (Serhan 1993: 165). For two decades after 1967, when Israel took control of the Occupied Territories, Palestinians had been denied the right to organize for socioeconomic and political goals. Despite this, a number of community groups grew, often clandestinely (1993: 180). By the late 1980s there were hundreds, involved in a variety of tasks, including Islamic education, community kitchens and urban growing of food (Fisher 1993: 25).

Over time, however, Israel's 'iron fist' approach in the West Bank and the Gaza Strip led to increasing tension with Palestinians: the *intifada* was the result. Its roots can be traced to a number of discrete developments, including the acquisition of Palestinian land for Jewish settlements, human rights concerns, high local unemployment and denial of water for Palestinians' land. In the West Bank, 12 Jewish settlements had been established between 1976 and 1977. By 1988 the Israeli government had confiscated 52 per cent of all land in the West Bank and established 135 settlements with over 65,000 inhabitants. By 1992 there were 212 settlements with 112,000 inhabitants in the Territories – almost 13 per cent of their population – that is, nearly 6 per cent of Israel's total people. But the issue of what to do with the Palestinians remained unresolved.

The Gaza Strip was home to 400,000 Palestinians in 1967, presenting a great demographic and security problem for the Israelis. Israel's orginal intention was to annex Gaza and to resettle Palestinians from there to the West Bank and the Sinai desert. In 1973 Prime Minister Rabin called for the population to be dispatched to Jordan. While this was not attempted, Jewish settlements grew in number, with the Jewish population increasing fivefold. Despite the fact that Gaza's Arab population in the early 1990s exceeded half a million people, crammed into 140 square miles – giving the area a greater population density than Hong Kong – the Israelis by 1992 had confiscated more than a third of the total area and awarded it to Jewish settlers who made up 0.5 per cent of the population. Settlers on average have 2.6 acres of land in Gaza, while Palestinians have 0.006 acres each, over 430 times less.

Just as land seizures in both Gaza and the West Bank and the implantation of settlements in the Territories paralleled previous patterns established in Israel after 1948, so other policies resembled those used to contain the Arabs left in Israel. Because of the very different demographic balance that obtains in the Territories, as well as greater levels of politicization among Palestinians living there, Israeli policies have been much more more severe than those used in Israel proper. Whereas demolition of houses, wanton disregard for civil rights, imprisonment without trial, torture, deportation and political killings seldom occur in Israel itself, they are commonplace in the Territories. Between 1967 and the *intifada* in December 1987 there were more than 500,000 detentions and arrests (an average of one arrest/detention for every three Palestinians); there were also over 2,000 deportations and 1,500 house demolitions. From 1982 to 1987 more than 130 Palestinians lost their lives at the hands of Israeli soldiers or settlers. By comparison, between 1968 and 1983 Israeli government statistics reveal that 14 Israeli citizens and 22 soldiers were killed by West Bank Palestinians. From April 1986 to May 1987 alone, Israeli forces killed 22 Palestinians, while armed attacks on Israel took two lives (Bill and Springborg 1994: 328).

The legal system, which even prior to the *intifada* allowed for arrest and detention without charges or trial for up to six months (renewable on request to a military court), was based on some 1,200 military regulations strictly regulating the lives of Palestinians. Tight censorship was also imposed (in 1985 alone, 1,600 books were banned), collective punishments were meted out (house destruction, collective curfews, mass arrests), all gatherings of more than ten people for 'political purposes' were prohibited and any displays of Palestinian nationalism were banned.

Palestinians were also denied material resources. Access to water was progressively denied to Palestinians and diverted to local Jewish settlements and Israel proper. Similarly, economic resources were siphoned out of the Territories into Israel. More than 100,000 Palestinians work in Israel, mainly in menial and badly paid jobs. In the first 20 years of occupation, $1 billion dollars were deducted from wages of Palestinians employed in Israel for employment benefits for which they were, in fact, ineligible. Over the same period, residents of the Occupied Territories paid $800 million in taxes, two-and-a-half times the total incoming investment from Israel over that period. As a result of the outflow of resources, the Palestinians' agriculture and industry stagnated. By the early 1990s half of the Palestinians of the Territories were unemployed. The average GNP per capita in the Territories in 1989 was $1,250, one-seventh that of Israel proper (World Bank 1995: 163, table 1).

These factors formed the background to the *intifada*, sparked by the – probably – accidental killing of four young Palestinians by an Israeli-driven truck. The *intifada* was met by a firm Israeli response. In 1988–9, 159 children under 16 years were killed by soldiers. Yet more than half of them were not near a demonstration when killed; fewer than a fifth of them were involved in stone-throwing. In addition, more than 60,000 children were gassed, beaten or wounded. In 1991, Israeli forces deported 8 Palestinians, killed 99, wounded 13,500, while at any one period 11,000 Palestinians were in prison (Bill and Springborg 1994: 331).

It must have seemed to many Arab inhabitants of the Gaza Strip and the West Bank that the main nationalist group, the Palestine Liberation Organization (PLO), was unable to help them. As a result, there was a greater need than ever for local organization. The Palestinian National Front (PNF), an umbrella organization coordinating political activities of various groups, operated from 1973 to 1978 in the West Bank and the Gaza Strip. Following strong Israeli pressure, the PNF was dissolved in late 1978. In the early 1980s a new organization emerged: the National Guidance Committee, which included leaders of trade unions and professional organizations, as well as municipal officials. It too was outlawed, in May 1982. A plethora of community groups survived, coordinated by the secretive Unified Command of the Uprising.

While Palestinian responses to what was widely perceived as oppressive Israeli rule initially centred on a range of secular groups, by the 1980s Islamist groups were enjoying growing popularity. The local Muslim Brotherhood, like its Egyptian counterpart rejecting nationalism as antithetical to Islam, is the oldest Islamist group in the Gaza Strip. It has been a force in Palestinian politics since the 1940s. During the late 1970s and early 1980s, however, it was encouraged by Israeli military commanders, who believed that its stance of non-violence and anti-nationalism made it a useful alternative to the PLO. As a result, Israel gave a partial *carte blanche*, allowing the Brotherhood to build mosques and charitable institutions. By the mid-1980s, however, Israeli officials were taking heed of indications that some of the Muslim Brotherhood supporters were preparing to abandon their principle of non-violence in favour of an anti-Israel *jihad*. As in Egypt, the moderation of the mainstream Brotherhood helped to stimulate militant offshoots, including Hamas.

The Movement for an Islamic Society – Hamas, which is also the Arabic acronym meaning 'zeal' – came into being in 1987, founded by Sheikh Ahmed Yassin, who was later imprisoned by the Israeli government. The Israelis recognized Hamas as a potential threat because unlike the Muslim Brotherhood it advocated violent tactics to achieve its goal of an Islamic state. Hamas refused to cooperate with nationalists on the grounds that it wanted to create an *Islamic* not a *secular* state, and because it refused compromises with Israel. The Hamas Covenant (1988) calls on all Palestinian Muslims to wage holy war against Israel as the only solution to the Palestinian problem. By 1988 it was calling for general strikes on days not designated by the Unified Command. Following the PLO's declaration of the establishment of a Palestinian state in 1988, Hamas distributed leaflets declaring: 'This independence is imaginary. It is a quick move by some of the Palestinian ranks to steal the fruits of the intifadah's victory.' As Morris notes, the political significance of Hamas and other Islamist groups such as Islamic Jihad suggests a 'discernible move among young Muslims of the West Bank and Gaza towards strident forms of Islam' (1989: 136).

Islamic Jihad is the second most prominent Islamist organization in the Territories, perpetrating knife, grenade and shooting attacks on Israeli troops and civilians since the early 1990s. Little is known about its leadership or membership, and it has no known links to other groups of the same name. It seems to be more concerned than Hamas with 'extremist politics' alone (Kershner 1995: 33).

Overall, the influence of the Islamist groups appears to vary over time. One poll in 1995 conducted by a Palestinian research institute put Hamas's support at 14 per cent. Others put support for the movement higher, at about 30 per cent. Mahmud Zahhar, Hamas spokesman for Gaza, dismissed the apparent discrepancy thus: 'It depends who you ask, people at the cinema or people in the refugee camps.' Hamas managed to poll 45–50 per cent in West Bank student and trade union elections in the early 1990s (1995: 34).

Such figures suggest that Hamas support comes primarily from the educated young and the most politically active section of Palestinian society, trade unionists. Hamas is undoubtedly the largest Islamist group, especially in the Gaza Strip, probably in part because of its sponsoring of community projects, including hospitals, clinics, sports clubs, youth centres, schools and kindergartens: two-thirds of West Bank kindergartens are thought to be Hamas 'affiliated' (Ya'ari and Horovitz 1994: 23). Support for Hamas also comes from the unemployed, probably the largest constituency in Gaza and the West Bank. *Jerusalem Report* (1995) detailed a survey conducted by Nablus's an-Najah University in May 1995 reporting that there was 58 per cent unemployment in the Gaza Strip and 50 per cent in the West Bank among Palestinians. These are some of the highest figures in the world.

The division between the largely secular PLO and its affiliates in the

Territories, on the one hand, and Hamas and other Islamist groups, on the other, was further widened by the decision reached in Autumn 1991 to participate in American-sponsored peace talks with the Israelis. As the PLO was preparing to declare its willingness to take part in the Madrid peace conference in 1991, Hamas was condemning the gathering as a 'conference for selling land'. It issued death threats to would-be participants, calling for the liberation of Palestine by force. As peace negotiations continued over the next few years, tensions between Islamists and secular nationalists boiled over in Gaza, where pitched battles were regularly fought. In one round of fighting between Hamas and PLO supporters in July 1992, about 150 people were injured and one killed (Bill and Springborg 1994: 353).

Hamas came very close to derailing the peace process. In late 1994 a bombing in Tel Aviv killed 22 people. In February and March 1996 further bombs killed another 63 Israelis. The leadership of the PLO-dominated Palestinian Authority arrested most of the Hamas leadership in June 1994; since then there has been an undeclared war between the Palestinian Authority and Hamas. The victory of the Likud leader, Binyamin Netanyahu – a sceptic of the peace process – in Israel's May 1996 elections is thought to have been assured by the Hamas bombs a few months before.

Conclusion

In this chapter, we have seen how Islamist groups in Nigeria, Egypt, Algeria and Israel's Occupied Territories have grown over the last two decades in conditions of economic hardship, unemployment, a lack of democracy, fears of both secularization and Westernization, and diminishing state legitimacy and authority. These factors underpin the rise of groups like the FIS or Hamas who have benefited in such a situation. Yet the Islamist groups mostly attract the young and alienated; they are much less attractive to the middle classes. It has to be borne in mind that there is a large number of people in the Muslim countries of the Middle East and Africa committed to secularism and modernity. Among the middle classes particularly, there is a strong desire to 'scramble for their market shares, learn how to compete in a merciless world economy, provide jobs, move out of poverty' (Ajami 1993: 5). For such people, the appeal for an Islamist state generally falls on deaf ears.

Ajami's words quoted here may well highlight the principal impediment to the long-term success of the Islamists. In advocating rejection of modernity and the secular, individualistic values which have underlain the modernization process in the West, Islamists provide an important focus for marginalized, excluded and alienated social groups. While appealing directly to the masses, however, Islamist leaders have excoriated the degeneracy of the group most closely associated with modernity, that is the urban middle class. As a result, it is unlikely that Islamist movements will succeed in uniting communities across the social division of class. In other words, their mass appeal is stymied by their targeting of one particular social group as the 'anti-Islamic' enemy.

On the other hand, the appeal, and potential, of Islamism cannot be dismissed. It provides a focus for popular identification and a highly developed moral and social code, legitimated by divine authority, which explicitly rejects Western cultural and ideological domination. However, while Islamism provides a substantial and immediate threat to governments in nearly all Muslim countries, its potential to develop into an ideology of government is much more doubtful.

Like other oppositional action groups we have examined in the chapters of this book, Islamists thrive when ordinary people who happen in this example to be Muslims – feel abandoned by the state, helpless in the face of conditions which they see as undermining already insecure lifestyles. Unpalatable though they may be to many in the West, Islamic groups offer a precious commodity to the dispossessed: the hope of a new order when things will improve for the ordinary man. Whether many ordinary female Muslims share the same optimism is debatable: where Islamic states have been instituted in recent times – Afghanistan, Iran and Sudan – there seems little evidence that the lot of women improves; unfortunately, most evidence points to a different interpretation. None the less, it is possible to see the Islamist groups as products of the same sets of circumstances as those which stimulated the rise of the other categories of action groups examined in this book.

8
Conclusion

In the book's conclusion I discuss the general arguments and comparative implications of the material presented in earlier chapters, consider the implications for our wider understanding of political change, outline a few suggested areas for further research and make some predictions as to the future for Third World action groups.

Generally, the book has been concerned with an examination of what happens when ordinary people in the Third World band together to attempt to deal with a range of material problems. Are their vehicles – action groups – unique, that is *sui generis*? Or are there any parallels in the political history of social and economic change in the West, or earlier in the Third World? Are there fundamental deeper principles that we can recognize from comparable times elsewhere? Or are such groups simply defensive reactions to rapid change, where the subordinate are especially damaged? What particular variations and features do the action groups demonstrate? Might this be how vigorous, dynamic civil societies get to be born? Are the action groups discussed in this book contributing to the slow emergence of the democratic process? These hypotheses provided an introduction to the chapters and cases I discussed; now, what has emerged?

The case studies presented aimed to offer a representative range of examples showing that there are many common threads and themes involved, even when they seem to be addressing quite different problems in different fields. A broad analytical framework seemed to me necessary given the pervasiveness and interdependence of the issues. I sought to show that a range of action group concerns are connected in a variety of ways and that successful approaches in one area are often of great relevance to another.

The main linking theme is that the emergence of tens of thousands of action groups over the last 20 years or so reflects growing dissatisfaction with the way that the vast majority of Third World states are run. The action groups I described generally aspire to act as the vehicles of the disempowered and subordinate; if they have anything else in common it is that they organize people around the issue of – broadly defined – *democratization*. This is the issue with the most symbolic effectiveness and mobilizing potential.

General Arguments and Comparative Implications

At the root of politics in whatever national context is the interactive relationship between the state and its people. After three decades or more of independence many Third World governments are not regarded by analysts as successes. Many have been unable to deliver security or sustained opportunities to the majority of their citizens to increase their well-being; in short, they are often not very good at providing what people want – development and democracy (Clapham 1985; Manor 1991; Cammack et al. 1993).

If measured by the stridently expressed demands for greater democracy so common in the 1990s across the Third World, it seems likely that the legitimacy and authority of many of those states have declined over time. While many states in Asia and Africa have at least one great success to their credit – the achievement of national independence from colonial rule – as an enduring vehicle for delivering all their people's aspirations they have been, in many cases, failures.

At independence, most Third World citizens believed that freedom from colonial rule would lead to greater political, economic and social justice than hitherto – for the simple reason that henceforward they would no longer be ruled by an alien government. Instead, leaders and bureaucratic personnel would be drawn from the indigenous people. However, popular aspirations, fanned by nationalist politicians anxious to be elected, were very often much greater than the ability of states to meet these ambitions. Incipient democracies were for the most part quickly replaced by one-party states and military dictatorships – that were very hard to dislodge. Very few – less than a dozen – Third World countries managed to maintain competitive electoral and party systems where the accountability of the government to its people was consistently a live issue (Pinkney 1993).

Power monopolies not only made it difficult for broad-based national political parties to develop but also for a species of democracy to evolve which would empower the poor and marginalized. Instead, postcolonial political systems by and large managed to develop a range of political capacities to enhance their longevity. According to Almond and Powell (1966), they included the ability to discourage or repress peasant discontent, a distributive capacity to improve the welfare of favoured groups of urban workers, an extractive capacity to obtain resources from rural areas through patron–client networks, and an ability to distract attention by massive public works or military adventurism. These policies often enabled non-democratic governments in the Third World to survive, sometimes for decades.

Another of the results of the entrenchment in power of unelected elites was that, for many people, the optimism of independence waned. The state was increasingly regarded, not as a champion of popular interests, but as a group of people driven by a primary desire to enrich themselves – often illegally – from national resources. This might not have been so bad, perhaps, if governments had been able to protect citizens from crime, terrorism, job losses, inflation and natural disasters, yet, few could consistently accomplish many of these things. Why, then, should citizens respect and support those in power? As conditions worsened during the 1970s and 1980s as a result of economic downturns, the widespread loss of respect for governments developed into strongly expressed demands – encouraged by international developments, particularly the end of the Cold War and the astonishingly rapid demise of the East European communist systems – for fundamental changes: for democracy, economic reforms and enhanced human rights.

The 'third wave' of democracy began in the mid-1970s in southern Europe, spreading first to Latin America and then to Asia and Africa, but failing to make much impact in the Middle East. While the numbers of democratically elected governments increased greatly, significant numbers of personalist dictatorships, one-party states and military regimes still remained. Non-democratic regimes almost invariably deny a range of rights and benefits to many of their citizens: human rights are widely ignored, women's demands are belittled and environmental safeguards – if they exist – are bypassed, while ethnic and religious minorities are routinely denied freedom of expression. When, on the other hand, a state's government is democratically accountable such issues are at least contested ground: that is, they appear on the political agenda; differing viewpoints are expressed, debated and contested. The emergence of a democratic system, then, is a key to putative improvements in relation to a range of issues; an essential step to wider social, political and economic reforms.

The literature on recent Third World democratization often gives the impression that regime change is more or less imposed by competing elites on a predominantly docile population inarticulate in political matters (for a survey see Hagopian 1993). I believe – and I see the case studies in this book as supporting this contention – that such a picture is often a caricature of reality. Even when elites do dominate the process of democratic transition, there is nearly always a large measure of popular activity underpinning the processes of change. 'Ordinary' men and women – workers, students, small-scale farmers and landless labourers – organize themselves into a variety of groups, sometimes illicit, even illegal, which collectively have the effect of directly or indirectly aiding the 'assaults on the seats of power', to use Linz's expression (1990: 152).

Sometimes such groups become part of a wider self-identified pro-democracy movement, where diverse groups from all parts of society consolidate into a greater whole – 'the people' – demanding democracy and the removal of their rulers. Yet, as the recent experiences of democratic transition in Eastern Europe, Latin America and Africa make clear, such expressions of popular unity frequently amount to a brief, intense outburst that quickly dies away (Bratton and van de Walle 1994; Hagopian 1993; Held 1993). In sum, popular mobilization behind transitions to democracy includes two elements: first, opposition groups emerging during authoritarian rule, and second, the overall flowering of civil society surfacing during the democratic transition.

All the action groups described in this book have appeared because of the circumstances created by authoritarian, economically unsuccessful rule. They are strategies of survival and the defence of group or community interests, encompassing a wide range of rural and urban associations. Some of them – particularly in Africa – are working outside the formal economy in an attempt to cater for basic needs locally, sometimes in cooperation with foreign agencies; others undertake a wide array of projects located in self-help initiatives and the defence of rural land rights; in short, they involve activities of protest and conflict, lobbying and pressurising government agencies and politicians. Some have provided settings for political learning, such as Latin America's Basic Christian Communities (discussed in chapter 2), serving as 'schools for educating the exploited in their inalienable rights' –

that is, a key conduit for the diffusion of democratic ideas (Bermeo 1992: 285–6), 'seedbeds of democracy' (Sandbrook 1988: 262). In Africa and Asia, a similar – although often less extensive and politically salient – array of groups, together with ethnic and religious associations, has also surfaced.

In the Middle East, Islamist groups – some of which, but not all, are contemptuous, even hostile to democracy – represent a region-wide phenomenon. Yet local modernizing middle classes and Western observers alike fear that the Islamic solution will turn out to be a variant of totalitarianism. While it is surely appropriate to emphasize Islamic concepts like *shura* (consultation), *ijma* (consensus) and *bay'a* (affirmations of communal loyalty), they do not collectively amount to a compelling theory of government. Unfortunately, others – like *hurriyya* (freedom) and *huquq insaniyya* (human rights) – rarely receive equal attention in the discourse of the Islamists (Esposito and Piscatori 1991). Certainly Islamist groups offer a substantive – and in many cases objectively necessary – critique of the authoritarian state in the Middle East. Yet there is no guarantee that a range of rights would be protected under Islamist rule. Recent and existing Islamic states – post-revolutionary Iran, Pakistan under Zia al-Haq, Sudan under National Islamic Front rule – have failed, according to Mayer (1991), to codify and implement an Islamic set of human rights principles. The result, she concludes, has been a systematic limitation rather than expansion of the civil and political rights found, for example, in the Universal Declaration of Human Rights and related international law. However, Mayer argues that the main explanation for this authoritarianism lies less in Islamic teachings – rather flexible on the issue of rights generally, although not, it seems, when it comes to those of women and non-Muslim minorities – than in the rulers' cynical manipulation of Islam.

Taken collectively, however, do the action groups examined in this book add to the vigour and dynamism of local civil societies? The answer, simply put, is 'yes'. The more societally representative groups there are, the better it is when it comes to democracy. When I refer to civil society I mean a set of organizations and associations in at least partial independence from the state, including those dimensions of social life which cannot be regarded as part of the state or swallowed up by it. Civil society comprises an array of entities in the Third World. What they have in common, however, is that they are demanding – in one form or another – a voice in politics. Often women's movements are at the cutting edge of democratization; they are especially noteworthy in Latin America and India, and of growing – although still embryonic – importance in Africa and perhaps in the Middle East

(Norton 1993: 209). During the transition-to-democracy phase, these and other groups in civil society play a crucially important role. Their collective critiques of the policies of authoritarian .regimes combine with demands for democracy and basic political, legal and social rights. Thus the transition-to-democracy phase is marked by a coalition between often ad hoc popular groups and the institutionalized bodies in civil society, often suppressed during authoritarian rule. These include trade unions, professional groups – lawyers, journalists, doctors and so on – and student associations. The collective goal of both sets of groups – in the short term – is simply democratic change. In short, transitions to democracy are accompanied by decisive upsurges in popular mobilization and organization. A strengthening of civil society takes place which 'improves the conditions for democracy and simultaneously makes the reversal to authoritarian rule more difficult' (Sørensen 1993: 60).

Studies of democratic transition have successfully identified the factors that prompted the various transitions from authoritarian rule, in particular explaining (1) how those transitions were sustained against resistance from, *inter alia*, hardliners in security services; and (2) how the opposition movements of civil society contributed to democratization. Such studies, especially that of O'Donnell, Schmitter and Whitehead (1986), provide a model of regime change that can be applied around the globe.

For the most part, civil society does not topple healthy regimes; usually, regimes crumble from within, victims of corruption, increasingly hollow claims to legitimacy and deepening economic failure. As Norton puts it, 'civil society [is] more the beneficiary than the wrecking ball' (1993: 211). Civil society is nearly always idealized as an uncomplicatedly beneficial entity. Yet it would be a mistake to see it as an always united, consensual thing, a focal point of interest groups and associations necessarily pursuing the same objectives. Like any social phenomenon, civil society may well have a negative side: self-interest, chauvinism and animosity dwell side by side with humanity, justice and affinity. None the less, as already stated, the development of civil society *is* a crucial step towards realizing a politically freer and more just Third World. It is very hard to imagine a participant political system that is capable of surviving for long without a vibrant civil society. But while the emergence of a dynamic and vigorous civil society is a necessary development, it is not on its own sufficient for the emergence and growth of substantive democracy – that is, where marginal groups have a full say in politics.

When the battle is won and the authoritarian ancien régime is gone, the struggle for the next phase – democratic consolidation – creates a new kind of political environment with novel challenges to civil society. The rallying point of the common enemy is no longer there. Instead, the challenge has shifted from cooperating in the common goal of removing unwelcome rulers to institutionalizing democratic competition between the interests and aspirations of various groups in the society. The demands put on the skills and commitments of leading actors to meet this challenge are different from those required during the transition phase itself. According to Karl the actors must henceforward show the 'ability to differentiate political forces rather than draw them into a grand coalition, the capacity to define and channel competing political projects rather than seek to keep potentially divisive reforms off the agenda, and the willingness to tackle incremental reforms . . . rather than defer them to some later date' (1990: 17). Thus, while popular mobilization and organization undoubtedly improve the prospects of democracy, it is how popular power is used *after* the transition that is the decisive element in the difficult – but wholly necessary – process to consolidate and extend democracy to previously excluded groups.

Between 1972 and 1994 – broadly the era of the third wave of democracy – the number of countries with 'democratic political systems' increased from 44 to 107. Put another way, the proportion of democracies grew from less than a quarter to nearly 60 per cent of the world's nearly 190 countries in just two decades (Shin 1994: 136). Many of the new democracies are in the Third World; yet nearly all of them have so far failed to extend democracy to include the previously marginalized. I do not believe that, for the most part, their emancipation and inclusion is simply a matter of time; rather, it is more a question involving regimes' willingness to allow subordinate groups to express – and pursue – their aspirations in the political arena.

While the transition-to-democracy phase has – rightly – attracted a great deal of attention, no Third World regions have been extensively focused on in terms of studying politics *after* regime change. In short, there has so far been relatively little discussion on why, after the institution of democratic regimes and at least partial macroeconomic recovery under structural adjustment, many of the new Third World democracies have 'barely managed to limp along in an unconsolidated state' (Hagopian 1993: 465), much less to deepen democratic consolidation.

One reason for this deficiency is that the literature on both democratic transition and consolidation has attempted to assess the present (and prospects for the future) without paying sufficient attention to the influence of the Third World's recent past on the present day organization of political interests and power. As Remmer notes in the case of Latin America, 'scholars moved from the study of democratic breakdown to the study of democratic transitions without pausing to analyze the authoritarian phase that came in between' (1989: 24). Without such analyses it has been necessary to assume that changes in political culture conducive to democratic consolidation have occurred. It is rarely discussed how the programmes and policies of authoritarian regimes worked to dismantle or restructure both the formal and informal institutions of representation that had supported democratic predecessors. I suggest that the design and strength of representative institutions and networks that emerged from the periods of authoritarian rule were moulded by policies then prevailing.

Nearly always in the Third World, 'politics' reflects competition or collaboration between politically and economically powerful elites. It matters little whether regimes are characterized as leftist or rightist authoritarian or as oligarchic democracies; the point is that power monopolies at the apex very often form the political superstructure in Third World countries. Thirty years ago, Organski (1965) identified such a power monopoly as comprising a 'syncratic alliance', that is, a concord uniting traditional agrarian interests, too strong to be destroyed, with a modernizing industrial elite. A bargain is struck: in exchange for obtaining the political support of agrarian interests, powerful urban sectors agree not to disturb the often semifeudal conditions of the countryside. Thus, even when a formal democracy operates, class structures remain more or less unchanged – that is, they remain largely traditional, with the impact of industrialization being in the main accommodated to traditional patterns of dominance and subordination.

In Latin America and parts of Asia, large landowners represent the rural side of the coalition. For example, successive postcolonial Indian governments, despite nearly always being legitimated through the ballot box, have failed to break with powerful allies, the rural elites. Although such ruling families were formally shorn of traditional powers after independence, they very often managed to maintain their position by a very successful alternative: the democratic route to power. Although Organski's description may be less relevant to Africa, support from those with wealth and power is more crucial to political decision-makers than support from other classes. There, Clapham argues, neopatrimonialism – that is, personal dictatorship – 'is the most salient type [of authority]' because it 'corresponds to the normal forms of social organization in precolonial societies' (1985: 49). In short, while the exact bases of power may differ, Third World elites control both the basis of economic wealth and the direction of political development.

Elitist coalitions are not restricted to non-democratic regimes. They may also define a pattern of political power in countries that regularly alternate between military and elected civilian rule. Or they may be a means of maintaining upper class power, as in Colombia, Argentina or the Philippines, even when formally democratic systems exist (Rueschemeyer et al. 1992: 174–5; Gills and Rocamara 1993). The crucial point is that dictatorial regimes may be overthrown – and replaced by nominally or partially substantively democratic alternatives – without defeating narrowly based monopolies. Thus oligarchical or syncratic democracies may have the outward characteristics of competitive constitutional regimes – that is, opposition groups are free to organize – yet monopolies of political power persist.

The literature on transitions in particular holds that civil societies that struggled against one-party and military dictatorships have the potential to weaken the cultural foundations of authoritarianism, and so to serve as a genuine base for democracy. What is needed, it is believed, is that the new democratic consensus must be strengthened and political instability reduced by electoral and institutional forms that make democratic government workable – that is, less at the mercy of the self-interested squabbles of politicians and incumbent elites. For this to come to pass, there must be a learning process: the destructive confrontations of the past must not be repeated by the new generation of politicians coming to power. They must seek to deepen democracy and extend it to previously excluded classes and groups.

A civil society implies a shared sense of identity through agreement over the rough boundaries of the shared political unit. Therefore a sense of citizenship, with associated rights and responsibilities, is central to the concept. Historically, citizens demonstrate their 'good citizenship' by exhibiting loyalty to both their local communities and to the state; in other words, the role of citizen is traditionally characterized by certain attitudes towards authority and legitimacy that are generally supportive both of the state and more generally of the status quo. The concept of 'citizen' implies the full participation of individuals in their local community life (Held 1989). Zolo explains, however, that full participation for some individuals in community life has historically been faced with obstacles of various kinds, related to gender, race, age or economic position (1993: 257). Such characteristics are those of contemporary subordinate groups in the Third World.

Subordinate groups in the Third World, concerned with, *inter alia*, the rights of women or of minority groups, are nearly always faced with apparently insuperable barriers when it comes to full participation in civil society. Moreover, the particular concerns such action groups represent are almost never reflected in the concerns of the mainstream political parties, other than rhetorically. What exists then is a kind of two-tier civil society, with the representative groups of existing or prospective elites inhabiting the top tier and the organizations of the subordinate and the marginalized located in the second, lower tier.

Subordinate people's action groups find it very difficult to place their concerns on the formal agendas of the institutionalized groups of either civil or political society. Yet they are asserting fundamental moral claims for the dignity of the person and the equality of the individual. It may be that action groups are indicators of a blossoming of civil society, demonstrations of vitality and assertiveness, a determined attempt to extend the range of its concerns. Since the claims of such groups are basic ones, they are not easily assailed, at least explicitly, by the authorities of the state or of the institutionalized groups in civil society. Thus they may enjoy more freedom of action than overtly political opponents or those wishing to affect the overall allocation of economic resources; they may also be less susceptible to cooptation, since their demands may not be so easily quenched by cash or privilege.

Implications for our Wider Understanding of Political Change

I have argued that action groups emerge in the Third World as a result, *inter alia*, of attempts by the state to impose its rule on increasingly unwilling citizens. Yet this does not explain the *timing* of their growth, particularly swift over the last two decades or so (Ergas 1986; Durning 1989: 55; Fisher 1993: 23; Omvedt 1994: 35). I am not suggesting that there were no action groups before the 1970s. For example, dozens of African independent churches, manifestations of anti-colonial feeling, appeared around the time of World War I, a response to the social destabilization and disruption caused by European colonization and exacerbated by the effects of the war (Haynes 1996a: ch. 1). In Brazil, 30 years later, hundreds of urban community associations emerged as a result of social stresses, urbanization and the failure of the state to provide a sufficiency of services during a period of intense modernization (Mainwaring and Viola 1984: 27). In short, groups synonymous with contemporary action groups have emerged in a variety of places, probably whenever there are massive political, social and economic disruptions to ordinary people's lives. Thus, in this sense, contemporary action groups are not unique. Yet what *is* novel about them is that societal destabilization, connected with the processes of modernization, has dovetailed with demands for democracy to produce something qualitatively different.

Societal destabilization has been caused by what might be called incomplete or truncated modernization. Politically, modernization is regarded as synonymous with the involvement of an ever larger number of people in the political process. Socially, it refers to the 'realignment and the restructuring of the social position of individuals and groups' in swiftly urbanizing environments (Gutkind 1970: 356). The end result of the process of modernization – modernity – is widely believed to be a consensual framework of values and a comprehension about the nature of order as exemplified by Western political systems. As Norgaard explains, what Western-style modernity promised Third World peoples was 'control over nature through science, material abundance through superior technology, effective government through rational social organization'; in other words, a transformation of the hitherto 'slow and precarious course of human progress onto the fast track' (1994: 1). In sum, modernity is associated with a particular way of 'organizing society, a distinct structure of accumulation, and a set of values and beliefs for regulating social behaviour and state systems' (Bangura 1994: 20).

Throughout the Third World, with the important exception of post-revolutionary states such as Iran and China, modernization is usually regarded as synonymous with Westernization. The advent of significant social change would result in a jettisoning of older, traditional values and the adoption of more 'rational', more 'realistic' social and political practices. The sociopolitical effects of modernization have not, however, been uniform throughout the Third World: generational, gender-related and state-minority conflicts are common due to the patchy, partial adoption of modern practices alongside the continuity of 'traditional' (that is, premodern) ways of doing things. In short, swift social change has radically destabilized many societies, creating a dichotomy between those who benefit – many of whom are connected to the state in some way – and those who do not. New social strata have arisen whose position in the new order is decidedly ambiguous, such as the rural–urban migrants throughout the Third World who find themselves, in effect, between two worlds, often without an effective or appropriate set of anchoring values. Truncated modernization is partly the consequence of mass population movements from the countryside to urban centres: the new environment is unfamilar and alien, simultaneously remote and impersonal, yet apparently full of opportunity. The search for an 'anchor', for 'rootedness' often manifests itself in the formation of self-help action groups devoted to a variety of objectives located in a nexus of developmental and democratic concerns. More and more rural dwellers migrate to the Third World's urban centres in search of paid employment, a consequence of deteriorating conditions in their home areas. The most urbanized Third World region is Latin America and the Caribbean, where 70 per cent of people live in towns and cities. Asia and Africa are expected to have at least 50 per cent of their people living in urban areas by the year 2025 (UNRISD 1995). The result is that there are tens of millions of people in transition between rural and urban self-identification; many are established, often precariously, in various 'informal' ways, gaining an income through various survival strategies. They cope – because they have to – in different ways, including community mobilization in action groups; they participate in social life through religious, occupational or neighbourhood mutual aid associations.

Action groups epitomize the core of what Beck (1994) calls 'subpolitics'. The core of the notion of subpolitics is that the personal is political. Whether opposing despoilation of the natural environment or fighting for greater women's rights or some other cause, Third World action groups both symbolize and signify the beginnings of a new form of association between the state and society which serves to synthesize the public and private spheres. When the personal becomes political the implication is that *social* power, by encountering, engaging and jousting with the state, is demanding a reformulation of *political* power.

'Subpolitics' is characterized by the emergence of various agents outside the political system appearing 'on the stage of social design compet[ing] . . . for the emerging shape of the political' (1994: 22). The association of what C. Wright Mills (1970) referred to as 'personal troubles' and 'public issues' is a consistent theme in subpolitics. That is, 'the personal is linked to the political both empirically – oppression shapes interpersonal relations – and morally – political commitment ought to be translated into behavioural changes' (J. Scott 1990: 21).

Discontent with the state's democratic and developmental abilities is not restricted to the Third World. During the 1980s and 1990s, it has been suggested, there have been historically high levels of societal discontent in the West (Gurr 1993; Beck 1994; Galbraith 1995). Why should this be the case? High levels of societal discontent are unexpected, Galbraith (1995) feels, because:

With the exception of the Balkans and the deeper depths of Africa, the world is at peace and the general economic situation is reasonably good. [As a result] the present state of social and political discontent calls for an explanation. Why in the United States, in Britain and Europe, even in Japan, is there such strongly expressed disaffection? Why are so many people so eloquently unhappy, and especially with the way they are governed?

Galbraith argues that widespread societal discontent in the West is the result of two developments. First, the absence of the tensions of the Cold War gives 'time and space for the routine distempers of everyday life' to manifest themselves. Second, there is 'an electorate dominated by relatively fortunate people' who no longer need the state 'as the buttress of their power and well-being as did the old-fashioned capitalists'. This is because many can personally provide many of the services which the state formerly almost exclusively delivered, such as housing, education, recreation, libraries and guards for personal security. As a result, he argues, many relatively wealthy people both dislike and distrust the state, deeply resenting the taxes they must pay for the upkeep of their less fortunate fellow citizens. The latter, lacking money and 'voice', are, politically speaking, out of sight.

While identifying an important phenomenon, Galbraith is wrong to assume that societal discontent in the West is exclusively expressed by middle-class individuals. Societal discontent is much wider than this – a characteristic of subordinate groups' grievances in relation to an array of concerns including women's rights, environmental protection and the socioeconomic position of minority groups. An example of the latter is Louis Farrakhan's Nation of Islam, an important vehicle of alienated African-Americans. The Nation of Islam's objective is nothing less than fundamental reform of the social and political arrangements of society. Its growing influence was demonstrated in October 1995 when it managed to mobilize around 1 million African-American men for the 'Million Man March' through the city of Washington to protest at the lowly socioeconomic position of most African-Americans. Preaching a volatile mixture of black separatism, anti-semitism, anti-corruption and self-help, the Nation of Islam sought to focus African-American males' existential frustrations (Fletcher 1994). Farrakhan's concern is for African-American men to work together in pursuit of their collective self-interest. To this end, the Nation of Islam runs both welfare agencies and businesses with the aim of empowering poor African-Americans; in short, the goal is self-emancipation (Haynes 1995a).

Farrakhan is not satisfied with making the Nation of Islam a formidable sociopolitical force only in the USA; he also aims to build links with alienated black men elsewhere. A January 1996 visit to South Africa by Farrakhan sought to present the Nation of Islam's message of black liberation from white domination to the volatile young men of the townships, where unemployment is at crisis levels and Islam an increasingly popular religion. Farrakhan's visit alarmed many South African whites, not least because his deputy made a speech in early 1994 – which Farrakhan endorsed – calling for the slaughter of white people by blacks (McGreal 1996). The significance of the Nation of Islam is that it does not wish to achieve political power through the ballot box; rather, it exists to focus the discontent of hundreds of thousands of ordinary people living under a political system which they believe does not benefit them significantly.

Beck argues that whereas the 1960s and 1970s in the West were about trying to change the world via revolution, politics in the 1980s and 1990s, especially for the poor and their idealist allies, is about trying to retrieve something tolerable from a postmodern chaos. In post-unification Germany, for example, 'the socially most astonishing and surprising – and perhaps the least understood – phenomenon of the 1980s was the unexpected renaissance of a political subjectivity, outside and inside the institutions. . . . it is no exaggeration to say that citizen-initiative groups have taken power politically' (1994: 18). Beck believes that the traditional actors of politics – the state, parliament, political parties and trade unions – are no longer of much *political* relevance to large numbers of people. Political parties have fallen victim to self-deception; the new themes of societal concern, such as protection of the natural environment, societal empowerment, feminism and human rights, 'have not originated from the farsightedness of the rulers or from the struggle in parliament or from business, science or the state' (1994: 19). Instead, 'the core of today's [sub]politics is the ability of self-organization . . . the state is confronted by all sorts of groups and minorities . . . constitut[ing] ten thousand different power agencies in . . . society' (Enzenberger, quoted in Beck 1994: 39).

The sociopolitical significance of the West's 'citizen-initiative' groups, like their action group counterparts in the Third World, is that they comprise new areas of societal concerns in which the established parties appear to show little real interest. A good example is that of environmental concerns, including the building of new motorways, the construction of nuclear power stations, the apparent inability to dispose of toxic waste acceptably, and so on. Because the established political parties have been very slow to accept that such issues are of widespread *political* concern, many people seem to believe that the only way to change things is to embark on lobbying and direct action campaigns. It is the apparent indifference with which the state and the established political parties seem to regard such concerns – the main raisons d'être of action groups in both the Third World and the West – that is their main stimulus to action.

Suggested Areas for Further Research

I hypothesize that the right not to be hungry or lacking in power is inextricably linked to the rise of civil societies and action groups in the Third World; the latter concern is important to the emergence of the citizen-initiative groups in the West. Yet at the moment these remain hypotheses. What is needed is not only more and better information about Third World action groups over time so as to perceive whether they are just a flash in the pan or whether they amount to something substantive; we also need more information for use in comparative assessment of the groups. Second, we need to know much more about their counterparts in the West: how, if at all, are they related? To what extent are their agendas comparable? Are links developing between them which might allow us to analyse them as global phenomena sharing ideas, ideologies, funds and personnel?

At the moment, such comparative issues are little more than a mass of contested concepts and competing approaches. Perhaps, once we have increased data, it will be timely to focus on salient models and to structure the emerging field of knowledge in terms of the formulation and testing of a number of them. Results might not only be of academic importance. Policy implications might also be drawn leading to better policies to include the concerns of the mass of the marginalized in government's agendas for development.

Action Groups and the Future

From the accounts of action groups' successes and failures presented in this book, it would not be appropriate to conclude that they are at this stage in their development the progenitors, foundations and manifestations of a new age, the impending advent of true participatory democracy in the Third World. Reality is more complex and, for the subordinate, often much grimmer. While it is true that in a large number of Third World countries new and unexpected spaces have opened for the kind of organized efforts that I discuss in this book, it is also the case that many relatively powerless people find it increasingly difficult to defend their livelihood and well-being, even through participatory initiatives.

Yet, in some respects, the collection of action groups that I described *does* amount to a 'quiet' revolution. Relative to what was there before, an organizational explosion *is* occurring in the Third World; very often, however, it is *defensive* in orientation. As Fisher puts it, 'relative to the magnitude of the . . . task [of empowerment and development], this is a revolution stumbling through its early stages. [Action groups] are making inroads but are still far from overthrowing the old order of poverty and inequality' (1993: 8).

I explored the impact of two of the most significant developments stimulating some kinds of action groups: macroeconomic decline and the spread of demands for democracy. The environmental protection groups I examined have as their main imperative the desire to hold back or at least slow down the pace of environmental damage to the places where they live. Yet very often the destruction of the natural environment is a direct consequence of industrialization. It is no coincidence that people most affected by damage to the natural environment are living in countries with very fast industrial growth rates, such as South-East Asia and Latin America. What is needed is a compromise between the needs of forest dwellers and others and the imperatives of industrial growth. This is a highly political question; there are entrenched interests on both sides. It seems unlikely, however, that the power of environmental protection groups is normally sufficient to cope with that of state and business interests. Only in India, of the countries examined, is there a record of recent successes for environmental action groups. Elsewhere the position looks quite bleak.

Turning to the position of women, the situation is complex; no clear conclusions can easily be drawn. In some places – Brazil and India are probably the best examples – there are quite a few examples of women empowering themselves, of increasing their socioeconomic position through their own efforts. In other places, especially Africa and the Middle East, there are no clear grounds for optimism in this regard at this stage. Part of the discrepancy between regions and countries is to do with the nearly ubiquitous cultural realities that Third World women must encounter and deal with. There is more social willingness in some places to allow women a greater social role than hitherto, yet for every Kerala there are hundreds of places where the prospects for women's liberation and emancipation look decidedly bleak at the current time. Thus, while women *must* do their own empowering, it helps if they are pushing at a relatively open door. What is clear, and what has generally been reckoned for decades, is that urbanization, education and industrialization are the keys to an amelioration of women's position. Yet, as we saw in the case of Kerala, perhaps of just as much importance is the willingness of governments to preside over policies which make women's empowerment plausible and achievable. In other words, women's action groups will only make progress where the governing authorities and the organizations of civil society do not unequivocally prevent it happening. Unfortunately, such supportive environments are uncommon in the great majority of the Third World countries, especially in most Middle Eastern and African states.

The general picture is that action groups are flourishing, multiplying and claiming new responsibilities in a wide variety of countries. It would be premature, however, to claim unreservedly that they represent the way of the future in the Third World. This conclusion represents, on the one hand, an unresolved tension between the possibility that something new and important is happening, that the participation of the subordinate is becoming more practicable as well as more self-evidently necessary for their well-being, and, on the other, the chances that, ultimately, such initiatives are destined to fail.

There are hundreds of millions of people in the Third World trying to follow risk-minimizing tactics of relations with local 'big men', landlords, money-lenders, commercial intermediaries and the state's functionaries. Increasingly large numbers of people are in contact with potential allies from national and international organizations introducing them to participatory ideals and techniques; sometimes, successfully. On the other hand, action groups with a variety of goals also continue to emerge as a result of entirely indigenous organizational imperatives; some of them also achieve palpable gains for their members. Yet, whatever their foundations, whether new or older, most action groups confront frequent threats to their viability.

In this book I have explored many kinds of participation. The precariousness of successful organized efforts, the needs of groups and movements for continual innovative coping with new challenges, and the capacity of economic and political changes to abrogate even what appear to be the most firmly established gains, are clear. It used to be thought that development would eventually incorporate most of the subordinate: the issue was, what were the terms of incorporation to be? Now, in many of the wealthier Third World countries as well as the more impoverished, exclusion of those lacking in power seems to be increasing rather than diminishing.

Previous sources of collective identity that formerly served as frames of reference for organized struggles – especially institutional politics and nation-state building – are mostly disintegrating; a groping towards new collective identities is apparent. It is also clear that if the subordinate cannot see their way to participate in development as an accessible and intelligible process, a proportion is prepared to pursue their goals through religious or ethnic means. Whether the totality of ordinary people's efforts will end in an adjustment of the broad economic and political picture in the Third World is not at all clear. The last two decades have seen huge changes in many Third World countries; perhaps the only certainty in this regard is that the next 20 years will bring even more surprises.

No doubt, political change will follow a variety of paths in the Third World. In some cases, people will be led in circles, only to find themselves where they began. In others, the rulers will adopt, or continue to utilize, what I have called facade democracy – that is, a system where only the vocabulary of democracy is employed. The pressures to open up political systems in the Third World will almost certainly not abate, and if civil society continues to develop – albeit in patchy, one step forward, two steps backward fashion – issues of accountability and performance will grow in importance in many countries. While many Third World countries continue to be characterized by regular encroachments on the dignity of individuals, it is to be hoped that the trajectory of politics in the Third World is towards a clear emphasis on the right of the individual to be free of arbitrary abuse at the hands of the state. The evidence is still mixed, but an optimist might conclude that there is enough in the pages of this book to suggest that the time has come when Third World governments – of whatever political and democratic stripe – must begin to take seriously demands for the dignity and the equality of the individual expressed collectively by the tens of thousands of action groups.

Notes

Chapter 1 Introduction

1 The term 'Third World' was invented in the 1950s to refer, on the one hand, to the large group of economically underdeveloped, then decolonizing, countries in Africa, Asia and the Middle East and, on the other, to Latin American states, mostly granted their freedom in the early nineteenth century, but still economically weak. Despite a shared history of colonization there are important differences between Third World states. For example, such economically diverse countries as the United Arab Emirates (1993 GNP per capita, $21,430), South Korea ($7,660) and Mozambique ($90), or politically singular polities such as Cuba (one-party communist state), Nigeria (military dictatorship) and India (multiparty democracy), are all members of the Third World. To many, the economic and political – not to mention cultural – differences between Third World countries outweigh their supposed similarities.

  While the blanket term 'Third World' obscures cultural, economic, social and political differences between states, it has advantages over alternatives like 'the South' or 'developing countries'. The expression 'the South' is essentially a geographic expression which ignores the fact that some 'Western' countries – Japan, Australia, New Zealand – are in the geographical south. The idea of the 'South' does, however, have the advantage of getting away from the connotation of developing towards some preordained end-state or goal which is explicit in the idea of *'developing* countries'. It is by no means clear, however, what the idea of a 'developed' state conveys: does it connote only a certain (high) degree of economic growth or is there an element of redistribution of the fruits of growth involved? What of widely divergent social conditions in a 'developed' country? In this book I will use the term 'Third World', still the standard terminology in the absence of a better alternative. (GNP figures from World Bank 1995: 162–3, table 1.)

2 I understand 'development' to be a process leading to increases in people's 'quality of life'. Lack of development, on the other hand, means that many

people have insufficient material resources and are 'obliged to struggle even to survive' (Hadjor 1993: 100).

3 Empowerment is a concept deriving from the work of Paulo Freire, a Brazilian educationist who died in 1997. It means acquiring the awareness and skills necessary to take charge of one's own life chances. Thus empowerment is about encouraging individuals and groups to make their own decisions and to take part in shaping their own destinies; people must be able to participate in decision-making.

4 Sethi (1993) uses the term 'action group' in a narrower way than I do, referring exclusively to political grassroots organizations.

5 Bill and Springborg argue that the 'most crucial units of interest aggregation in the Middle East [are] informal groups' (1994: 93). The point is that the politicized action groups – Islamist organizations – are opposed to the state. In many Middle Eastern countries, however, where the state is nearly always powerful, many people calculate that their best interests will be served by seeking to exploit the opportunities the 'system' offers within informal groups. In Iraq, such goal-oriented informal groups are known as *shilla* or *jama'at*, and in Saudi Arabia, *bashka*. In Egypt, groups of between two and 12 members form a *shilla*. They not only socialize together but also help one another advance politically and economically.

Chapter 2 Action Groups in Regional Focus

1 The core of the concept of sustainable development is the use of renewable resources, such as solar power and waste recycling, as well as the design and implementation of new technologies and changes in consumption by those in the West and the rich in the Third World. The aim of sustainable development is to forge a form of development which maintains an appropriate balance, one which is environmentally tolerable over a long period.

Chapter 3 Macroeconomic Decline and Action Groups

1 Bangladesh has nearly 70,000 villages, a population of 115 million in 1993, and some 65 million landless people (World Bank 1995: 162, table 1; Ekins 1992: 123).

Chapter 4 Democracy and Indigeous Peoples

1 The first wave was in the late nineteenth century, manifested by the emergence of democratic governments in Western Europe and North America; the second came immediately after World War II with the demise of fascist regimes in Italy, Japan and West Germany and the introduction or reintroduction of democracy in those countries.

2 The EZLN calls itself the Zapatistas after the legendary Mexican guerrilla hero Emiliano Zapata, leader of a forgotten rural peasantry in Morelos region

in opposition to the opportunist politicans of Mexico City, from 1910 until his assassination in 1919.

Chapter 5 Environmental Protection

1 Although one major cause of deforestation is said to be 'shifting cultivation', it is not clear that this is necessarily destructive of forest cover. Cammack et al. argue that slash-and-burn agriculture 'has historically proved to be compatible with sustainable exploitation and natural regeneration' (1993: 312). Nevertheless, fires are sometimes started by 'careless tribesmen or other nomadic farmers, destroying precious resources which need to be harvested instead of thrown away' (Cohen 1994: 44).
2 This may or may not be a sign of the emergence of what is known as a 'primary environmental care' policy in Indonesia. An emerging scheme for eco-labelling promises to add safeguards. In order to sell tropical timber in markets of developed countries like Sweden, Australia, Canada and the US, it is increasingly necessary to demonstrate that timber comes from sustainable sources.

Chapter 6 Women and Empowerment

1 The Roman Catholic Church is the leading religious organization in all countries in the Latin American region.

Chapter 7 Islamist Action Groups

1 Such groups are often referred to as Islamic fundamentalist organizations; yet such a nomenclature is an oxymoron. *All* Muslims believe in the fundamentals of Islam; thus the use of the term to depict Islamist radicals makes no sense.

Bibliography

Abubakr, M. (1986): 'BUK mosque and divisive sermons', *The Triumph* (Lagos), 5 May.

Africa Confidential (1995): 'Ken and the soja boys', 36.6 (17 Mar.), pp. 3–4.

—— (1996): 'Press on the button', 37.1 (5 Jan.), pp. 4–5.

Africa Research Bulletin 1991–2: Report, 16 Dec.–5 Jan., p. 10656.

Afshar, A. (1994): 'Commentaries on Muslim women', *Third World Quarterly*, 15.4, pp. 789–92.

Ahmad, Z. H. (1989): 'Malaysia: quasi-democracy in a divided society', in L. Diamond, J. Linz and S. M. Lipset (eds), *Democracy in Developing Countries*, vol. 3: *Asia*, London: Adamantine Press, pp. 347–82.

Ahmed, L. (1992): *Women and Gender in Islam*, New Haven: Yale University Press.

Ajami, F. (1993): 'The summoning', *Foreign Affairs*, Sept.–Oct. pp. 2–9.

Ake, C. (1995): 'The New World Order: a view from Africa', in H.-H. Holm and G. Sørensen (eds), *Whose World Order? Uneven Globalization and the End of the Cold War*, Boulder: Westview, pp. 19–42.

Allegretti, A. (1990): 'Extractive reserves: an alternative for reconciling development and conservation in Amazonia', in A. Anderson, *Alternatives to Deforestation in Amazonia*, New York: Columbia University Press, pp. 3–23.

Almond, G. and Powell, Bingham G. (1966): *Comparative Politics: A Developmental Approach*, New York: Little Brown.

Alvarez, S. (1990): *Engendering Democracy in Brazil*, Princeton: Princeton University Press.

Amin, S., Frank, A. G. and Wallerstein, I. (1990): *Transforming the Revolution*, New York: Monthly Review Press.

Anderson, B. (1991): *Imagined Communities: Reflections on the Origin and Spread of Nationalism*, 2nd rev. edn, London: Verso.

Andreas, P. (1995): 'Free market reform and drug market prohibition: US policies at cross-purposes in Latin America', *Third World Quarterly*, 16.1, pp. 75–87.

Arrighi, G. (1991): 'World income inequalities and the future of socialism', *New Left Review*, no. 189, pp. 39–65.

Attina, A. (1989): 'The study of international relations in Italy', in H. Dyer and L. Mangasarian (eds), *The Study of International Relations: The State of the Art*, London: Macmillan, pp. 344–57.

Auda, G. (1991): 'An uncertain response: the Islamic movement in Egypt', in J. Piscatori (ed.), *Islamic Fundamentalisms and the Gulf Crisis*, London: Cambridge University Press, pp. 109–30.

—— (1993): 'The Islamic movement and resource mobilization in Egypt: a political culture perspective', in L. Diamond (ed.), *Political Culture and Democracy in Developing Countries*, Boulder: Lynne Rienner, pp. 379–407.

Augelli, E. and Murphy C. (1988): *America's Quest for Supremacy and the Third World: A Gramscian Analysis*, London: Pinter.

Ayoade, J. A. (1988): 'States without citizens: an emerging African phenomenon', in D. Rothchild and N. Chazan (eds), *The Precarious Balance: State and Society in Africa*, Boulder: Lynne Rienner, pp. 100–18.

Ayoob, M. (1995): 'The new-old disorder in the Third World', *Global Governance*, 1.1, pp. 59–78.

Ayubi, N. (1991): *Political Islam: Religion and Politics in the Arab World*, London: Routledge.

Balandier, G. (1971): *Sens et Puissance*, Paris: Presses Universitaires de France.

Balls, E. (1995): 'Learning hard lessons from Mexico's crisis', *Guardian*, 10 July.

Bangura, Y. (1994): *Economic Restructuring, Coping Strategies and Social Change: Implications for Institutional Development in Africa*, Discussion Paper 52, Geneva: United Nations Research Institute for Social Development.

Bates, R. (1993): 'The politics of economic policy reform: a review article', *Journal of African Economies*, 2.3, pp. 417–33.

Bayart, J.-F. (1983): 'La revanche des sociétés africaines', *Politique Africaine*, no. 11, pp. 95–127.

—— (1991): 'Finishing with the idea of the Third World: the concept of the political trajectory', in J. Manor (ed.), *Rethinking Third World Politics*, Harlow: Longman, pp. 51–71.

—— (1993): *The State in Africa*, Harlow: Longman.

Beck, U. (1994): 'The reinvention of politics: towards a theory of reflexive modernization', in U. Beck, A. Giddens and S. Lash, *Reflexive Modernization: Politics, Tradition and Aesthetics in the Modern Social Order*, Cambridge: Polity, pp. 37–66.

Beeley, B. (1992): 'Islam as a global political force', in A. McGrew and P. Lewis (eds), *Global Politics: Globalization and the Nation State*, Cambridge: Polity Press, pp. 293–311.

Benhabib, S. and Cornell, D. (1987): 'Introduction: beyond the politics of gender', in S. Benhabib and D. Cornell (eds), *Feminism as Critique*, Minneapolis: University of Minnesota Press.

Bennett, V. (1992): 'The evolution of urban popular movements in Mexico between 1968 and 1988', in A. Escobar and S. Alvarez (eds), *The Making of Social Movements in Latin America: Identity, Strategy and Democracy*, Boulder: Westview, pp. 240–59.

Beresford, D. (1995): 'Cheery Kaunda plots his return', *Guardian*, 10 July.

Berg, R. (1987): 'Non-governmental organizations: new force in Third World development and politics', CASID Distinguished Speakers Series 2, Center for Advanced Study of International Development, Michigan State University.

Bermeo, N. (1992): 'Democracy and the lessons of dictatorship', *Comparative Politics*, 24, pp. 273–91.

Bernal, V. (1994): 'Gender, culture and capitalism', *Comparative Studies in Society and History*, 36.1, pp. 36–67.

Beyer, P. (1994): *Religion and Globalization*, London: Sage.

Bienefeld, M. (1994): 'The new world order: echoes of a new imperialism', *Third World Quarterly*, 15.1, pp. 31–48.

Bill, J. and Springborg, R. (1994): *Politics in the Middle East*, 4th edn, New York: Harper Collins.

Birai, U. M. (1993): 'Islamic tajdid and the political process in Nigeria', in M. Marty and R. Scott Appleby (eds), *Fundamentalisms and the State: Remaking Politics, Economics and Militance*, Chicago: University of Chicago Press, pp. 184–203.

Black, I., Bowcott, O. and Vidal, J. (1995): 'Nigeria defies world with writer's "judicial murder"', *Guardian*, 11 Nov.

Blom Hansen, T. (1995): 'Democratisation, mass-politics and Hindu identity: the communalisation of Bombay', paper presented to the workshop 'Political Culture and Religion in the Third World', European Consortium for Political Research Joint Sessions, Bordeaux, 27 Apr.–2 May.

Body Shop nd (*c*.mid-Nov. 1995): 'Ken Saro-Wiwa and the Ogoni: Fact sheet'.

Boer, L. and Koekkoek, A. (1994): 'Development and human security', *Third World Quarterly*, 15.3 pp. 555–73.

Booth, J. and Seligson, M. (1993): 'Paths to democracy and the political culture of Costa Rica, Mexico, and Nicaragua', in L. Diamond (ed.), *Political Culture and Democracy in Developing Countries*, Boulder: Lynne Rienner, pp. 107–38.

Boserup, E. (1970): *Women's Role in Economic Development*, London: Allen and Unwin.

Bowen, M. (1992): 'Beyond reform: adjustment and political power in contemporary Mozambique', *Journal of Modern African Studies*, 30.2, pp. 255–79.

BRAC (Bangladesh Rural Action Committee) (1988): *A Brief on BRAC*, Dhaka: BRAC.

Bradbury, M. (1995): 'Let's do the Popomo a-go-go', *Guardian*, 9 Dec.

Braid, M. (1995): 'How quality of life matches up to global sisterhood', *Independent*, 18 Aug.

Bratton, M. (1989): 'Beyond the state: civil society and associational life in Africa', *World Politics*, 41.3, pp. 407–30.

—— (1994a): 'International versus domestic pressures for "democratization" in Africa', paper presented at the conference on 'The End of the Cold War: Effects and Prospects for Asia and Africa', School of Oriental and African Studies, University of London, 21–2 Oct.

—— (1994b): 'Micro-democracy? The merger of farmer unions in Zimbabwe', *African Studies Review*, 37.1, pp. 9–38.

Bratton, M. and van der Walle, N. (1994): 'Neopatrimonial regimes and political transitions in Africa', *World Politics*, 46, pp. 453–89.

Bretherton, C. (1996): 'Contemporary sources of armed conflict', in C. Bretherton and G. Poynton (eds), *Global Politics: An Introduction*, Oxford: Blackwell, pp. 100–25.

Breyman, S. (1993): 'Knowledge as power: ecology movements and global environmental problems', in R. Lipschutz and K. Conca (eds), *The State and Social Power in Global Environmental Politics*, New York: Columbia University Press, pp. 124–57.

Brittain, V. (1994): 'Victims from birth', *Observer*, 16 Oct., special supplement, p. 12.
—— (1995): ' "Count the cost of women's work" ', *Guardian*, 18 Aug.
Bromley, S. (1993): 'The prospects for democracy in the Middle East', in D. Held (ed.), *Prospects for Democracy*, Cambridge: Polity, pp. 380–406.
—— (1994): *Rethinking Middle East Politics*, Cambridge: Polity.
Brown, N. (1990): *'Peasant Politics in Modern Egypt: The Struggle against the State*, New Haven: Yale University Press.
Brydon, L. and Chant, S. (1989): *Women in the Third World*, Aldershot: Edward Elgar.
Bull, H. (1977): *The Anarchical Society: A Study of Order in World Politics*, London: Macmillan.
Bush, R. and Szeftel, M. (1994): 'Commentary: states, markets and Africa's crisis', *Review of African Political Economy*, no. 60, pp. 147–56.
Callaghy, T. (1993): 'Vision and politics in the transformation of the global political economy: lessons from the Second and Third Worlds', in R. Slater, B. Schutz and S. Dorr (eds), *Global Transformation and the Third World*, Boulder: Lynne Rienner, pp. 161–258.
Callaghy, T. and Ravenhill, J. (1993): 'How hemmed in? Lessons and prospects of Africa's responses to decline', in T. Callaghy and J. Ravenhill (eds), *Hemmed In: Responses to Africa's Economic Decline*, New York: Columbia University Press, pp. 521–60.
Callaway, B. and Creevey, L. (1994): *The Heritage of Islam: Women, Religion and Politics in West Africa*, Boulder and London: Lynne Rienner.
Callick, R. (1991): 'No blue skies yet in the South Pacific', *Pacific Economic Bulletin*, 6.2, pp. 1–19.
Calvert, S. and Calvert, P. (1996): *Politics and Society in the Third World*, Hemel Hempstead: Prentice Hall.
Camilleri, J. and Falk, J. (1992): *The End of Sovereignty? The Politics of a Shrinking and Fragmented World*, Aldershot: Edward Elgar.
Cammack, P., Pool, D. and Tordoff, W. (1993): *Third World Politics: A Comparative Introduction*, 2nd edn, London: Macmillan.
Cardenal, R. (1990): 'The martyrdom of the Salvadorean church', in D. Keogh (ed.), *Church and Politics in Latin America*, London: Macmillan, pp. 172–85.
Carnoy, M. (1984): *The State and Political Theory*, Princeton: Princeton University Press.
Carrim, Y. (1993): 'ANC as a mass political organisation', in A. Johnston, S. Shezi and G. Bradshaw (eds), *Constitution-Making in the New South Africa*, London: Leicester University Press, pp. 89–114.
Casanova, J. (1994): *Public Religions in the Modern World*, Chicago and London: University of Chicago Press.
Case, W. (1993): 'Semi-democracy in Malaysia: withstanding the pressures for regime change', *Pacific Affairs*, 66.2, pp. 183–205.
Castaneda, J. (1993): *Utopia Unarmed: The Latin American Left after the Cold War*, New York: Knopf.
Chabal, P. (1986): 'Introduction: thinking about politics in Africa', in P. Chabal (ed.), *Political Domination in Africa*, Cambridge: Cambridge University Press, pp. 1–16.
—— (1992): *Power in Africa: An Essay in Political Interpretation*, London: Macmillan.

Chambers, R. (1985): *The Working Women's Forum: a Counter-Culture by Poor Women*, New York: UNICEF.

Charlton, R., May, R. and Cleobury, T. (1994): 'From BINGO to TANGO: NGOs and development in Africa', paper presented at African Studies of the UK biennial conference, University of Lancaster, Sept.

—— (1995): 'NGOs in the politics of development: projects as policy', *Contemporary Politics*, 1.1, pp. 19–42.

Chazan, N. (1993): 'Between liberalism and statism: African political cultures and democracy', in L. Diamond (ed.), *Political Culture and Democracy in Developing Countries*, Boulder: Lynne Rienner, pp. 67–106.

Chen, M. A. (1983): *A Quiet Revolution: Women in Transition in Rural Bangladesh*, Cambridge, Mass.: Schenkman.

Chilton, P. (1995): 'Mechanics of change: social movements, transnational coalitions, and the transformation processes in Eastern Europe', in T. Risse-Kappen (ed.), *Bringing Transnational Relations Back In*, Cambridge: Cambridge University Press, pp. 189–226.

Clapham, C. (1985): *Third World Politics: An Introduction*, London: Routledge.

Clapham, C. and Wiseman, J. (1995): 'Conclusion: assessing the prospects for the consolidation of democracy in Africa', in J. Wiseman (ed.), *Democracy and Political Change in Africa*, London: Routledge, pp. 220–32.

Clark, C. and Chan, S. (1995): 'MNCs and developmentalism: domestic structure as an explanation for East Asian dynamism', in T. Risse-Kappen (ed.), *Bringing Transnational Relations Back In*, Cambridge: Cambridge University Press, pp. 112–45.

Clark, J. (1991): *Democratizing Development*, London: Earthscan.

Cohen, J. (1985): 'Strategy or identity: new theoretical paradigms and contemporary social movements', *Social Research*, 52.4, pp. 663–716.

Cohen, M. (1994): 'Culture of awareness', *Far Eastern Economic Review*, 17 Nov., p. 44.

Coles, M. (1994): 'Women of Iran "treated as sub-humans"', *Observer*, 4 Dec.

Conca, K. (1993): 'Environmental change and the deep structure of world politics', in R. Lipschutz and K. Conca (eds), *The State and Social Power in Global Environmental Politics*, New York: Columbia University Press, pp. 306–26.

Corcoran-Nantes, Y. (1990): 'Women and popular urban social movements in São Paulo, Brazil', *Bulletin of Latin American Research*, 9.2, pp. 249–64.

—— (1993): 'Female consciousness or feminist consciousness: women's consciousness raising in community-based struggles in Brazil', in S. Radcliffe and S. Westwood (eds), *'Viva': Women and Popular Protest in Latin America*, London and New York: Routledge, pp. 136–55.

Cornia, G. A., van der Hoeven, R. and Mkandawire, T. (eds) (1992): *Africa's Recovery in the 1990s*, London: UNICEF/Macmillan.

Coulon, C. (1983): *Les Musulmans et le Pouvoir en Afrique Noire*, Paris: Karthala.

Crook, R. (1995): 'Côte d'Ivoire: multi-party democracy and political change: surviving the crisis', in J. Wiseman (ed.), *Democracy and Political Change in Africa*, London: Routledge, pp. 11–44.

Crook, R. and Manor, J. (1995): 'Democratic decentralisation and institutional performance: four Asian and African experiences compared', *Journal of Commonwealth and Comparative Politics*, 33.3, pp. 309–34.

Crystal, J. (1991): 'The human rights movement in the Arab world', *American–Arab Affairs*, Spring, pp. 14–16.

Cumming-Bruce, N. (1995): 'Thailand's voters may be swayed by the devil with deep pockets rather than devil they know', *Guardian*, 30 June.

Danevad, A. (1995): 'Responsiveness in Botswana politics: do elections matter?', *Journal of Modern African Studies*, 33.3, pp. 381–402.

Danielsson, B. and Danielsson, M.-T. (1986): *Poisoned Reign: French Nuclear Colonialism*, 2nd rev. edn, Ringwood: Penguin.

Dasgupta, P. (1993): *An Inquiry into Well-being and Destitution*, Oxford: Clarendon Press.

de Waal, A. and Omaar, R. (1995): 'Sowing the seeds of famine and war', *Guardian*, 1 Feb.

Deeb, M. (1989): 'Egypt', in S. Mews (ed.), *Religion in Politics: A World Guide*, Harlow: Longman, pp. 62–6.

Deeb, M.-J. (1989a. 'Algeria', in S. Mews (ed.), *Religion in Politics: A World Guide*, Harlow: Longman, pp. 6–8.

—— (1989b): 'Morocco', in S. Mews (ed.), *Religion in Politics: A World Guide*, Harlow: Longman, p. 185.

Dessouki, A. H. (ed.) (1982): *Islamic Resurgence in the Arab World*, New York: Praeger.

Di Palma, G. (1990): *To Craft Democracies*, Berkeley: University of California Press.

Diamond, L. (1993a): 'The globalization of democracy', in R. Slater, B. Schutz and S. Dorr (eds), *Global Transformation and the Third World*, Boulder: Lynne Rienner, pp. 91–112.

—— (1993b): 'Introduction: political culture and democracy', in L. Diamond (ed.), *Political Culture and Democracy in Developing Countries*, Boulder: Lynne Rienner, pp. 1–33.

Diamond, L., Linz, J. and Lipset, S. (eds) (1989): *Democracy in Developing Countries*, vol. 3: *Asia*, London: Adamantine Press.

Dichter, T. and Zesch, S. (1989): *Savings and Credit Societies in Kenya: Insights into Management Transformation and Institutional Modernization*, Sector Study Series, New York: Technoserve.

Dicker, R. (1991): 'Monitoring human rights in Africa', *Journal of Modern African Studies*, 29.3, pp. 505–10.

Diegues, A. C. (1992): *The Social Dynamics of Deforestation in the Brazilian Amazon: An Overview*, Discussion Paper 36, Geneva, United Nations Research Institute for Social Development.

Dolan, M. (1993): 'Global economic transformation and less developed countries', in R. Slater, B. Schutz and S. Dorr (eds), *Global Transformation and the Third World*, Boulder: Lynne Rienner, pp. 259–82.

Dorr, S. (1993): 'Democratization in the Middle East', in R. Slater, B. Schutz and S. Dorr (eds), *Global Transformation and the Third World*, Boulder: Lynne Rienner, pp. 131–57.

Duodu, C. (1996): 'Nigerian troops shoot six dead as Ogoni mourn Saro-Wiwa', *Observer*, 7 Jan.

Durning, A. (1989): *Action at the Grassroots*, Worldwatch Papers 88, Washington, D.C.: Worldwatch Institute.

Dyson-Hudson, N. (1985): 'Pastoral production systems and livestock development projects: an East African perspective', in M. Cernea (ed.), *Putting People First: Sociological Variables in Rural Development*, New York: Oxford University Press, pp. 157–86.

192 *Bibliography*

The Economist (1995a): 'A kept woman', 15 July, p. 61.

—— (1995b): 'France's other blast', 16 Sept. p. 88.

Edie, C. (1991): *Democracy by Default: Dependency and Clientelism in Jamaica*, Boulder: Lynne Rienner.

Ekins, P. (1992): *A New World Order: Grassroots Movements for Global Change*, London: Routledge.

Elliot, L. (1994): 'New welfare plan to turn clock forward', *Guardian*, 25 Oct.

Ellis, S. (1994): 'Politics and nature conservation in South Africa', *Journal of Southern African Studies*, 20.1, pp. 53–69.

—— (1995): 'Liberia 1989–1994: a study of ethnic and spiritual violence', *African Affairs*, 94.375, pp. 165–97.

Elshtain, J. B. (1995): 'Exporting feminism', *Journal of International Affairs*, 48.2, pp. 541–58.

Engels, D. and Marks, S. (eds) (1994): *Contesting Colonial Hegemony: State and Society in Africa and India*, London: I. B. Tauris.

Enzenberger, H. (1991): *Mittelmas und Wahn*, Frankfurt: Suhrkamp.

Ergas, Z. (1986): 'In search of development: some directions for further investigation', *Journal of Modern African Studies*, 24.2, pp. 303–34.

Escobar, A. and Alvarez, S. (1992a): 'Introduction: theory and protest in Latin America today', in A. Escobar and S. Alvarez (eds), *The Making of Social Movements in Latin America: Identity, Strategy and Democracy*, Boulder: Westview, pp. 1–15.

—— (1992b): 'Conclusion: theoretical and political horizons of change in contemporary Latin American social movements', in A. Escobar and S. Alvarez (eds), *The Making of Social Movements in Latin America: Identity, Strategy and Democracy*, Boulder: Westview, pp. 317–30.

Esman, M. and Uphoff, N. (1984): *Local Organizations: Intermediaries in Local Development*, Ithaca: Cornell University Press.

Esposito, J. and Piscatori, J. (1991): 'Democratization and Islam', *Middle East Journal*, 45.3, pp. 427–40.

Etienne, B. and Tozy, M. (1981): 'Le glissement des obligations islamiques vers le phenomene associatif à Casablanca', in *Le Maghreb Musulman en 1979*, Paris: Karthala, pp. 243–61.

Etzioni, A. (1990): *The Moral Dimension: Towards a New Economics*, New York: Free Press.

Evans, P., Rueshemeyer, D. and Skocpol, T. (eds) (1985): *Bringing the State Back In*, Cambridge: Cambridge University Press.

Ezard, J. (1995): 'Secret rape of Cambodia's dwindling forest', *Guardian*, 20 Mar.

Fals Borda, O. (1992): 'Social movements and political power in Latin America', in A. Escobar and S. Alvarez (eds), *The Making of Social Movements in Latin America: Identity, Strategy and Democracy*, Boulder: Westview, pp. 303–16.

Fatton, R. (1990): 'Gender, class and state in Africa', in J. Parpart and K. Staudt (eds), *Women and the State in Africa*, Boulder: Rienner, pp. 47–66.

Feijoo, M. C., and Gogna, M. (1990): 'Women in the transition to democracy', in E. Jelin (ed.), *Women and Social Change in Latin America*, London: Zed Books, pp. 79–114.

Femia, J. (1981): *Gramsci's Political Thought: Hegemony, Consciousness and the Revolutionary Process*, Oxford: Clarendon Press.

Fieldhouse, D. (1992): 'War and the origins of the Gold Coast Cocoa Marketing Board, 1939–40', in M. Twaddle (ed.), *Imperialism, the State and the Third World*, London: British Academic Press, pp. 153–82.

Fisher, J. (1993): *The Road from Rio: Sustainable Development and Nongovernmental Movements in the Third World*, Westport: Praeger.
—— (1994): 'Is the iron law of oligarchy rusting away in the Third World?', *World Development*, 22.2, pp. 129–43.
Fletcher, M. (1994): 'Mullah of Chicago's mean streets', *Guardian*, 17 Feb.
Forrest, J. (1988): 'The quest for state "hardness" in Africa', *Comparative Politics*, 20.4, pp. 423–42.
Fossaert, R. (1978): *La Société*, vol. 5 *Les États*, Paris: Le Seuil.
French, H. (1995): 'Africa lingers off-line', *Guardian*, 24 Nov.
Fry, G. (1993): 'At the margin: the South Pacific and changing world order', in R. Leaver and J. Richardson (eds), *Charting the Post-Cold War Order*, Boulder: Westview, pp. 224–42.
Fuentes, M. and Gunder Frank, A. (1989): 'Ten theses on social movements', *World Development*, 17.2, pp. 179–91.
Fukuyama, F. (1989): 'The end of history', *National Interest*, no. 16, pp. 3–18.
—— (1992): *The End of History and the Last Man*, London: Penguin.
Furedi, F. (1994): *Colonial Wars and the Politics of Third World Nationalism*, London: I. B. Tauris.
Gaffney, P. (1994): *The Prophet's Pulpit: Islamic Preaching in Contemporary Egypt*, Berkeley: University of California Press.
Galbraith, J. K. (1995): 'To have and have not', *Observer*, 29 Oct.
Garreton, M. (1991): 'Political democratisation in Latin America and the crisis of paradigms', in J. Manor (ed.), *Rethinking Third World Politics*, Harlow: Longman, pp. 100–17.
Gayama, P. (1993): 'Africa's marginalisation: a perception, not a process', in A. Adedeji (ed.), *Africa within the World*, London: Zed Books.
Geisler, G. (1995): 'Troubled sisterhood: women and politics in southern Africa', *African Affairs*, 94.377, pp. 545–78.
George, S. (1993): 'Uses and abuses of African Debt', in A. Adedeji (ed.), *Africa within the World: Beyond Dispossession and Dependence*, London: Zed Books/ACDESS, pp. 59–72.
Gerschenkron, A. (1962): *Economic Backwardness in Historical Perspective*, Cambridge: Harvard University Press.
Ghazi, P. (1995): 'Rainbow warriors defy French guns', *Observer*, 9 July.
Gifford, P. (1989): 'Tanzania', in S. Mews (ed.), *Religion in Politics: A World Guide*, Harlow: Longman.
—— (1991): 'Christian fundamentalism and development in Africa', *Review of African Political Economy*, no. 52, pp. 9–20.
—— (1996): 'Chiluba's Christian nation: the churches in Zambian politics', paper presented at the biennial conference of the African Studies Association of the UK, University of Bristol, 9–11 Sept.
Gills, B. (1993): 'Korean capitalism and democracy', in B. Gills, J. Rocamara and R. Wilson (eds), *Low Intensity Democracy*, London: Pluto Press, pp. 226–57.
Gills, B. and Rocamara, J. (1992): 'Low intensity democracy', *Third World Quarterly*, 13.3, pp. 501–24.
Gills, B., Rocamara, J. and Wilson, R. (eds) (1993): *Low Intensity Democracy*, London: Pluto Press.
Gittings, J. (1994): 'Homelessness in the name of aid', *Guardian*, 18 Mar.
—— (1995): 'Solitude of freedom now awaits Burma's stubborn champion of democratic reform', *Guardian*, 11 July.
—— (1996): 'Famine haunts the isolated nation', *Guardian*, 8 Jan.

Global Witness (1995): *Forests, Famine and War: The Key to Cambodia's Future*, London: Global Witness.

Goldenberg, S. (1996): 'India's pariahs scent power', *Observer*, 12 May.

Gott, R. (1973): *Rural Guerrillas in Latin America*, Harmondsworth: Penguin.

Gray, J. (1996): 'If the fez fits', *Guardian*, 8 Jan.

Grayson, J. (1989): 'Korea', in S. Mews (ed.), *Religion in Politics*, Harlow: Longman, pp. 153–9.

Greenpeace USA (1990): *The International Trade in Wastes: A Greenpeace Inventory*, Washington, D.C.: Greenpeace USA.

Guadilla, M.-P. (1993): '*Ecologica*: women, environment and politics in Venezuela', in S. Radcliffe and S. Westwood (eds), '*Viva*': *Women and Popular Protest in Latin America*, London and New York: Routledge, pp. 65–87.

Gumbel, A. (1994): 'Outlawed Islamic front delivers warning on Algerian agreements with the IMF', *Guardian*, 13 Apr.

Gunder Frank, A. (1993): 'Marketing democracy in an undemocratic market', in B. Gills, J. Rocamara and R. Wilson (eds), *Low Intensity Democracy*, London: Pluto Press, pp. 35–58.

Gunson, P. (1996): 'Casual jailing of two Zapatistas', *Guardian*, 10 May.

Gurr, T. R. (1993): 'Why minorities rebel: a global analysis of communal mobilization and conflict since 1945', *International Political Science Review*, 14.2, pp. 161–201.

Gutkind, P. (1970): *The Poor in Urban Africa: A Prologue to Modernization, Conflict, and the Unfinished Revolution*, Montreal and Quebec: Centre for Developing-Area Studies, McGill University.

Habermas, J. (1988): *Legitimation Crisis*, Cambridge: Polity.

Hadjor, K. (1993): *Dictionary of Third World Terms*, London: Penguin.

Haggard, S. (1990): *Pathways from the Periphery: The Politics of Growth in the Newly Industrializing Countries*, Ithaca: Cornell University Press.

Hagopian, F. (1993): 'After regime change: authoritarian legacies, political representation, and the democratic future of Latin America', *World Politics*, 45, pp. 464–500.

Hailey, W. M. (1954): *African Survey*, New York: Oxford University Press.

Hall, J. (1993): 'Consolidations of democracy', in D. Held (ed.), *Prospects for Democracy*, Cambridge: Polity, pp. 271–90.

Hamer, J. (1984): 'Preconditions and limits in the formation of associations: the self-help and cooperative movement in sub-Saharan Africa', *Associations Transnationales*, no. 5, pp. 276–83.

Hanlon, J. (1991): *Mozambique: Who Calls the Shots?*, London: Zed Books.

Hansen, K. T. (1990): 'The black market and women traders in Lusaka, Zambia', in J. Parpart and K. Staudt (eds), *Women and the State in Africa*, Boulder and London: Lynne Rienner.

Harbeson, J. (1994): 'Civil society and political renaissance in Africa', in J. Harbeson, D. Rothchild and N. Chazan (eds), *Civil Society and the State in Africa*, Boulder and London: Lynne Rienner.

Harris, A. (1990): 'Race and essentialism in feminist legal theory', *Stanford Law Review*, 42, pp. 581–616.

Harrison, P. (1993): *The Third Revolution: Population, Environment and a Sustainable World*, London: Penguin.

Harsch, E. (1996): 'Global coalition debates Africa's future', *Africa Recovery*, 10.1, pp. 24–31.

Harvey, N. (1995): 'Rebellion in Chiapas: rural reforms and popular struggle', *Third World Quarterly*, 16.1, pp. 39–73.

Hawthorn, G. (1991): ' "Waiting for a text?" Comparing Third World politics', in J. Manor (ed.), *Rethinking Third World Politics*, Harlow: Longman, pp. 24–50.

—— (1993): 'Sub-Saharan Africa', in D. Held (ed.), *Prospects for Democracy*, Cambridge: Polity, pp. 330–53.

—— (1994): 'Liberalization and "modern liberty" ', *World Development*, 21.8, pp 1299–312.

Haynes, J. (1993a): *Religion in Third World Politics*, Buckingham: Open University Press.

—— (1993b): 'The state, good governance and democracy in sub-Saharan Africa', *Journal of Modern African Studies*, 31.3, pp. 535–9.

—— (1993c): 'Sustainable democracy in Ghana? Problems and prospects', *Third World Quarterly*, 14.3, pp. 451–67.

—— (1995a): *Religion, Fundamentalism and Identity: A Global Perspective*, Discussion Paper 65, Geneva: United Nations Research Institute for Social Development.

—— (1995b): 'Ghana: from personalistic to democratic rule', in J. Wiseman (ed.), *Democracy and Political Change in Africa*, London: Routledge, pp. 92–115.

—— (1995c): 'The renaissance of "political" religion in the Third World in the context of global change', paper for conference on 'Religion and Global Order', University of Wales conference centre, 1–3 Nov.

—— (1996a): *Religion and Politics in Africa*, London: Zed Books.

—— (1996b): *Third World Politics: A Concise Introduction*, Oxford: Blackwell.

—— (1996c): 'Politics of the Natural Environment in the Third World', *Journal of Contemporary Politics*, 2.2, pp. 19–42.

Healey, J., Ketley, R. and Robinson, M. (1992): 'Political regimes and economic policy in developing countries, 1978–88', ODI Working Paper 67, London.

Heikal, M. (1995): *Secret Channels: The Inside Story of Arab-Israeli Peace*, London: HarperCollins.

Held, D. (1987): *Models of Democracy*, Cambridge: Polity.

—— (1989): *Political Theory and the Modern State*, Cambridge: Polity.

—— (1993): 'Democracy: from city-states to a cosmopolitan order?', in D. Held (ed.), *Prospects for Democracy*, Cambridge: Polity, pp. 13–52.

Helmore, K. (1985): 'Working for survival', part 3 of 'The neglected resource: women in the developing world', *Christian Science Monitor*, 19 Dec.

Hettne, B. (1995): *Development Theory and the Three Worlds*, Harlow: Longman.

Hewitt, W. E. (1990): 'Religion and the consolidation of democracy in Brazil: the role of the communidades eclesias de base (CEBs)', *Sociological Analysis*, 50.2, pp. 139–52.

Higgins, A. (1996): 'Values change, cant doesn't', *Guardian*, 5 Jan.

Higson, A. (1995): 'France's poisoned paradise lost', *Guardian*, 30 Dec.

Hintjens, H. (1996): 'Comparing local development organisations in the context of structural adjustment: grassroots organisations in Burkina Faso and Senegal', in I. Hampsher-Monk and J. Stanyer (eds), *Contemporary Political Studies 1996*, vol. 1: *Proceedings of the Annual Conference of the Political Studies Association Held at Glasgow, 10–12 April, 1996*, pp. 598–609.

Hirst, D. (1995a): 'Algeria leads by its flawed example', *Guardian*, 24 Nov.

—— (1995b): 'Righteous murder', *Guardian*, 15 Dec.

Hobbes, J. (1969): *Leviathan*, London: Fontana.

Hoebel, A. (1972): *Anthropology: The Study of Man*, 4th edn, New York: McGraw-Hill.

Hong, K. K. (ed.) (1991): *Jeux et enjeux de l'auto-promotion*, Paris: Presse Universitaire de France.

Hugill, B. (1996): 'Asia's tiger economies earn their stripes', *Observer*, 7 Jan.

Hunter, A. and von der Mehden, F. (1989): 'Singapore', in S. Mews (ed.), *Religion in Politics: A World Guide*, Harlow: Longman.

Huntington, S. (1968): *Political Order in Changing Societies*, New Haven: Yale University Press.

—— (1991): *The Third Wave: Democratization in the Late Twentieth Century*, Norman: University of Oklahoma Press.

—— (1993): 'The clash of civilizations?', *Foreign Affairs*, 72.3, pp. 22–49.

Huus, K. (1994): 'A question of economy', *Far Eastern Economic Review*, 17 Nov., pp. 52–3.

Hutton, W. (1995): 'Myth that sets the world to right', *Guardian*, 12 June.

Hyden, G. (1980): *Beyond Ujamaa in Tanzania: Underdevelopment and an Uncaptured Peasantry*, London: Heinemann.

—— (1983): *No Shortcuts to Progress: African Development Management in Perspective*, Berkeley: University of California Press.

—— (1992): 'Governance and the study of politics', in G. Hyden and M. Bratton (eds), *Governance and Politics in Africa*, Boulder: Lynne Rienner, pp. 1–26.

Hyden, G. and Bratton, M. (1992): 'Preface', in G. Hyden and M. Bratton (eds), *Governance and Politics in Africa*, Boulder: Lynne Rienner, pp. ix–xii.

Ibrahim, J. (1991): 'Religion and political turbulence in Nigeria', *Journal of Modern African Studies*, 29.1, pp. 115–36.

Ihonvbere, J. and Vaughan, O. (1995): 'Nigeria: democracy and civil society: the Nigerian transition programme, 1985–93', in J. Wiseman (ed.), *Democracy and Political Change in Africa*, London: Routledge, pp. 71–91.

ILO (International Labour Organization) (1994): *World Labour Report 1994*, Geneva: ILO.

IMF Survey (1993): 'Seminar explores links between macro policy and the environment', 14 June, pp. 177, 187.

Inglehart, Ronald (1990): *Culture Shift in Advanced Industrial Society*, Princeton: Princeton University Press.

Inoguchi, T. (1995): 'A view from Pacific Asia', in H.-H. Holm and G. Sørensen (eds), *Whose World Order? Uneven Globalization and the End of the Cold War*, Boulder: Westview, pp. 119–36.

Jackson, R. (1990): *Quasi-states: Sovereignty, International Relations and the Third World*, Cambridge: Cambridge University Press.

Jaquette, J. (1982): 'Women and modernization theory: a decade of feminist criticism', *World Politics*, 34.2, pp. 267–84.

—— (ed.) (1989): *The Women's Movement in Latin America*, Boston: Unwin Hyman.

Jayasankaran, S. (1994): 'Air of concern', *Far Eastern Economic Review*, 17 Nov., pp. 51–2.

Jelin, E. (ed.) (1990): *Women and Social Change in Latin America*, London: Zed/ UNRISD.

Jerusalem Report (1995): 'Jobless in Gaza', 18 May, p. 8.

Jesudason, J. (1995): 'Statist democracy and the limits to civil society in Malaysia', *Journal of Commonwealth and Comparative Politics*, 33.3, pp. 335–56.

Joshi, V. (1995): 'Democracy and development in India', *Roundtable*, no. 333, pp. 73–80.

Jowitt, K. (1993): 'A world without Leninism', in R. Slater, B. Schutz and S. Dorr (eds), *Global Transformation and the Third World*, Boulder: Lynne Rienner, pp. 9–27.

Kamrava, M. (1993): *Politics and Society in the Third World*, London: Routledge.

Kane, O. (1990): 'Les mouvements religieux et le champ politique au Nigeria septentrional', *Islam et Societés au Sud du Sahara*, no. 4, pp. 7–24.

Karl, T. L. (1990): 'Dilemmas of democratization in Latin America', *Comparative Politics*, 23.1, pp. 1–21.

Karl, T. L. and Schmitter, P. (1993): 'Democratization around the globe: the opportunities and risk', in M. Klare and D. Thomas (eds), *World Security: Trends and Challenges at Century's End*, New York: St. Martin's Press, pp. 270–94.

Kaviraj, S. (1991): 'On state, society and discourse in India', in J. Manor (ed.), *Rethinking Third World Politics*, Harlow: Longman, pp. 72–99.

Keane, J. (1988): *Democracy and Civil Society*, London: Verso.

Kees van Donge, J. (1995): 'Zambia: Kaunda and Chiluba: enduring patterns of political culture', in J. Wiseman (ed.), *Democracy and Political Change in Africa*, London: Routledge, pp. 193–219.

Kepel, G. (1994): *The Revenge of God: The Resurgence of Islam, Christianity and Judaism in the Modern World*, Cambridge: Polity.

Kershner, I. (1995): 'No guarantees from Hamas', *Jerusalem Post*, 14 Dec.

King, A. Y. C. (1993): 'A nonparadigmatic search for democracy in post-Confucian culture: the case of Taiwan, R. O. C.', in L. Diamond (ed.), *Political Culture and Democracy in Developing Countries*, Boulder: Lynne Rienner, pp. 139–62.

Klein, E. (1984): *Gender Politics: From Consciousness to Mass Politics*, Cambridge: Harvard University Press.

Knippers Black, J. (1993): 'Elections and other trivial pursuits: Latin America and the New World Order', *Third World Quarterly*, 14.3, pp. 545–54.

Krasner, S. (1995): 'Power politics, institutions, and transnational relations', in T. Risse-Kappen (ed.), *Bringing Transnational Relations Back In*, Cambridge: Cambridge University Press, pp. 257–79.

Laitin, D. (1986): *Hegemony and Culture: Politics and Religious Change among the Yoruba*, Chicago: University of Chicago Press.

Lamb, R. (1996): 'Not young but fresh and green', *Guardian*, 25 Sept.

Lancaster, C. (1993): 'Governance and development: the views from Washington', *IDS Bulletin*, 24.1, pp. 9–15.

Lane, J.-E. and Ersson, S. (1994): *Comparative Politics*, Cambridge: Polity.

Lean, M. (1996): 'Working in good faith', *Guardian*, 18 Sept.

Lecomte, B. (1986): *Project Aid: Limitations and Alternatives*, Paris: OECD Development Centre Studies.

Leftwich, A. (1993): 'Governance, democracy and development in the Third World', *Third World Quarterly*, 14.3, pp. 605–24.

Lehmann, D. (1990): *Democracy and Development in Latin America*, Cambridge: Cambridge University Press.

Levine, D. (1984): 'Religion and politics: dimensions of renewal', *Renewal*, 59.233, pp. 117–35.

—— (1990): 'The Catholic church and politics in Latin America', in D. Keogh (ed.), *Church and Politics in Latin America*, London: Macmillan, pp. 8–32.

Linklater, A. (1981): 'Men and citizens in international relations', *Review of International Studies*, 7.1, pp. 23–37.

Linz, J. (1990): 'Transitions to democracy', *Washington Quarterly*, 13.3, pp. 143–64.

Lipschutz, R. (1992): 'Reconstructing world politics: the emergence of global civil society', *Millennium*, 21.3, pp. 389–420.

Lipschutz, R. and Conca, K. (eds) (1993): *The State and Social Power in Global Environmental Politics*, New York: Columbia University Press.

Lipset, S. M. (1963): 'Economic development and democracy', in S. M. Lipset (ed.), *Political Man*, Garden City, N.Y.: Anchor, pp. 27–63.

Litfin, K. (1993): 'Eco-regimes: playing tug of war with the nation-state', in R. Lipschutz and K. Conca (eds), *The State and Social Power in Global Environmental Politics*, New York: Columbia University Press, pp. 94–118.

McCargo, D. (1992): 'The political ramifications of the 1989 "Santi Asoke" case in Thailand', paper presented at the annual conference of the Association of South-East Asian Studies, School of Oriental and African Studies, University of London, 8–10 Apr.

McCormick, J. (1989): *Reclaiming Paradise: The Global Environmental Movement*, Bloomington: Indiana University Press.

McGreal, C. (1996): 'Racist leader plans SA trip', *Guardian*, 20 Jan.

McGrew, A. (1992a): 'Conceptualizing global politics', in A. McGrew and P. Lewis (eds), *Global Politics*, Cambridge: Polity, pp. 1–28.

—— (1992b): 'Global politics in a transnational era', in A. McGrew and P. Lewis (eds), *Global Politics*, Cambridge: Polity, pp. 312–30.

Maier, K. (1991): 'Blood flows in Kano streets in Christian–Muslim battles', *Independent*, 16 Oct.

Mainwaring, S. and Viola, E. (1984): 'New social movements, political culture and democracy: Brazil and Argentina in the 1980s', *Telos*, no. 61, pp. 17–54.

Mallow, J. (1987): 'Bolivia's economic crisis', *Current History*, Jan, pp. 9–12.

Mann, M. (1986): *The Sources of Social Power*, vol. 1, Cambridge: Cambridge University Press.

Manor, J. (1991): 'Introduction', in J. Manor (ed.), *Rethinking Third World Politics*, Harlow: Longman, pp. 1–11.

Marchand, M. (1995): 'Latin American women speak on development', in M. Marchand and J. Parpart, *Feminism/Postmodernism/Development*, London: Routledge, pp. 56–72.

Marty, M. and Appleby, R. S. (1993): 'Introduction', in M. Marty and R. Scott Appleby (eds), *Fundamentalism and the State: Remaking Polities, Economies, and Militance*, Chicago: University of Chicago Press, pp. 1–9.

Mason, W. (1994): 'What is new in neostructuralism?', in B. Gills and R. Palan (eds), *Transcending the State–Global Divide: A Neostructuralist Agenda in International Relations*, Boulder: Lynne Rienner, pp. 15–22.

Mayer, A. E. (1991): *Islam and Human Rights: Tradition and Politics*, Boulder: Westview Press.

—— (1993): 'The fundamentalist impact on law, politics and constitutions in Iran, Pakistan, and the Sudan', in M. Marty and R. Scott Appleby (eds), *Fundamentalism and the State: Remaking Polities, Economies, and Militance*, Chicago: University of Chicago Press, pp. 110–51.

Mearsheimer, J. (1990): 'Why we will soon miss the Cold War', *Atlantic Monthly*, 266.2, pp. 35–50.

Medard, J.-F. (1991): 'The historical trajectories of the Ivorian and Kenyan states', in J. Manor (ed.), *Rethinking Third World Politics*, Harlow: Longman, pp. 185–212.

Medhurst, K. (1989): 'Brazil', in S. Mews (ed.), *Religion in Politics: A World Guide*, Harlow: Longman, pp. 25–9.

Melucci, A. (1981): 'Ten hypotheses for the analysis of new movements', in D. Pinto (ed.), *Contemporary Italian Sociology*, Cambridge: Cambridge University Press, pp. 173–94.

—— (1985): 'The symbolic challenge of contemporary movements', *Social Research*, 52.4, pp. 789–816.

Mendes, C. (1992): 'Peasants speak: Chico Mendes – the defence of life', *Journal of Peasant Studies*, 20.1, pp. 160–76.

Migdal, J. (1988): *Strong Societies and Weak States: State–Society Relations and State Capabilities in the Third World*, Princeton: Princeton University Press.

Mikell, G. (1991): 'Equity issues in Ghana's rural development', in D. Rothchild (ed.), *Ghana: The Political Economy of Recovery*, Boulder and London: Lynne Rienner, pp. 85–100.

Miller, L. (1990): *Global Order: Values and Power in International Politics*, 2nd edn, Boulder: Westview.

Miller, M. (1995): *The Third World in Global Environmental Politics*, Buckingham: Open University Press.

Mills, C. Wright (1970): *The Sociological Imagination*, 2nd edn, London: Penguin.

Milne, S. (1996): 'Exiled Saudi dissidents seek television licence', *Guardian*, 15 Jan.

Mitra, S. (1990): 'Introduction', in S. Mitra (ed.), *The Post-Colonial State in Asia*, Hemel Hempstead: Wheatsheaf, pp. 1–17.

—— (1992): 'Democracy and political change in India', *Journal of Commonwealth and Comparative Politics*, 30.1, pp. 9–38.

Mittelman, J. (1994): 'The globalisation challenge: surviving at the margins', *Third World Quarterly*, 15.3, pp. 427–41.

Molyneux, M. (1985): 'Mobilization without emancipation? Women's interests, the state, and revolution in Nicaragua', *Feminist Studies*, 11.2, pp. 227–54.

Monbiot, G. (1994a): 'Hero and victims', *Guardian*, 18 Mar.

—— (1994b): *No Man's Land, an Investigative Journey through Kenya and Tanzania*, London: Macmillan.

—— (1996a): 'You don't give us the earth, we'll take it', *Guardian*, 11 Jan.

—— (1996b): 'Nice and easy does it', *Guardian*, 8 May.

Monga, C. (1995): 'Civil society and democratisation in Francophone Africa', *Journal of Modern African Studies*, 33.3, pp. 359–80.

Moore, B. (1966): *Social Origins of Dictatorship and Democracy: Lord and Peasant in the Making of the Modern World*, Boston: Beacon Press.

Moore, Michael (1995): Book review of L. Jayasuriya, *The Changing Face of Sri Lankan Politics: The Background to the 1994 General Election* (Perth: Edith Cowan University), *Journal of Commonwealth and Comparative Politics*, 33.3, pp. 421–3.

Moore, Molly (1994): 'Indian films fight cable TV with "sexy, sexy" songs', *Guardian*, 5 Aug.

Morales, W. (1994): 'US intervention and the new world order: lessons from Cold War and post-Cold War cases', *Third World Quarterly*, 15.1, pp. 77–101.

Morris, P. (1989): 'Israel', in S. Mews (ed.), *Religion in Politics: A World Guide*, Harlow: Longman, pp. 123–37.

Morris-Jones, W. (1992): 'Shaping the post-imperial state: Nehru's letters to chief ministers', in M. Twaddle (ed.), *Imperialism, the State and the Third World*, London: British Academic Press, pp. 220–41.

Mosley, P. (1991): 'Kenya', in P. Mosley, J. Harringtan and J. Toye, *Aid and Power: The World Bank and Policy-Based Lending*, vol. 2: *Case Studies*, London and New York: Routledge, pp. 270–310.

Mosley, P., Harringan, J. and Toye, J. (1991a): *Aid and Power: The World Bank and Policy-Based Lending*, vol. 1: *Analysis and Policy Proposals*, London and New York: Routledge.

—— (1991b): *Aid and Power: The World Bank and Policy-Based Lending*, vol. 2: *Case Studies*, London and New York: Routledge.

Mouzelis, N. (1986): *Politics in the Semi-Periphery*, London: Macmillan.

Moyser, G. (1991): 'Politics and religion in the modern world: an overview', in G. Moyser (ed.), *Politics and Religion in the Modern World*, London: Routledge, pp. 3–20.

Murphy, C. (1994): *International Organization and Industrial Change: Global Governance since 1850*, Cambridge: Polity.

Naanen, B. (1995): 'Oil-producing minorities and the restructuring of Nigerian federalism: the case of the Ogoni people', *Journal of Commonwealth and Comparative Politics*, 33.1, pp. 46–78.

Nakamura, A. and Koike, O. (1992): 'Responsible governance and problems of administrative reform: experiences of developing countries in Asia', *Governance*, 5.4, pp. 484–92.

Navarro, M. (1989): 'The personal is political: Las Madres de Plazo de Mayo', in S. Eckstein (ed.), *Power and Popular Protest in Latin America*, London: University of California Press, pp. 241–58.

Navarro, R. (1996): 'Give us earth, water and air', *Guardian*, 25 Sept.

Nelson, J. (1993): 'The politics of economic transformation', *World Politics*, 45, pp. 433–63.

Norgaard, R. (1994): *Development Betrayed: The End of Progress and a Coevalutionary Revisioning of the Future*, London: Routledge.

Norton, A. R. (1993): 'The future of civil society in the Middle East', *Middle East Journal*, 47.2, pp. 205–16.

O'Connell, J. (1989): 'Nigeria', in S. Mews (ed.), *Religion in Politics: A World Guide*, Harlow: Longman, pp. 196–201.

O'Donnell, G. (1979): *Modernization and Bureaucratic-Authoritarianism: Studies in South American Politics*, 2nd edn, Berkeley: Institute of International Studies, University of California.

O'Donnell, G., Schmitter, P. and Whitehead, L. (eds) (1986): *Transitions from Auhoritarian Rule: Prospects for Democracy*, Baltimore: Johns Hopkins University Press.

Ogoni Community Association UK (1995): 'Ogoni campaign builds internationally', press release, 13 Nov.

O'Hagan, J. (1995): 'Civilisational conflict? Looking for cultural enemies', *Third World Quarterly*, 16.1, pp. 19–38.

Okin, S. M. (1994): 'Gender inequality and cultural differences', *Political Theory*, 22.1, pp. 5–24.

Omvedt, G. (1994): 'Peasants, dalits and women: democracy and India's new social movements', *Journal of Contemporary Asia*, 24.1, pp. 35–48.

Organski, A. (1965): *The Stages of Political Development*, New York: Knopf.

Osaghae, E. (1995): 'The Ogoni uprising: oil politics, minority agitation and the future of the Nigerian state', *African Affairs*, 94.376, pp. 325–44.

Ould-Mey, M. (1994): 'Global adjustment: implications for peripheral states', *Third World Quarterly*, 15.2, pp. 319–36.

Owen, R. (1992): *State, Power and Politics in the Making of the Modern Middle East*, London: Routledge.

Parpart, J. (1988): 'Women and the state in Africa', in D. Rothchild and N. Chazan (eds.), *The Precarious Balance: State and Society in Africa*, Westview: Boulder, pp. 208–30.

Pateman, C. (1988): *The Sexual Contract*, Cambridge: Polity.

Payne, T. (1988): 'Multi-party politics in Jamaica', in V. Randall (ed.), *Political Parties in the Third World*, London: Sage, pp. 135–54.

Peluso, N. L. (1993): 'Coercing conservation: the politics of state resource control', in R. Lipschutz and K. Conca (eds), *The State and Social Power in Global Environmental Politics*, New York: Columbia University Press, pp. 46–70.

Pendle, G. (1976): *A History of Latin America*, Harmondsworth: Penguin.

Perry, E. (1989): 'State and society in contemporary China', *World Politics*, 41.4, pp. 578–91.

Peterson, M. J. (1992): 'Transnational activity, international society and world politics', *Millennium*, 21.3, pp. 371–88.

Philip, G. (1993): 'The new economic liberalism and democracy in Latin America: friends or enemies?', *Third World Quarterly*, 14.3, pp. 555–72.

Phillips, A. (1991): *Engendering Democracy*, Cambridge: Polity.

—— (1992): 'Must feminists give up on liberal democracy', in D. Held (ed.), *Prospects for Democracy*, Cambridge: Polity, pp. 93–111.

Piel, M. with Sada, P. (1984): *African Urban Society*, Chichester: Wiley.

Pinkney, R. (1993): *Democracy in the Third World*, Buckingham: Open University Press.

Plank, D. (1993): 'Aid, debt, and the end of sovereignty: Mozambique and its donors', *Journal of Modern African Studies*, 31.3, pp. 407–30.

Plommer, L. and Mosteshar, C. (1994): 'Bringing a beam of delight to the closed world of Iran', *Guardian*, 5 Aug.

Poggi, G. (1978): *The Development of the Modern State: A Sociological Introduction*, Stanford: Stanford University Press.

Potter, D. (1993): 'Democratization in Asia', in D. Held (ed.), *Prospects for Democracy*, Cambridge: Polity, pp. 355–79.

Pradervand, P. (1988): 'Afrique noire: la victoire du courage', *IFDA Dossier*, no. 64, pp. 3–12.

—— (1989): *Listening to Africa: Developing Africa from the Grassroots*, Westport: Praeger.

Pridham, G. (1994): 'The international dimension of democratisation: theory, practice and inter-regional comparisons', in G. Pridham, E. Herring and G. Sanford (eds), *Building Democracy? The International Dimension of Democratisation in Eastern Europe*, London: Leicester University Press, pp. 7–31.

Princen, T. (1994): 'NGOs: creating a niche in environmental diplomacy', in T. Princen and M. Finger, *Environmental NGOs in World Politics. Linking the Local and the Global*, London: Routledge, pp. 29–47.

—— (1995): 'Ivory, conservation, and environmental transnational coalitions', in T. Risse-Kappen (ed.), *Bringing Transnational Relations Back In*, Cambridge: Cambridge University Press, pp. 227–53.

Princen, T. and Finger, M. (1994): *Environmental NGOs in World Politics: Linking the Local and the Global*, London: Routledge.
Pye, L. (1991): *China: An Introduction*, 4th. edn, New York: HarperCollins.
Pye, L. with Pye, M. (1985): *Asian Power and Politics: The Cultural Dimensions of Authority*, Cambridge: Harvard University Press.
Radcliffe, S. and Westwood, S. (1993a): 'Gender, racism and the politics of identity in Latin America', in S. Radcliffe and S. Westwood (eds), *'Viva': Women and Popular Protest in Latin America*, London and New York: Routledge, pp. 1–29.
—— (eds) (1993b): *'Viva': Women and Popular Protest in Latin America*, London: Routledge.
Rahman, A. (1988): *Glimpses of the Other Africa*, Geneva: International Labour Organisation.
Rai, S. (1994): 'Towards empowerment of South Asian women', *Third World Quarterly*, 15.3, pp. 532–47.
Randall, V. (1993): 'The media and democratisation in the Third World', *Third World Quarterly*, 14.3, pp. 625–46.
—— (1995): 'The media and religion in Third World politics', paper presented at the workshop, 'Political Culture and Religion in the Third World', European Consortium for Political Research Joint Sessions, Bordeaux, 27 Apr.–2 May.
Randall, V. and Theobald R. (1985): *Political Change and Underdevelopment: A Critical Introduction to Third World Politics*, London: Macmillan.
Rau, B. (1991): *From Feast to Famine*, London: Zed Books.
Rawnsley, A. (1995): 'The billionaire dissident', *Observer*, 29 Oct.
Redclift, M. (1988): 'Introduction: agrarian social movements in contemporary Mexico', *Bulletin of Latin America Research*, 7.2, pp. 249–56.
Reeves, G. (1993): *Communications and the 'Third World'*, London: Sage.
Remmer, K. (1989): *Military Rule in Latin America*, Boston: Unwin Hyman.
—— (1993): 'Democratization in Latin America', in R. O. Slater, B. M. Schutz and S. R. Dorr (eds), *Global Transformation and the Third World*, Boulder: Lynne Rienner, pp. 91–112.
Rettie, J. (1994): 'Out of sight, out of mind', *Guardian*, 14 Mar.
Reveyrand-Coulon, O. (1993): 'Les énoncés féminins de l'islam' in J.-F. Bayart (ed.), *Religion et Modernité. Politique en Afrique Noire*, Paris: Karthala, pp. 63–100.
Rich, B. (1990): 'The emperor's new clothes: the World Bank and environmental reform', *World Policy Journal*, Spring, pp. 305–29.
—— (1994): *Mortgaging the Earth: The World Bank, Environmental Impoverishment, and the Crisis of Development*, Boston: Beacon Press.
Risse-Kappen, T. (1995): 'What have we learnt?', in T. Risse-Kappen (ed.), *Bringing Transnational Relations Back In*, Cambridge: Cambridge University Press, pp. 280–313.
Roberts, H. (1991): 'A trial of strength: Algerian Islamism', in J. Piscatori (ed.), *Islamic Fundamentalisms and the Gulf Crisis*, London: Cambridge University Press, pp. 131–54.
—— (1992): 'The Algerian state and the challenge of democracy', *Government and Opposition*, 27.4, pp. 433–54.
Robison, R. (1988): 'Authoritarian states, capital-owning classes, and the politics of newly industrialising countries: the case of Indonesia', *World Politics*, 40, pp. 52–74.

Roniger, L. (1994): 'Conclusions: the transformation of clientelism and civil society' in L. Roniger and A. Günes-Ayata (eds), *Democracy, Clientelism, and Civil Society*, Boulder: Lynne Rienner, pp. 207–14.

Roniger, L. and Günes-Ayata, A. (eds) (1994): *Democracy, Clientelism, and Civil Society*, Boulder: Lynne Rienner.

Rood, D., James, C. and Sakamati, S. (1995): 'Collateral damage', *Far Eastern Economic Review*, 21 Sept., pp. 16–17.

Rose, D. (1996): 'The man they had to silence', *Observer*, 7 Jan.

Rosenau, J. (1990): *Turbulence in World Politics: A Theory of Change and Continuity*, Princeton: Princeton University Press.

—— (1993): 'Environmental challenges in a turbulent world', in R. Lipschutz and K. Conca (eds),*The State and Social Power in Global Environmental Politics*, New York: Columbia University Press, pp. 71–93.

Rothchild, D. and Chazan, N. (eds) (1988): *The Precarious Balance: State and Society in Africa*, Boulder: Westview.

Roy, O. (1985): *L'Afghanistan: Islam et modernité politique*, Paris: Seuil.

Rudebeck, L. (1990): 'The effects of structural adjustment in Kandjadja, Guinea-Bissau', *Review of African Political Economy*, no. 49, pp. 73–8.

Rudolph, S. (1987): 'State formation in Asia – prolegemon to a comparative study', *Journal of Asian Studies*, 46.4, pp. 731–46.

Rueschemeyer, D., Stephens, E. and Stephens, J. (1992): *Capitalist Development and Democracy*, Cambridge: Polity.

Ruggie, J. G. (1993): 'Territoriality and beyond: problematizing modernity in international relations', *International Organization*, 47.1, pp. 141–76.

Sabbagh, R. (1994): 'Jordanian women pay the violent price of traditional male "honour"', *Guardian*, 28 Dec.

Safa, H. (1990): 'Women and social movements in Latin America', *Gender and Society*, 14.4, pp. 354–69.

Sage, A. (1995): 'Cracked dreams turn boys into real terrorists', *Observer*, 17 Sept.

Sahliyeh, E. (1990): 'Introduction', in E. Sahliyeh (ed.), *Religious Resurgence and Politics in the Contemporary World*, Albany: State University of New York Press, pp. 1–20.

Said, E. (1996): 'War babies', *Observer*, 14 Jan.

Saif, W. (1994): 'Human rights and Islamic revivalism', *Islam and Christian–Muslim Relations*, 5.1, pp. 57–65.

Salame, G. (1993): 'Islam and the West', *Foreign Policy*, Spring, pp. 22–37.

Samudavanija, C.-A. (1993): 'The new military and democracy in Thailand', in L. Diamond (ed.), *Political Culture and Democracy in Developing Countries*, Boulder: Lynne Rienner, pp. 269–94.

Sandbrook, R. (1988): 'Liberal democracy in Africa: a socialist-revisionist perspective', *Canadian Journal of African Studies*, 22.2, pp. 240–67.

Saro-Wiwa, K. (1992): *Genocide in Nigeria: the Ogoni tragedy*, London: Saros International.

Saurin, J. (1995): 'The end of international relations? The state and international theory in the age of globalization', in J. Macmillan and A. Linklater (eds), *Boundaries in Question: New Directions in International Relations*, London: Pinter, pp. 244–61.

Schatzberg, M. (1988): *The Dialectics of Oppression in Zaire*, Bloomington: Indiana University Press.

Schirmer, J. (1993): 'The seeking of the truth and the gendering of consciousness: the comadres of El Salvador and the Conavigua Widows of Guatemala', in S. Radcliffe and S. Westwood (eds), *'Viva': Women and Popular Protest in Latin America*, London: Routledge, pp. 30–64.

Scholte, J. Aart (1993): *International Relations of Social Change*, Buckingham: Open University Press.

Scott, A. (1990): *Ideology and the New Social Movements*, London: Unwin Hyman.

Scott, J. (1977): 'Hegemony and the peasant', *Politics and Society*, 7.3. pp. 267–96.

—— (1985): *Weapons of the Weak: Everyday Forms of Peasant Resistance*, New Haven: Yale University Press.

—— (1990): *Domination and the Arts of Resistance: Hidden Transcipts*, New Haven: Yale University Press.

Scott, M. (1990): 'Dishing the rules', *Far Eastern Economic Review*, 14 June, pp. 34–9.

Scott, N. (1995a): 'Mexico blazes path to ruin', *Guardian*, 14 Jan.

—— (1995b): 'Argentines strike against job cuts', *Guardian*, 11 Aug.

Serhan, B. (1993): 'The Palestinian social movement', in P. Wignaraja (ed.), *New Social Movements in the South*, London; Zed Books, pp. 164–82.

Serra, L. (1985): 'Ideology, religion and class struggle in the Nicaraguan revolution', in R. Harris and C. Vilas (eds), *Nicaragua: A Revolution under Siege*, London: Zed, pp. 74–96.

Sethi, H. (1993): 'Survival and democracy: ecological struggles in India', in P. Wignaraja (ed.), *New Social Movements in the South*, London: Zed Books, pp. 122–48.

Shah, G. (1988): 'Grass-roots mobilization in Indian politics', in A. Kohli (ed.), *India's Democracy: An Analysis of Changing State–Society Relations*, Princeton: Princeton University Press, pp. 262–304.

Shaikh, F. (ed.) (1992): *Islam and Islamic Groups: A Worldwide Reference Guide*, Harlow: Longman.

Shaw, T. (1993): 'Africa in the New World Order: marginal and/or central?', in A. Adedeji (ed.), *Africa within the World: Beyond Dispossession and Dependence*, London: Zed Books/ACDESS, pp. 78–93.

Shillington, K. (1992): *Ghana and the Rawlings Factor*, London: Macmillan.

Shils, E. (1991): 'The virtue of civil society', *Government and Opposition*, 26.1, pp. 3–20.

Shin, D. C. (1994): 'On the third wave of democratization: a synthesis and evaluation of recent theory and research', *World Politics*, 47, pp. 135–70.

Shupe, A. (1990): 'The stubborn persistence of religion in the global arena', in E. Sahliyeh (ed.), *Religious Resurgence and Politics in the Contemporary World*, Albany: State University of New York Press, pp. 17–26.

Sigmund, P. (1993): 'Christian democracy, liberation theology, and political culture in Latin America', in L. Diamond (ed.), *Political Culture and Democracy in Developing Countries*, Boulder: Lynne Rienner, pp. 329–46.

Simon, R. (1982): *Gramsci's Political Thought*, London: Lawrence and Wishart.

Sisson, R. (1993): 'Culture and democratization in India', in L. Diamond (ed.), *Political Culture and Democracy in Developing Countries*, Boulder: Lynne Rienner, pp. 37–66.

Skocpol, T. (1979): *States and Social Revolution*, Cambridge: Cambridge University Press.

Slater, D. (1985): *New Social Movements and the State in Latin America*, CEDLA Latin American Studies 25, Amsterdam: Floris.

Smith, B. (1982): *The Church and Politics in Chile*, Princeton: Princeton University Press.

—— (1990): *More than Altruism: The Politics of Private Foreign Aid*, Princeton: Princeton University Press.

Smith, M. (1992): 'Modernization, globalization and the nation-state', in A. McGrew and P. Lewis, *Global Politics*, Cambridge: Polity, pp. 253–68.

So, A. (1990): *Social Change and Development*, London: Sage.

Sørensen, G. (1993): *Democracy and Democratization*, Boulder: Westview.

Sparr, P. (1994): 'Feminist critiques of structural adjustment', in P. Sparr (ed.), *Mortgaging Women's Lives*, London: United Nations/Zed Books, pp. 20–35.

Spelman, E. (1988): *Inessential Woman: Problems of Exclusion in Feminist Thought*, Boston: Beacon.

Staniland, M. (1985): *What is Political Economy?*, New Haven: Yale University Press.

Stavenhagen, R. (1992): 'Challenging the nation-state in Latin America', *Journal of International Affairs*, 45.2 , pp. 421–40.

Stepan, A. (1988): *Rethinking Military Politics: Brazil and the Southern Cone*, Princeton: Princeton University Press.

Stiefel, M. and Wolfe, M. (1994): *A Voice for the Excluded: Popular Participation in Development: Utopia or Necessity?*, London and Geneva: Zed/UNRISD.

Sylvester, C. (1995): 'Whither opposition in Zimbabwe', *Journal of Modern African Studies*, 33.3, pp. 403–24.

Tahi, M. S. (1992): 'The arduous democratisation process in Algeria', *Journal of Modern African Studies*, 30.3, pp. 400–20.

Tai, H. (1989): 'The oriental alternative: a hypothesis on East Asian culture and economy', *Issues and Studies*, 25, pp. 10–36.

Tarock, A. (1995): 'Civilisational conflict? Fighting the enemy under a new banner', *Third World Quarterly*, 16.1, pp. 5–18.

Tehranian, M. (1990): *Technologies of Power*, Norwood, N.J.: Ablex.

Theodoulou, M. (1994): 'Zero Tolerance' and 'Uncensored', in special supplement on censorship, *Observer*, 24 Apr.

Thomas, A. et al. (1994): *Third World Atlas*, 2nd edn, Buckingham: Open University Press.

Thomas, R. (1995): 'World Bank embraces radical message of social partnership between governments and unions', *Guardian*, 30 June.

Thompson, M. (1993): 'The limits of democratisation in ASEAN', *Third World Quarterly*, 14.3, pp. 469–84.

Thomson, R. and Armer, M. (1980): 'Respecifying the effects of voluntary associations on individuals in a traditional society', *International Journal of Comparative Sociology*, 21.3–4, pp. 288–302.

Touraine, A. (1985): 'An introduction to the study of social movements', *Social Research*, 52.4, pp. 749–88.

Tran, M. (1994): 'World Bank sees Nepal project as test of credibility', *Guardian*, 17 Nov.

Tsikata, E. (1989): 'Women's political organisations, 1951–87', in E. Hansen and K. Ninsin (eds), *The State, Development and Politics in Ghana*, London: CODESRIA. pp. 73–93.

Turner, V. (1969): *The Ritual Process: Structure and Anti-Structure*, Ithaca: Cornell University Press.

Turton, A. (1987): *Production, Power and Participation in Rural Thailand*, Geneva: UNRISD.

Twaddle, M. (1992): 'Imperialism and the state in the Third World', in M. Twaddle (ed.), *Imperialism, the State and the Third World*, London: British Academic Press, pp. 1–22.

UNDP (United Nations Development Programme) (1993): *Human Development Report 1993*, Oxford: Oxford University Press for the UNDP.

—— (1995): *Human Development Report 1995*, Oxford: Oxford University Press for the UNDP.

—— (1996): *Human Development Report 1996*, Oxford: Oxford University Press for the UNDP.

United Nations (1991): *World's Women: Trends and Statistics 1970–90*, New York: United Nations.

UNRISD (United Nations Research Institute for Social Development) (1995): *States of Disarray*, Geneva: UNRISD.

Uphoff, N. (1993): 'Grassroots organizations and NGOs in rural development: opportunities with diminishing states and expanding markets', *World Development*, 21.4, pp. 607–22.

Vaughan, O. (1995): 'Assessing grassroots politics and community development in Nigeria', *African Affairs*, 94.377, pp. 501–18.

Vetter, S. (1986): 'Building the infrastructure for progress: private development organizations in the Dominican Republic', *Grassroots Development*, 10.1, pp. 2–9.

Vidal, J. (1995a): 'Nepalese hail move to scrap huge dam', *Guardian*, 5 Aug.

—— (1995b): 'Rats of the rubbish society fight back', *Guardian*, 9 Sept.

—— (1995c): 'Localism vs globalism', *Guardian*, 15 Nov.

—— (1996): 'Harmed and dangerous', *Guardian*, 8 May.

Villalón, L. (1995): *Islamic Society and State Power in Senegal: Disciples and Citizens in Fatick*, Cambridge: Cambridge University Press.

Vincent, R. J. (1986): *Human Rights and International Relations*, Cambridge: Cambridge University Press.

Vogler, J. (1992): 'Regimes and the global commons: space, atmosphere and oceans', in A. McGrew and P. Lewis (eds), *Global Politics*, Cambridge: Polity, pp. 118–37.

Voll, J. (1991): 'Fundamentalism in the Sunni Arab world: Egypt and the Sudan', in M. Marty and R. Scott Appleby (eds), *Fundamentalisms Observed*, Chicago and London: University of Chicago Press, pp. 345–402.

von der Mehden, F. (1989): 'Malaysia', in S. Mews (ed.), *Religion in Politics: A World Guide*, Harlow: Longman.

Walker, M. (1995): 'How the existing consensus on foreign policy goals is collapsing', *Guardian*, 21 Feb.

Wanyande, P. (1987): 'Women's groups in participatory development', *Development: Seeds of Change*, nos 2–3, pp. 94–102.

Waylen, G. (1992): 'Rethinking women's political participation and protest: Chile 1970–90', *Political Studies*, 40.2, pp. 299–314.

—— (1993): 'Women's movements and democratisation in Latin America', *Third World Quarterly*, 14.3, pp. 573–87.

Weber, M. (1947): *The Theory of Social and Economic Organization*, New York: Free Press.

—— (1969): 'Major features of world religions', in R. Robertson (ed.), *The Sociology of Religion*, Baltimore: Penguin, pp. 19–41.

Webster, P. (1995): 'Capital of terror', *Guardian*, 6 Sept.
Whitehead, L. (1993): 'The alternatives to "liberal democracy": a Latin American perspective', in D. Held (ed.), *Prospects for Democracy*, Cambridge: Polity, pp. 312–29.
Wignaraja, P. (1993a): 'Preface', in P. Wignaraja (ed.), *New Social Movements in the South*, London: Zed Books, pp. xv–xviii.
—— (ed.) (1993b): *New Social Movements in the South*, London: Zed Books.
Williams, D. (1994): 'The World Bank, "governance", and the ideology of transformation', paper presented at the conference on 'The End of the Cold War: Effects and Prospects for Asia and Africa', School of Oriental and African Studies, University of London, 21–2 Oct.
Williams, G. (1994): 'Why structural adjustment is necessary and why it doesn't work', *Review of African Political Economy*, no. 60, pp. 214–25.
Williams, P. and Falola, T. (1995): *Religious Impact on the Nation State: The Nigerian Predicament*, Aldershot: Avebury.
Winans, E. and Haugerud, A. (1977): 'Rural self-help in Kenya: the harambee movement', *Human Organisation*, no. 36, pp. 334–51.
Wiseman, J. (1990): *Democracy in Black Africa*, New York, Paragon House.
—— (1995): 'Introduction', in J. Wiseman (ed.), *Democracy and Political Change in Africa*, London: Routledge, pp. 1–10.
Woollacott, M. (1995): 'A rage for peace and power', *Guardian*, 9 Sept.
—— (1996): 'Crude deals that buy silence', *Guardian*, 6 Jan.
World Bank (1986): *World Development Report 1986*, Oxford: Oxford University Press for the World Bank.
—— (1991): *World Development Report 1991*, Oxford: Oxford University Press for the World Bank.
—— (1994): *Adjustment in Africa: Reforms, Results and the Road Ahead*, Oxford: Oxford University Press for the World Bank.
—— (1995): *World Development Report 1995*, Oxford: Oxford University Press for the World Bank.
World Commission on Environment and Development (1987): *Our Common Future*, Oxford: Oxford University Press.
Ya'ari, E. and Horovitz, D. (1994): 'Can Hamas blow up the peace process?', *Jerusalem Post*, 17 Nov.
Zinn, C. and Bowcott, O. (1995): 'Storm of anti-nuclear protests mark Bastille Day', *Guardian*, 15 July.
Zolo, D. (1993): 'Citizenship in a post-communist era', in D. Held (ed.), *Prospects for Democracy*, Cambridge: Polity, pp. 254–68.
Zubaida, S. (1989): *Islam, the People and the State*, London: Routledge.

Index

31 December Women's Movement, 52, 69–72, 73, 120

Abed, F., 34
action groups,
  and civil society, 166–74
  and democracy, 2, 39–40, 75–94, 166–74
  and development, 6–8, 19, 24, 51–74
  and indigenous peoples, 75–94, 173
  and natural environment, 11–12, 95–119, 180
  and new social movements, 13–14
  and politics, 8–12, 24, 38
  and religion, 142–64; see also religious opposition
  and socialism, 15
  and the state, 6–7, 99–100
  and women's empowerment, 24–5, 120–41, 173, 180; see also Islamist groups; women
Algeria,
  Islamist groups, 154–8, 163
Alvarez, S., 129
ANAI, 42–3

Bangladesh, 36, 52, 60, 73
Bangladesh Rural Advancement Committee, 36–7

Basic Christian Communities, 33–5, 168
Beck, U., 176–8
  and sub-politics, 176–7
Brazil, 33, 35, 41, 55, 93–4, 101, 174
  Indians, 87–90
  Indigenous People's Union, 89
  National Council of Rubber Tappers, 89–90
  women's groups, 130, 134–8, 140, 180; see also favela groups

Cambodia, 96, 102, 110, 118
  forest destruction, 107–8
Catholic Church, 41
Chile, 34, 35, 41
Chipko movement, 102–3, 119
civil society, 3, 19–21, 78–9, 118–19
  and action groups, 13, 15–18; see also action groups and civil society
  in Africa, 18, 25, 28, 96
  in Asia, 18, 96
  in India, 4, 25, 96, 102
  in Latin America, 18–19, 33
  in the Middle East, 18
  and political society, 16–17
  and women, 141
Cohen, J., 14
communications revolution, impact of, 78

Conavigua, 41
Coordinating Council for Human
    Rights, 100
credit provision,
    in Africa, 29–30
    in India, 139–40

Da'wa, 149
democracy,
    in Africa, 75–6, 82, 168
    in Asia, 75–6
    facade, 82–5
    formal, 81–2
    in global context, 76–8
    and indigenous peoples, 75–94
    in Latin America, 34–5, 75–6, 82–3,
        132, 168
    low intensity, 83–4
    in the Middle East, 82
    substantive, 80, 85–7
development action groups
    in Latin America, 32–3
    in sub-Saharan Africa, 25–32

Earth Summit (1992), 97–9
economic growth rates in the Third
    World, 53–7
Egypt,
    Islamist groups, 143, 151–2, 163
    Muslim Brotherhood, 152–4
environmental protection, 94, 95–100
    and deforestation, 101–2
    in Latin America, 42–3
Escobar, A. and Alvarez, S., 14, 40

favela (slum development) groups,
    35, 134–8
    São Paulo Shantytown Movement
    and Unemployed Movement,
    135–8
Federation of Environmental
    Organizations, 43
Fisher, J., 5, 6, 7, 28, 30, 39, 96, 100,
    130, 139, 180
French Polynesia, 96
    and economic role of France,
    111–12
    and nuclear testing, 110–14
    see also Tahiti

Fuentes, M. and Gunder Frank, A.,
    15

Galbraith, J. K., 177
Garreton, M., 86
Ghana, 28
    see also 31 December Women's
    Movement
Gills, B., Rocamara, J. and Wilson,
    R., 83–4
Grameen Bank, 60–2
Greenpeace, 104, 110
Group of Forestation Engineering
    and Habitat, 43

Hall, J., 78–9
Helsinki Conference on Security and
    Cooperation in Europe, 77
Huntington, S., 1, 76, 144

India, 36, 96
    economy, 55
    women's rights, 44–5, 140, 180; *see
    also* women in India
Indonesia, 96, 102
    Wanana Lingkungan Hidap
    Indonesia, 106–7, 118–19
International Monetary Fund, 64–5,
    78
Islamic Movement (Nigeria),
    149–50
Islamic Party of Kenya, 46–7, 144
Islamist groups, 142–64
    and Iran, 144–5
    and liberal democracy, 142–3
    political programme, 142–7
    see also religious opposition;
    individual countries
Israel's Occupied Territories,
    Islamist groups, 159–63

Kamrava, M., 126
Kenya, 28, 30, 96, 99, 102, 108–10,
    118, 144
    Green Belt movement, 108–10
    harambee groups, 30–1, 120
    see also Islamic Party of Kenya
Kerala, *see* women in Kerala

Leton, G., 116–17

Maathai, W., 109–10
Madres de la Plaza de Mayo, 41,
    133–4, 140
Malaysia, 81–2, 96, 101
    Sahabat Alam Malaysia, 105–6,
    118–19
Mendes, C., 90
Mexico, 93–4
    impact of NAFTA, 92
    rule by PRI, 91
    politics in Chiapas, 91
Mikell, G., 71
modernization, impact of, 175–6
Muslim Students Society (Nigeria),
    150

Narmada Valley Project, 103–5
Nation of Islam, 177–8
Nigeria, 96, 102, 114–18
    economic growth, 56
    Islamist groups, 147–51, 163
    Women in Nigeria, 45–6
    see also Ogoni people

Ogoni people, 25, 114–19
    actions against the state, 114–17
    and environmental degradation,
    114–17
    impact of oil exploitation, 116
    Movement for the Survival of the
    Ogoni People, 115–17
Organski, A., 79
Ouédraogo, B. L., 58, 62

political conditions in the Third
    World, 79–80

religious opposition,
    in Algeria, 72
    in colonial Africa, 174
    in Kenya, 46
    in the Middle East, 48–9, 169
    in Tanzania, 47–8
    see also Islamist groups
Rincón, E. R., 93

Saro-Wiwa, K., 115–17
Sarvodaya Shramadana Movement,
    37
Scott, J., 81–2

Self-Employed Women's
    Association, 37, 44
Six-S movement (Association for
    Self-Help during the Dry Season
    in the Savannahs and the Sahel),
    28, 31–2, 57–60, 73
Socio-Legal Aid, Research and
    Training Centre, 44–5
South Korea, economic growth, 55–6
Stepan, A., 16–17
Stockholm Conference (1972), 97
structural adjustment programmes,
    51–2
    in Algeria, 72–3
    in Egypt, 67
    in Ghana, 68–9
    impact on women, 124–8
    in Mexico, 68, 73
    social costs, 63–4, 65–8, 73
sustainable development, 43

Tahiti, 25, 118
    independence movement, 110–14
    women, 113
Tanzania, 28, 46
    Islamist groups, 144
Thailand, 52
    rural development, 62–3
Touraine, A., 13, 49
Tsikata, E., 70, 71

United Nations Development
    Programme, 128
Unrepresented Nations and Peoples
    Organisation, 114–15

Waylen, G., 129
women,
    in Cuba, 121
    in East and South-East Asia, 126–7
    feminist and feminine groups, 128
    general socio-economic position in
    India, 120, 141, 169
    in Kerala (India), 121, 122–4, 140
    in Latin America, 120, 122, 131–3,
    140, 169
    in the Middle East, 48, 169, 180
    in South Asia, 36
    in sub-Saharan Africa, 45–6, 141,
    169

women, *Cont'd*
  in the Third World, 121–2
  see also structural adjustment
    programmes, impact on women;
    individual countries
Working Women's Forum, 138–40
World Bank, 65–6, 78, 104–5

Yan Izala, 149

Yewwi Yewwu, 46
Yunus, M., 60, 62

Zapatistas, 73, 90–3
  see also Mexico
Zedillo, E., 93
Zimbabwe, 30, 81–2, 127
  women, 130–1

Lightning Source UK Ltd.
Milton Keynes UK
UKHW020956241022
410996UK00009B/334

9 780745 616476